ANTIQUE COLLECTING FOR EVERYONE

ANTIQUE COLLECTING FOR

EVERYONE

BY KATHARINE MORRISON McCLINTON

ILLUSTRATED WITH OVER TWO HUNDRED PHOTOGRAPHS

BONANZA BOOKS · NEW YORK

ANTIQUE COLLECTING FOR EVERYONE

This edition published by Bonanza Books,
a division of Crown Publishers,
by arrangement with the copyright owner

(B)

Preface

THE STORY OF ANTIQUES will be many years in the writing and no present-day author can give the complete answer no matter how authoritative his contribution. However, in old newspapers and old documents such as inventories, account books, diaries, and letters, new light is constantly shed on the subject. I have tried to add authentic material, obtained from these sources, on the various subjects treated in the twenty-four chapters of this book, and I have tried to answer some specific questions about the objects, such as what objects to collect, the availability of certain antiques, and what one can expect to pay for them, not in dollars, but in comparative values. Again, I have stressed good taste as the most important factor in forming a valuable collection and in getting the most for one's money.

The objects I have chosen are those most popular with collectors today. I have noted the growing interest in folk arts and I have, I think, explored a bit of ground not covered by other writers on the subject.

For their interest and assistance I wish especially to thank Miss Dorothy C. Barck, librarian at the New York Historical Society, and her staff; Miss Carolyn Scoon, assistant to the curator of the New York Historical Society; and William H. Distin, librarian, The Edison Institute Museum, Dearborn, Michigan. I also wish to thank Miss Alice Winchester, editor of *The Magazine Antiques,* for her interest and encouragement and for permission to include material previously published in that periodical; and *McCall's* and *The American Collector* for material which appeared in issues of other magazines.

I also wish to thank Miss Edith Blum, whose collection of Mocha ware made that chapter possible, and Mrs. Alfred Mackenzie of Mamaroneck, who kept me in touch with the present collecting market through her shop and active participation in current antique shows.

Katharine Morrison McClinton

Contents

———

Good Taste in Collecting

―――――――

THE collector who is endowed with innate good taste or who has trained his appreciation to note the beauty of fine line, significant form, and harmonious color has a sounder basis of judgment than the one who knows the number of diamonds in the pattern or the factory where such and such an article was made. Indeed the collector who arms himself with an appreciation of artistic values will never be cheated, for even if he buys a reproduction it will be beautiful in itself. For beauty is not a thing of antiquity but a living element, being created anew with each artist's conception, and in our ability to judge the best of today's decorative art we train our taste to appreciate the finest treasures of other days. Lady Charlotte Schreiber had such discriminating taste that her collection of pottery, porcelain, and enamels is now in the Victoria and Albert Museum, but from her journals we catch the fun and romance of collecting rather than an attitude of calculated bargaining. However, Lady Charlotte had rare good taste and aesthetic judgment. The average American collector seems to be more interested in the historical or sentimental value of an object, or in the mark which tells him that the object is genuine, than in its actual beauty. If this were not true many objects which are now collected, such as story buttons, bisque figures, mechanical banks, shaving mugs, and Gibson Girl plates, would not be collected. These objects do not require the use of aesthetic judgment, for they have little art value; instead their values are social and historical. However, when a collector chooses silver, china, or furniture as his field for collecting, if he expects to assemble a fine collection which will increase in value and bring credit to him as a discriminating collector, he needs both natural good taste and an acquired knowledge of aesthetic values. Now, some people are born with good taste and it crops out all over. But everyone thinks he has good taste whether he has or not, or at least he reserves the right to "like what he likes." However, if one has an open mind and the desire he can improve his taste. This knowledge cannot be imparted like information or acquired by reading. It is best developed by actually working with materials and learning to put a few harmonious lines together on paper or by mixing paints. It can be acquired to a certain degree by comparing good and poor examples of glass, china, and other objects and by visits to museums where only the best is displayed, thus gradually developing a knowledge of good line and fine proportions. Indeed, anyone who spends much time with fine art objects cannot fail to develop a taste for them and an abhorrence of the poorly designed.

Your collecting interest will determine the direction of your study. For example, a knowledge of Greek, Roman, Gothic, and modern sculpture and of carving of all kinds will be of aid in collecting such objects as cameos, wax portraits, ivories, netsukes, chalk figures, and pottery and porcelain figures.

A study of paintings, etchings, and other prints will develop a knowledge of values which will be of great assistance to the collector of Currier and Ives prints, glass paintings, or any form of the graphic arts. Many other collectors' interests, such as china, needlework, and certain varieties of glassware, have color as their chief factor, and thus a knowledge of color harmony will be of value to the collector to these objects. Color is something that gets more fascinating the more you know about it and you begin seeing subtle harmonies that you were never conscious of before.

Of course there are certain factors in judging and knowing antiques which are not based on aesthetic value but are learned by actually handling the objects themselves. To judge glassware you must know the sound or ring, and there is a certain intangible "feel" about old glass and old china. There is also a quality of color which has nothing to do with color harmony; it is a certain mellowness of old color that gives an added aesthetic quality.

There is beauty of workmanship and finish about a fine object, whether it be evenly executed stitches in a rare old sampler, fine carving in wood or ivory, good brushwork, or beautifully executed inlay, and this beauty of execution increases the aesthetic value of an object. There is also a beauty which arises from the process itself. Thus the technical process of weaving changes the character and outline of a design and makes it different from the same design painted on paper.

An understanding of color and design can be of help when you are arranging your collection of antiques in your house or in a shop. Objects with dominant colors should be grouped against harmonious backgrounds, but the effect of color also depends to a certain extent upon light. Intense, brilliant colors are toned down by sunshine. Sunlight also brings other colors together because it adds a certain amount of yellow to all colors. Light reduces the intensity of red, improves greens and blues, and makes black less somber. The old English potteries were certainly thinking of the effect of sunlight on colors when they made gaudy-colored wares for African and West Indian trade. Grayed light is more suited for colors of medium tones. These factors may be applied when making a display for a sunny window or for an arrangement of articles in a room with medium light. In dark rooms articles require a contrast of tone if they are to show up. Shapes must also be large and simple; thus intricate designs or fine carvings cannot be expected to show up in poor light, and a delicate piece of glass or china may pass unseen in a dark corner. The colors which appear best in dark situations are those which have the most light themselves. Against a dark background yellow shows up best; then orange, red, green, and blue in diminishing order. Against a light background objects of blue will show up best, with those of green, red, orange, and yellow in diminishing order. A background of complementary color in the proper tone also helps to set off an object. However, when using a warm color as the background you must be careful to reduce its intensity or it will detract from the object of cool color displayed against it. This factor of contrasting color backgrounds is being used in exhibit rooms of modern museums throughout the country. Even the Metropolitan Museum has discarded the old neutral-background-good-for-everything theory, and paintings as well as collections of decorative arts are shown against colored backgrounds.

Design may also be used as an aid in arranging your collection, and you will find that small articles, such as snuff boxes or a collection of trivets, will be more effectively displayed if grouped about a center which is formed by the dominant object in the collection. Arranging your collection of glass, china, or whatever your collecting hobby may be can be fun if you follow a few of the rules. Indeed your collection can and should become the main feature of the room in which it is displayed. A collection just stored away on shelves doesn't mean much to anyone but the collector himself. I know of two collectors of old blue Staffordshire. One collector has an example of every rare piece ever made, but the pieces are crowded together on the shelves of a small room. The other collector, whose collection will not compare in value to that of the first, has placed her collection in two corner cupboards in her dining room against shelves of pale daffodil yellow, and the collection becomes a thing of delight to all her friends.

A collection of brass or copper is greatly enhanced against a dull-green background, and I remember a charming bedroom with snow-white walls and a fireplace of old blue-and-white Dutch tiles. Indeed if you want to make your antiques livable consider them when you plan the decoration and color scheme of your rooms.

All that I have said about color and backgrounds for antiques could also be of practical use to the antique shopkeeper or the dealer interested in the display of his wares in a booth at the antique show. Any exhibition booth will be more successful if one object or a group of objects such as a tea set is made the dominant feature. On the other hand, if the display consists of a heterogeneous conglomeration of objects, the spectator may pass on to the next booth without stopping. For the dominant feature choose an object whose colors and contours will carry at a distance.

Of course, association and sentimentality have their place in arranging an exhibit, and one who can recreate the atmosphere of an old New England kitchen or the country store or a table set up for tea goes a long way toward selling his wares. One dealer I know disposes of her cracked and chipped china cups and pitchers and teapots because she has the ingenuity to plant ivy and other growing greens in them. Another dealer who specializes in pewter displays his old pewter in an old cupboard against a painted background of deep gray-blue.

Katharine Morrison McClinton

Illustration Credits

The author wishes to thank the following persons and institutions for permission to reproduce the illustrations on the pages listed below:

ANTIQUE COLLECTING FOR EVERYONE

Mocha Ware

MOCHA WARE is one of those things that has been regarded with scorn and labeled kitchen ware, but it has come into the collector's field during the last five years. Although at one time Mocha ware was a common household pottery it is now supposed to be sophisticated to collect it. There is not a great deal of Mocha ware on the market today, because Mocha is a soft pottery and much has been broken, and of that left, many pieces are damaged and browned with usage, and these pieces are not desirable to discriminating collectors. The collections which I have studied were acquired within the last few years, but just enough ahead of the popular interest in Mocha ware so that their acquisition did not involve a great deal of money. Prices have tripled now and good pieces are much more difficult to find. Mocha ware looks like, and in fact it is related to, your old yellow mixing bowls.

Actually it is a creamware decorated with seaweed or tree silhouettes and other dipped brush patterns and bands of black, white, or other colors on backgrounds of tan, terra cotta, and blue. Mocha ware is sometimes called "banded creamware" or "Leeds ware" by modern collectors. In the old potteries it was always referred to as Mocha or dipped ware.

Mocha ware was first made by William Adams of Tunstall, England (1787–1805), and continued to be made by his descendant William Adams until 1831, and according to Edwin Atlee Barber was still being made by Adams in 1903. In the book *William Adams, an Old English Potter* by William Turner, a Mocha-ware mug is illustrated as belonging to the period 1787–1805 and described as follows: "Cream Ware—Mocha Mug, decorated in characteristic style with impressed diaper pattern around the rim —Height 6 in." The interesting feature of the mug is that both the tree silhouette design and the wave and loop pattern are found on the same article and thus we have a key to two patterns made at the same pottery, but we cannot be sure that all tree patterns and all wave and loop patterns were made by Adams. Adams did not mark this ware.

Lakin and Poole (1792–1796) made "mocha tumblers," and Leeds Pottery and many others who worked potteries about this time also undoubtedly made Mocha ware. However, it did not appear in America until later.

I have become addicted to looking up my favorite antiques in the old newspapers of the time, and much can be gleaned in this way about the pottery and chinaware imported into America from these early records. Especially is this true about Mocha ware. However, it often took several weeks of newspaper reading to discover even one advertisement relating to Mocha ware. The day I found an advertisement with not only a list of Mocha-ware articles but a maker's name as well I was as excited as a new father passing out cigars. The earliest mention of Mocha ware that I have found in American newspapers is in the *Boston Daily Advertiser* in 1815: "53 doz. Moco Bowls, 24 doz. check do, 23 doz. Painted do—B & G edged dishes. 21 Moco Mugs, 18 doz. Pitchers various patterns; gold neck Landscape, Hunting, Fluted gold Lions—Blue printed Turkish & Roman patterns."

In the same newspaper on January 19, 1816, Blake and Cunningham have the following notice: "C.C. Dishes, plates flat & soup Bowls, Moco Mugs, Salad bowls, chambers. Also an assortment of fine Blue printed ware. Hunting Jugs."

In the *New York Commercial Advertiser*, January 2, 1823, Wm. M. Shirley advertises: "10 crates new chequ'd or dipt bowls and jugs."

The most gratifying notice appears August 2, 1823, because it actually gives us the name of a maker of Mocha ware and associates the ware with other wares made at the same time.

Andrew Stevenson, 58 Broadway (Cobridge 1808–29)

> 50 crates edged plates, blue & green;
> 50 crated assorted painted tea ware;
> 100 crates C.C. ware assorted of every description;
> 100 hhds and crates blueprinted Tea and Table ware.
> 30 crates Mocho and col'd Pitchers and Bowls.
> 40 crates ass'd Willow Pattern plates Twiflers and Muffins.

For Sale by package from Liverpool. Manufacturers of goods they bring to market.

In the *New York Commercial Advertiser* for May 30, 1825, the following notice appears: "8 crates C.C. Chambers, filled with Mocho Bowls." And in the same newspaper on June 28: "Mocha and green banded Jugs and Mugs," and on August 13 the same firm, Fish and Grinnell, advertise: "Mocho, Marble, and Fancy Jugs, Mugs, Cups and Saucers, Bowls, Teapots, Sugar Boxes and Milk Jugs."

Mocha ware was still popular a few years later, for in the *New York Commercial Advertiser* for March 18, 1828, the following advertisement contains a reference to Mocha ware: "Earthenware—75 crates containing edged plates, dishes, tureens, painted chocolate mugs, handled cups and saucers, Moco Bowls, Mugs, Pitchers, Chambers etc." This Mocha ware was later sold for "measure ware" and used in inns, taverns, and hotels.

In the Boston Museum of Fine Arts is an agate bowl with a checkered molded border. It is labeled "Wedgwood." This design is similar to the marbled and mottled designs on Mocha ware and the border is impressed as those on Mocha ware, so it seems safe to call this piece Mocha and establish the fact that Mocha ware was made by Wedgwood. Undoubtedly the inspiration for many of the patterns, such as the marbled, came from Whieldon or Wedgwood, but I do not believe that any was actually made by Whieldon. The geometric patterns are also similar to the engine-lathe work used by Wedgwood on Egyptian Black ware. We know that jugs and mugs of creamware were turned on the lathe at Leeds and several of the molds for ornamenting Leeds Black Egyptian ware are identical with the molded designs on the borders and spouts of pitchers of Mocha ware. There are, however, no pieces with the Leeds mark. The mugs and jugs of checkered or other geometric patterns were turned on the lathe, the perfection of the design being too regular for handwork.

Various patterns of mocha or dipped ware were made at the Cambrian Pottery in Swansea between 1831 and 1850, and also at the South Wales Pottery at Llanelly.

Fragments of pieces dug up at the Cambrian Pottery include marbled designs with colored slips, mugs and jugs with lines and bands of color and impressed bands, a pattern with crude stars and wavy lines, and the seaweed pattern. The pieces are seldom marked, but jugs and mugs have been found with a raised crest with a crown and plumes and the word "Imperial" impressed. These were made in about 1834, according to E. Morton Nance in *The Pottery and Porcelain of Swansea and Nantgarw*.

Mocha, tortoise shell, and dipped ware was also made in various Scottish potteries. Common drinking cups, bowls, and mugs were made as early as 1823. The grounds were usually brown, green, or yellow decorated with ornamental rings.

Enoch Wood (1759–1840) made Mocha ware in about 1790. A barrel-shaped mug decorated with translucent green at the top and base and a diaper pattern stamped and colored brown and lines of gray is illustrated in Arthur Hayden's *Chats on Old English Earthenware*.

Types of decoration on Mocha ware include:

1. Tree pattern
2. Seaweed or dandelion pattern
3. Rope or wave and loop
4. Cat's-eye
5. Agate or marbled
6. Twigs
7. Checkered or other engine-turned geometric designs
8. Plain banded
9. Slip decoration of rings, dots, and wavy lines
10. Cream color with engine-turned bands

Often the same article has several types of decoration combined, such as tree and cat's-eye, or twig and cat's-eye, or tree and rope. Many pieces have a combination of impressed and painted horizontal bands as their only decoration.

Patterns were made on Mocha ware by the following process. The thrower or man at the potter's wheel first formed the vessel by hand, after which it was sent to the turner, who put it on the lathe and shaved the surface smooth, and often even gave it a pattern by engine turning; the white parts were thus tooled or turned out. The ground color or tint was then blown on the article from a bottle or atomizer by the turner, and while the surface was still wet, the piece was handed to an assistant, who placed it top downward and with a camel's-hair brush or feather or sponge, dipped into a prepared color solution composed of tobacco, turpentine, and acid, then touched the top of the moist zone so that the pigment flowed down and spread out in delicate mosslike tracery. This is the ingenious process that produced the curious arborescent effect and explains the seaweed and tree patterns. Some are set against a background of blue and pink tints that suggest the silhouette of trees against a winter sunset, and we wonder if the potter had some such impressionistic idea in mind. Rings of colored slip were trailed on from a vessel with a spout while the piece turned on the lathe.

TOP: Mocha urns, seaweed design, lion's head handles. Rope, agate, seaweed design mugs. CENTER: Seaweed and tree designs, black and molded bandings. BOTTOM: Pitchers and tavern mugs: dot and wavy lines, rope, and tree designs, colored bands, molded borders.

The dots and cat's-eye and rope or wave and loop designs were painted on in a different manner. The brush must have been charged with paint the consistency of heavy cream, for the surface of the patterns seems raised. As we said before, the plaid and checkered patterns are molded or engine-turned, while the various raised borders of herringbone, crescents, dots, guilloche, and horizontal lines are impressed, as are the foliaged decorations on spouts of pitchers and handles of teapots and pitchers.

The articles found in Mocha ware include large and small mugs, pitchers of various sizes, mustard pots, pepper pots, open salts, slop bowls, vases, teapots, covered sugar bowls, cups and saucers, mantel urns, chambers, double vases, and covered bowls.

One of the most interesting articles for the collector is the pepper pot, since it is more available than many of the others and is comparatively inexpensive. All types of patterns and characteristic decoration are found on pepper pots, including marbleized patterns and lathe-turned and impressed borders. Often the tree or moss silhouettes are especially fine, such as those on terra-cotta, blue, or dull-pink backgrounds. The shapes of pepper pots are equally as interesting as their design. They vary from large to small and from pear shape and cylinder shape to vase shape. The tops are flat or domed, with various patterns of pierced designs. One collector I know has several hundred pepper pots, all different. Pepper pots are usually footed, and the open salts which may be found to match are also footed.

Pitchers or jugs are also available for the collector. Although they are found in various sizes and shapes, the most common is the barrel shape. Many jug shapes are similar to those of Liverpool jugs, which were made at about the same time.

Perhaps the most popular article made in Mocha ware is the mug. Mugs are of various sizes, from the large heavy tavern size almost 9 inches in height to the small child's mug. Because of its size and area the mug affords the best opportunity for a study of the various designs. Handles are simple curves, but usually there is a foliation where the handle joins the body of the mug. Many mugs have engine-turned geometric designs.

The most refined articles of Mocha ware are the coffeepots or teapots, the cups and saucers—which are very rare—the covered sugar bowls, and the covered urns. These articles have molded detail on their handles and the finials of the teapot and the urn covers are molded flowers. Some Mocha urns have molded lions' heads as handles.

One of the most interesting features of Mocha ware is its color. Its subtle coloring appeals to the artist and to the sophisticated collector. Generally speaking, it is low in color intensity, the gray or drab tones such as buff, chocolate, terra cotta, and olive green predominating. These colors are given character by the use of contrasting black and white and strong intense blue and orange. Some of the colorings are as subtle as those of Japanese prints; others remind one of modern decoration in the use of buffs, browns, grays, and dull greens. Lavender-and-tan and pink-and-gray combinations are also beautiful—but rare. Perhaps the dull greens are the most beautiful, although the pieces with trees silhouetted against blue and rose washes on a tan ground have a special aesthetic value.

Since Mocha ware was made as recently as the early 20th century, the collector must be careful in his choice of pieces for his collection. If he does not have that rare ability of "feeling" the age of an antique, he must analyze each piece carefully before buying. Shapes indicate age. The more simple contours and the thinner weights are earlier than the heavy pieces. Subtle, fine coloring usually dates earlier than cruder colors and is also rarer. Pieces with refinements of decoration on the spouts and handles are a clue to better workmanship and to an earlier date.

Although Mocha was always a cottage or tavern ware and was usually made in such forms as jugs and mugs, some of the earlier pieces include teacups, covered urns, and coffee or teapots.

BIBLIOGRAPHY

"Mocha Ware," by Edwin Atlee Barber. *Old China*, vol. 2, January, 1903.
"Banded Cream Ware," by Robert J. Sim. *The Magazine Antiques*, August, 1945, pp. 82–83.
Collections of Miss Edith Blum and Mr. Edward Hewett.

Leeds Pottery

IN SPITE OF the popularity of Leeds ware and the aura that surrounds it, most people are unfamiliar with the great variety of types made by Leeds Pottery. To some, Leeds means blue or green shell- or featheredge ware with a flower painted under the glaze in characteristic blues, greens, and yellows; to others it means the Willow pattern; while to others Leeds means only the rare and expensive hand-painted pieces with names and dates. Indeed Leeds Pottery made all of these wares, and to tell the story of Leeds is to give a picture of the pottery industry in England from 1760 to 1820. The wares made at Leeds followed the styles and patterns of the pottery industry in general, and the factory made almost all of the wares currently popular. However Leeds Pottery pieces were better than average and their wares even rivaled some of Wedgwood's pottery. Leeds Pottery was also successful commercially and carried on a flourishing trade with America. Although the Leeds factory first established by the Green brothers may have made a more primitive pottery, the ware we know today as Leeds is a decorated creamware. It is thin and delicate in texture, with a heavy glaze which has a greenish cast. The variations in the different types of Leeds ware are in the decoration rather than in the pottery itself.

Although Leeds pottery does vary in weight and texture, some of the finest early pieces have sheen, are soft to the touch and creamy white in color, and have the exquisite shape of old Chinese pottery. The methods of decoration include painting, both under and overglaze; piercing; transfer printing; applied molded decoration; dipped decoration; and luster. The pieces with underglaze painting are heavier and darker in color, while those with the hand-painted names and dates have an eggshell texture and color. Leeds also made black basalt ware which did not have a soft paste base.

TOP: Leeds mug and teapot, molded design. CENTER: Green-and-white teapot with flower finial and braided handle. Plate with openwork and painted flower sprays. BOTTOM: Jug and teapot with painted designs.

The earliest type that we associate with the Leeds Pottery is that decorated with hand-painted oriental scenes and Chinese figures or primitive houses, in red, green, and black. Tea sets were painted with this sort of decoration up until 1800 or 1815. Sometimes a rose or some other flower is used together with an oriental figure.

The teapots, jugs, and loving cups with painted names, dates, and verses, together with flowers and feather or rococo scroll decoration, were made before and after 1775. This is the rarest and most expensive Leeds pottery. The name and date or verse are usually painted in front under the spout of the tea or coffeepot or jug and on the sides of the mugs and loving cups. The inscription is in black surrounded by a feather and scroll decoration in black and red and the flowers are in orange-red, lilac, yellow, and green. Sometimes a Chinese decoration is combined with the names and dates. One such coffeepot has the name "Ann Laws 1769" together with Chinese scenery, and another pot has a Chinese figure and a red rose and the inscription "William DWE 1774." These names, dates, and designs were put on at the order of the customer and usually celebrated a marriage or some other aniversary. The verses used were typical of the times and were the same as those used by Bristol, Liverpool, and other potteries at about the same dates.

Typical verses found on Leeds ware are:

> Let Virtue be one's Guide. I.B.
>
> Let love abide, Till death divide.
>
> When this you see remember me tho many miles we distant be.
>
> Beauty and riches will faid and fly away,
> But true love and virtue never will decay.
>
> Friendship without interest, Love without deceit.
>
> Love Unites Us.

Other verses have patriotic inscriptions such as "Britannia for Ever," and the farmer's jug has the inscription "God speed the Plough," while the drinker's mug has the familiar "One pott more and then." The religious inscription was also popular:

> Be present at our table Lord:
> Be here and everywhere adored,
> Thy creatures bless and grant that we
> May feast in Paradise with thee.

At a little later date Leeds Pottery made tea sets for the Dutch market with male and female portraits and an orange tree, or Dutch landscapes with the inscription "P.V.O.R."

Certain characteristics distinguish these Leeds pieces with inscriptions from those of other potteries and also serve as a means of identifying all of the early pieces of creamware made by Leeds Pottery. Identical shapes were made by other potters both in England and on the Continent, for the shapes were characteristic of the date, but Leeds Pottery can be identified by the blue-greenish color of the heavy glaze and by the typical beadwork border or beaded rim. The double twisted handle that ends in a molded flower and leaf where the handle is attached to the body is also characteristic, but the Leeds Pottery catalogue also shows several other types of handles, such as twisted-rope and hound handles. The molded rose knob is frequently found on Leeds Pottery teaware, but a plain round or teardrop knob was also used. The feather and scroll decoration in black and red is, however, typically Leeds, while the rococo scrolls and lacework borders are used by other potters as well. The large red or lilac rose alone or with tulips, fuchsias, and other flowers is another characteristic of the Leeds Pottery of this date. Leeds Pottery also made cups and saucers with blue and white chintz flowers painted under the glaze similar to those made by Caughley and Worcester. The cups were small and without handles.

Transfer printing as a means of decoration was also employed at an early date by Leeds Pottery. The transfer in black, red, or purple is the earliest, but multicolors in brilliant enamel are also found. The blue transfer came later. Early transfer patterns include the rare Exotic Birds printed by Sadler for Leeds Pottery. A similar transfer was also printed for Wedgwood. Other transfer patterns on Leeds pottery include a pastoral scene with shepherd and shepherdess and a garden tea-party scene, which was usually printed in black transfer but is also found in brilliant colors. The plates on this teaware have a featheredge and floral sprays almost identical with Wedgwood transfer pieces. Transfer prints also include a view of Kirkstall Abbey; a portrait of John Wesley; the Death of General Wolfe; a Masonic pattern; figures of Faith, Hope, and Charity; a ship; and a scene with mother and child.

Transfers were also made at a later date for the Dutch market. These often read, "For Liberty and Fatherland." In 1810 a Jubilee plate was made to celebrate the anniversary of George III. In 1820 Leeds Pottery made a plate for the coronation of George IV, which was decorated with a crown, a rose, a thistle, and a shamrock.

Blue transfer printing was made after 1790. The blue printed Willow pattern is the best known. Most pieces of Leeds Pottery Willow are marked. There are several variations in the design, but the darker print is the earlier.

The later light-blue or lilac print is inferior in body. Green, brown, and black was also used, and the Chinese Tower or Pagoda pattern was made about 1825. About 1820 children's plates and mugs were printed with maxims from Dr. Watts and Franklin, scripture subjects, and lines from Dillworth's book *Reading Made Easy*.

However, it was in the making of creamware with pierced designs and perforated borders that Leeds Pottery excelled all others, including Wedgwood. The openwork diamonds, hearts, ovals, and squares were hand punched. These lacelike piercings were especially fine in the large centerpieces, fruit baskets, chestnut bowls, cruets, and candelabra.

The pierced centerpieces are built up in three tiers of shells and baskets supported by dolphins, figures such as Pomona, Ceres, or Flora, and ornamental brackets. Chestnut bowls or tureens were set on stands and had ladles and a typical Leeds flower knob or finial.

Urns on pedestals are decorated with fluting and molded decoration in the form of human figures or goats' heads and drapery and swags of husks in the style of Adam. The finials were pineapple-shaped. Cruet stands holding pepper and other condiment castors with pierced tops sometimes had the names painted on in blue. Fruit baskets had pierced designs or basket-weave patterns and twisted or braided handles ending in a molded leaf or leaf and flower. Small leaf-shaped dishes and large covered melon-shaped dishes with flutings and molded leaf decorations are other well-known pieces of Leeds cream-colored ware. Another large piece was the cistern for water which was urn-shaped. Candlesticks were fluted columns on square bases; sometimes a Grecian figure serves as a column for a candlestick. Fluting, molded decorations, and perforations are found on candlesticks and more elaborate candelabra such as the vase candelabrum. Several types of vases for flowers (including the quintal flower horn vases) were also made. Inkstands, puzzle jugs, frog mugs, and figures were also made in creamware. The rare figures included Hygeia; Andromache; a boy with a dog; a market woman; Cupid; a lamb; a woman playing a guitar; a man with a tambourine; Wesley; Shakespeare; a warrior on a horse; and a fox-head stirrup cup. A small pottery house with crude painted decoration is

TOP: Leeds bowl, painted flowers; teapot, feather design. CENTER: Pitcher inscribed 1774; teapot with Tea Party transfer. BOTTOM: Pitcher, bird transfer; teapot, green and white with flower finial.

marked with the impressed "Leeds Pottery." And a creamware puzzle jug
has the mark "Leeds Pottery" and the impressed verse:

> Gentlemen come try your skill
> I'll Hould you sixpence if you will
> You cannot drink unless you spill.

Creamware dessert services included the elaborate centerpieces, fruit
baskets, and plates. Dinner services, a little thicker, had plates made with
Royal, Queens, shell, and feather edges. These plates were plain or with
perforated borders. The dinnerware was made plain but could be ordered
with crests and red lines on the edge or with laurel-wreath or other painted
borders. Cups and saucers are rare today, but were made in several shapes
both with and without twisted handles. Leaf-shaped dishes had molded
decoration and sometimes blue shell edges.

Teapots and coffeepots have plain or fluted bodies, plain or twisted
handles, a round or a flower knob, and a curved spout with embossed acanthus leaf. Some round teapots have a pierced border at the top. Creamware
with vertical stripes of green on the cream was early and was made by
Wedgwood as well as Leeds Pottery.

Around 1800 and later Leeds Pottery also made agate, tortoise-shell,
and Mocha ware. The pieces included mugs of several sizes, jugs, spill
vases, covered bowls and pepper pots, and mustard jars. They may also
have made tea sets. The characteristic beaded edge is found on these wares,
but handles and finials are usually plain and the pottery is heavy. At about
this same date, various types of lusterware was also made at Leeds. Goblets,
mugs, and jugs were the most common pieces. Some were made with hand-
painted names and dates. Luster borders enclosing transfer-printed classical
scenes were also popular. Silver, silver-resist patterns, gold, copper, and
purple luster were made from about 1790 to 1825. The early Leeds lusterware was made over a brown pottery surface, the later over a cream-
colored base.

Leeds Pottery also made black basalt ware from about 1780 to 1820.
Tea and coffee services, including cups and saucers, teapots, milk jugs, tea
canisters, coffeepots, slop and sugar basins, were made in a variety of patterns, with bas-reliefs of classic figures, the strawberry pattern, and
engine-turned geometric patterns. This ware varies from other Leeds ware
in shape and other characteristics. The handles are plain and the finials of
tea and coffeepots are of seated figures, swans, or a flower. The strawberry

pattern, which has heavy gadroon borders, imitates the shape and contour of silver services then popular, and was also made in silver luster. When marked, Leeds black basalt ware is impressed "Leeds Pottery" or "Hartley, Greens & Co, Leeds Pottery," usually under the spout or handle.

Although Leeds Pottery did a thriving business, much of the pottery sold as Leeds today is not Leeds. Few pieces are marked, and to judge an unmarked piece we must carefully check the weight, glaze, handles, finials, and general shape as well as the type of decoration. Blue and green shell- or featheredge creamware was made by all potteries, so it is incorrect to call it Leeds or even Leeds type, although of course some was also made by Leeds Pottery. It is also incorrect to call all old Mocha ware "Leeds," although some of the best was probably made at Leeds Pottery.

The best way to learn about Leeds Pottery is to seek out the marked pieces, of which there are still a few on the market, and study them. When Leeds is marked, it may have one of several markings, as follows:

Leeds Pottery.   HARTLEY GREEN & Cᵒ
                        LEEDS·POTTERY

Impressed marks   "Leeds Pottery"—scratched

The Swinton and Don Potteries were also owned by Leeds Pottery; and Ferrybridge, Hunsle Hall, Rothwell Pottery, Swansea, Castleford, and Wedgwood also made similar creamware. The Castleford catalogue in the Metropolitan Museum may be compared with that of Leeds Pottery if one has any doubt as to the similarity of the shapes and decoration. Castleford pottery made many pieces of creamware that are identical in design with those made at Leeds Pottery; and the familiar sectional teapot of sandy texture with lines of blue, which means Castleford to most people, was also made by Leeds. Indeed the Castleford pattern catalogue which was put out in 1796 has so many designs identical with the Leeds Pottery catalogue designs of 1783 that it would seem that the two factories might have had a connection. Some of the hand-painted work is also similar. The hand-painted blue or black scalloped lines, lacework, and sprigs of flowers may also be found on Bristol and Liverpool creamware of the same date. The title page of the Leeds Pottery catalogue of 1783 reads:

> Designs of Sundry Articles of Queen's or Cream colour'd Earthen-Ware manufactured by Hartley, Greens & Co: at Leeds Pottery with a great variety of other articles. The same Enamell'd, Printed or Ornamented with gold to any pattern; also with Coats of Arms, Cyphers, Landscapes, etc. etc.

BIBLIOGRAPHY

Historical Notices of Old Leeds Pottery, by Joseph R. & Frank Kidson. J. R. Kidson, Leeds, 1892.
Connoisseur, September, 1904, pp. 30–35; October, 1904, pp. 100–104; September, 1915, pp. 17–20; February, 1921, pp. 67–74.
Catalogue of Leeds Pottery, 1783, 1794.
Catalogue of Castleford Pottery, 1796.

Wedgwood Queensware and Its Imitators

QUEENSWARE, OR CREAMWARE, is a creamy white pottery which was made in the last half of the 18th and the early 19th century. It was a utilitarian ware made in complete dinner sets and is available today in its various forms either pierced and gilt, transfer printed, or hand painted. You may collect the fine old pierced or perforated pieces, the popular transfer historical-event Liverpool ware, or plates with hand-painted borders; a more modest collector may be interested in the jelly or blancmange molds. There are also many other variations in the decoration of creamware, including luster, which is made on a creamware base, and Mocha ware, but these are discussed elsewhere.

Queensware was so important to Wedgwood that in 1770 he published a catalogue illustrating his Queensware. This later went into several editions and was followed by a similar catalogue put out by Leeds Pottery in 1783 and by one from the Castleford Pottery in 1796. These catalogues were also printed in French, German, and Spanish for the various export markets. They contained illustrations of dinnerware, including plates, cups and saucers, coffeepots, jugs, salts, sugar bowls, fish trowels, casters, covered vegetable dishes, candlesticks, candelabra, and fancy dessert dishes; pierced fruit bowls and baskets, chestnut bowls and elaborate centerpieces of pierced work with pineapple centers. There were also spittoons, jelly molds, and other articles including crucifixes and holy-water fonts. The illustrations in the catalogues are either plain or with pierced decoration. There are embossed borders on plates and the finials of covers are molded in flower, fruit, or urn shapes. Plates are shown with Royal, shell, feather, or Queen's edges. Although no printed designs are shown, these shapes could all be had gilded, enameled, or marked with crests, according to order.

Of course there were various differences in the designs in the catalogues of each factory, and the collector will want to study them carefully.
However, all the factories followed Wedgwood leadership and tried to
match their pottery with Wedgwood wares.

Wedgwood did not invent creamware or Queensware, but the changes
which he made in the body and glaze about 1759 created a revolution in
the potters' trade and made earthenware popular for daily table use. Several
changes had already been made in the formula, and there was a gradual
transition from salt glaze to a creamy glaze or creamware, but, before
Wedgwood, creamware was still coarse, of uneven glaze, of a dirty yellow
color, and clumsy in shape. The story goes that Wedgwood gave a caudle
cup of this improved creamware to Queen Charlotte and she was so pleased
with it that in 1762 she ordered Wedgwood to make a set of dinnerware
in creamware, and because she objected to the raised barleycorn pattern,
the plates were made plain with only raised bands, or compartments, on
the edge and called Queen's Pattern. It was at this time that Wedgwood
changed the name of his creamware to Queensware. Several other factories
also used the name Queensware, and Queensware was the general name for
all creamware imported into America after 1771.

Creamware was first made in raised patterns of basket weave and in
pierced and perforated leaf and diamond and rice-grain designs similar to
those on the earlier salt glaze. Shellwork, fluting, and raised beaded borders
were also used. Wedgwood made some of the finest pierced creamware.
Edges and rims were embossed with ridges, lines, gadroon, and feather-
work. The more elaborate pieces such as pierced fruit baskets, centerpieces,
candelabra and candlesticks were fluted, scalloped, and decorated with
festoons and other raised decoration as well as pierced patterns. The pierced
creamware of Leeds is considered as fine as or finer than that of Wedgwood.
The perforations are made by hand and the hearts, diamonds, ovals, and
squares are more interesting than the perforations on Wedgwood's pieces,
but Wedgwood pieces usually have a finer shape and the glaze is creamy,
while Leeds has the characteristic greenish glaze. Leeds melon-shaped
dishes are especialy fine, as are the candlesticks, cruets, and chestnut dishes.

Although the catalogue of the Castleford Pottery illustrates shapes
similar to those of Wedgwood and Leeds, the products of the Castleford
Pottery were cruder in workmanship than those of either Wedgwood or
Leeds. When marked they are impressed "D.D. & Co. Castleford" or
"D.D. & Co" with "Castleford Pottery" impressed below.

Centerpieces, chestnut, and fruit bowls of pierced creamware are rare and expensive. Plates and pepper pots, however, are available and within the price range of the average collector.

In 1756, John Sadler of Liverpool applied transfer printing to Liverpool Delft tiles and other Liverpool ware, and by 1765 Wedgwood was sending his Queensware for Sadler to print. At first the designs were printed in black and were similar to the fable designs printed on tiles. Landscape scenes and ruins were also printed in black; the familiar tea-party scene in a garden was printed in red; and the pheasant designs were printed in purple and black. The borders were molded or impressed and often a flower border or a swag was painted by hand in addition to the transfer. By 1784 Wedgwood had his own transfers printed at Etruria, and by 1795 the designs were more realistic and lost much of the charm of the old designs.

Similar designs of transfer printing was also done by Sadler and Green for Leeds Pottery.

Adams also made transfer-printed creamware with openwork edges and perforations in about 1780. The mark is "Adams & Co" impressed.

Swansea creamware was printed in black, blue, green, or purple transfer designs. The earliest designs were of oriental inspiration, but later a series of transfer ship designs were made.

Richard Frank and Joseph Ring of Bristol employed a workman from Staffordshire to assist in the manufacture of creamware, and in the Bristol newspaper of 1786 an advertisement read: "Joseph Ring takes this opportunity to inform merchants and others that he has established a manufactory of Queen's and other earthenware which he will sell at low terms Wholesale and Retail as any of the best manufactories in Staffordshire can render same to Bristol."

Ring's son carried on the business with Henry Carter, and in 1802 an advertisement read: "Bristol Pottery, Temple Banks, Henry Carter, manufacturer of Blue Printed, Enamelled Table services. Blue, Green, and Coloured Edges, Painted and Cream coloured wares."

This factory employed 100 workmen and supplied foreign markets and made "table and Dessert service enamelled with Arms, Crests, and Cyphers." In 1813 the firm name was Carter, Ring & Pountney, and they made "painted, printed, enamelled and cream coloured earthenware." In 1821 they were making imitations of Etruscan ware, and from 1816 to about 1830, when the firm name was Pountney & Allies, William Fifield

TOP: Liverpool creamware with George Washington transfers. CENTERS AND BOTTOM: Wedgwood Queensware with black transfers.

was employed as a painter and painted creamware with floral designs and dates.

Queensware was also made in Liverpool in 1773 at Okill & Company and later the Etruscan decoration was used. From about 1783 through 1830, the popular black-transfer bowls, mugs, and jugs with American patriotic designs were made. These included portraits of Washington, Franklin, Jefferson, John Adams, John Hancock, and others, battle scenes of the War of 1812, the Death of General Wolfe, early sailing ships, political cartoons, and Masonic emblems. Transfer prints of the tea party, garden scene and jugs with Farmer's Arms are early. Transfers were also made with Liverpool views, Duke of York, and "Tar's Return." This ware is popular with present-day collectors, and for this reason it is more expensive than some of the earlier creamware.

Wedgwood Queensware was also painted to order with crests and other heraldic devices, together with borders of classic inspiration. However, as early as 1763 Queensware with hand-painted borders copied from Greek and Etruscan vases and reliefs, such as meander, dart and tongue, helix, and ivy, laurel, myrtle, vines, and other naturalistic designs, was available to the average purchaser. Designs for hand-painted borders included calico, purple flower, shagreen, sprig, green husk, purple laurel, Etruscan, and green fern leaf. In 1769 fifty dinner services of Queensware were sent to Amsterdam in one cargo. The *Pennsylvania Packet*, January 23, 1771, advertises "Queen's Ware—Feather edged oval dishes in sets." In the *Pennsylvania Chronicle*, September 26, 1772, a notice reads, "A large and general assortment of enamelled and plain Queen's Ware," and in the *Pennsylvania Evening Post* of July 11, 1776, the notice reads, "Enamelled, striped, fluted, pierced and plain Queen's Ware teapots, sugar dishes and bowls of several sizes, and plain, gilt, fluted and enamelled Queen's Ware coffee pots of the urn shape."

In 1774 the list of Wedgwood Queensware patterns included a printed bird pattern with feather edge, and the following hand-painted border patterns: oat, arrow, green flowers, green husks, strawberry leaf, black flowers, blue shell edge, ivy border with sprigs, purple arrowheads, purple antique, Etruscan red and black, Etruscan green and black, marine pattern with purple edge, calico pattern and sprigs, green double lines, brown double lines, laurel border, black antique music, Greek border, enameled shagreen, Queen's pattern, red birds, green feather edge and flower, purple flowers, and green oat-leaf border. Wedgwood made up pattern boxes of the plates which we assume had proved the most popular. In 1775 the box included purple or blue antique border, grape border, purple shell edge, green feather edge, purple flower, laurel border purple, and blue ivy pattern.

A pattern with trophies and music and a brown grape border was introduced in 1787, and the Dairy pattern with laurel-leaf border was also made then. Also listed in the books for 1787 were honeysuckle, red Etruscan, black and red spike, rose-color bell drops, red and black strawberry leaf with drop, double laurel, brown Etruscan, dotted border, green and shaded purple, brown edge inside brown husk, blue convolvulus with green leaves, brown drop, light-green bell drops, broad pea green and mauve, and brown lines. In 1789 the husk border and the vermicelli border were introduced, and in 1790 the red and black dotted border, green and black Etruscan, brown strawberry leaf, moss border, green oat, blue lines, green and purple grape, Royal pattern penciled, and landscapes were listed. After 1787 many of these patterns were printed and only filled in by hand. In about 1800 the cottage and naval patterns, both with autumnal leaf borders, were made.

Many variations of these patterns are also found, some made by Wedgwood, but many others by his imitators, for at the end of the 18th century there were about a hundred factories making creamware and most of them were copying Wedgwood's successful Queensware. Other well-known makers of creamware include Wilson, Adams, John Turner, Elijah Mayer, Warburton, Baddeley, Neale, Leeds Pottery, Castleford Pottery, and Cambrian Pottery at Swansea. Some of these factories copied the Wedgwood designs directly and others made variations, such as the Neale plate with the oak-leaf pattern, which is more interesting than the Wedgwood oak-and-acorn border. Swansea, however, copied many patterns direct and called their creamware Queensware from 1777. In weight, color, and style of decoration Swansea creamware resembled Wedgwood. The purple and green grape pattern imitated Wedgwood's green and purple grape border of 1790, and the black and red spike is also a Wedgwood pattern.

In 1774 Wedgwood made a creamware dinner set consisting of 952 pieces for Catherine II of Russia. It was painted with views of British country seats, ruins, gardens, and landscapes and had oak-leaf and acorn borders. A great many artists were employed to paint the scenes and borders, and the list includes not only men and women who were in the regular employ of the Wedgwood factory but outside artists as well.

TOP: Plates, painted in underglaze blue. CENTER: Teapot, black, painted. BOTTOM: Cream-ware plates, painted borders. Small plate, transfer. All Swansea pottery.

Mr. Stringer was in charge of painting the views and was assisted by Ralph Unwin, Mrs. Wilcox, and James Blakewell. Samuel Armstrong painted the lined edges. Nathaniel Cooper painted the frogs and also worked on borders. Joseph Linley, Mr. Wilcox, William Mence, Thomas Mills, Miss Glisson, Miss Pars, Catherine Dent, Ann Mills, Grace Roberts, and Ann Roberts are listed as border painters. John Englefield, Joseph Barret, William Quirk, Sam Armstrong, William Henshaw, Nat Wallace, William Thomas, John Roberts, George Simons, George Seigmund, Thomas Simcock, and Thomas Hutchins are listed as painters. The list is interesting because it probably included Wedgwood's best painters, but the number which he employed at this time must have been much greater because he was also making ware with hand-painted borders for the general public, and hand painting was used not only for dinnerware but also for such common articles as jelly molds, which were made in the form of corn, fir cones, roses, thistles, and shells and pyramids.

A great deal of Wedgwood Queensware is marked, but often many pieces in a dinner set are not marked. Leeds, Castleford, and Swansea Queensware are seldom marked, and few markings appear on creamware from other English factories.

Leeds made dinnerware with hand-painted crests and simple beadwork borders. Hand-painted scenes are sometimes set in round or oval medallions and surrounded by beadwork borders in black or brown with the flower finials painted to match. Crests were also painted within a circle of laurel and with red line borders. Wheat borders and other patterns similar to Wedgwood were made at Leeds. Leeds also made a type of creamware which is decorated with hand-painted flowers and names, dates, verses, and inscriptions. This is the Leeds pottery most sought after and the rarest. Most of it was made between about 1775 and 1800, although some pieces have been found with both earlier and later dates. Mugs, jugs, and teapots were the pieces usually decorated in this manner and they were made to order as presentation pieces. The decoration besides the date or verse consisted of red and black feather decoration or a large red or lilac rose alone or together with other flowers, the usual colors being red, yellow, and green, together with black lettering within a framework of rococo scrolls in black. Other features are the characteristic beaded work at the top of the rims and the double twisted handle ending in a raised flower or leaf and the rose knob on the teaware. Sometimes just the initials or name and date appear, such as on the rose-decorated mug labeled "Hugh Hughes 1775";

and again a verse is added, as on the teapot which reads "Mary Martin 1776. Let Virtue be one's Guide I.B."; or the rose-decorated jug with the lacelike border which reads "T.N. 1784. Let Love Abide, Till death divide." A popular mug reads "One pott more and then."

The perforated puzzle jug with or without inscription was also popular, as was the farmer's jug or teapot, which often had a painting of a plow and the inscription, "God Speed the Plough." These dated and inscribed pieces are the most sought-after type of Leeds creamware, and thus the rarest and most expensive on the market. Similar pieces with rose decoration, but without the inscription, and hand-painted oriental patterns with Chinese figures were also made at Leeds up until about 1810, and similar jugs and mugs were made at several Staffordshire potteries.

A simple cottage type of Leeds with feather edge and a hand-painted aster or a basket of flowers in the center has endeared itself to the present-day American collector. These are painted in green, orange, and yellow and date from about 1800 to 1830. Festoons in green and orange are also hand painted and a coarser teaware was later decorated in underglaze blue flowers, rustic figures, and cottages.

Featheredge plates with underglaze flower painting were also made at Swansea, and plates marked "Rogers" impressed with an aster painted in blue, yellow, green, and pink were made in about 1830.

The value of a collection of Queensware or creamware is to be judged according to the type collected. That with pierced designs should be chosen for the beauty of shape of the individual piece and for the design of the pierced perforations.

If a piece is marked Wedgwood, or Leeds Pottery, or D.D. & Co. Castleford, its value is increased a hundredfold. Creamware with transfer designs is especially valuable if the work was done by Sadler at Liverpool.

Creamware with hand-painted borders or medallions is valued according to the fineness of the painting. Although Wedgwood employed good painters, the work was often hastily done and by comparison with the excellent workmanship on his Russian service we see what really fine painting of this type should be. However, the borders are often in delicate brushwork and the execution of each stroke is refined and clean. The painting, although freehand, follows a set pattern so that we do not have the naïve spontaneous brushwork of inscribed and dated pieces or the finer spontaneity of brushwork found on old English Delft.

Creamware continued in great demand until 1825 or 1830, when many of the patterns first introduced as hand painted were then printed and filled in by hand. The same patterns continued to be made, even down to the present day, so that one cannot judge age from the pattern or design but must consider the texture and actual painting of each individual piece.

So far, the Queensware or creamware with the hand-painted borders has not found much favor with collectors. There is, however, enough of it on the market to make collecting interesting. The prices are right, but much of it is in poor condition.

BIBLIOGRAPHY

Historical Notices of Old Leeds Pottery, by Joseph R. Kidson and Frank Kidson. J. R. Kidson, Leeds, 1892.
Old Bristol Potteries, by W. J. Pountney. J. W. Arrowsmith, Ltd., London.
Handbook of Wedgwood Ware, by Eliza Meteyard. George Bell & Sons, Ltd., London, 1875.
Catalogue of Leeds Pottery, 1794.
Catalogue of Castleford Pottery, 1796.
Liverpool Transfer Designs on Anglo-American Pottery, by Robert H. McCauley. Southworth Anthoensen Press, Portland, Maine, 1942.
The Imperial Russian Dinner Service, by George Charles Williamson. George Bell & Sons, Ltd., London, 1909.

4

Some Popular 19th-Century Pottery

FLOWING BLUE

YOU CAN PICK up odd pieces of Flowing Blue in almost any antique shop, but it takes some patience to assemble a tea set. However, once you get a few pieces together you will feel the charm and you'll be off on a new hobby. Flowing Blue (also called Flow or Flown) china is available and within the price range of the average collector's purse. Perhaps Flowing Blue, because of the similarity of its patterns, is not so interesting to collect as some other kinds of china, but it is decorative for the dining table and with patient search it is possible to assemble a complete dinner service.

Flowing Blue is a stone china decorated with oriental patterns. It was first made in Staffordshire from about 1825, while the old blue china with historical scenes was still being made and before light-toned scenic china became popular. The stone china base of Flowing Blue distinguished it from the softer pottery base of old blue or light-toned scenic china. Flowing color is produced by action of volatile chlorides upon ceramic colors. The designs are applied to the china surface with ceramic colors, and in the kiln they are exposed to a chloridated atmosphere. The vapor causes the color to spread and blur. The value of the piece is determined by the depth of color and the way the color spreads. Sometimes the pattern is too blurred to be attractive. Although Flowing Blue is the popular and most pleasing color, many of the same patterns were also made in Flowing Brown and Flowing Purple. Cobalt oxide is used for blue, and nickel oxide for brown. The china base for flowing color was stone, usually ironstone, and thus pieces are often marked "Pearl Stone" or "Stone China" or something similar, in addition to the name of the pattern and the maker.

The design motifs of the various Flowing Blue patterns are of oriental inspiration. The majority of the patterns include a temple, a bridge, and a tree. The tree may be a bamboo, a willow, or a flowering tree. Often a boat is included. The motifs are assembled and arranged differently by each designer, and thus the patterns of the various manufacturers vary although they include similar motifs. Also, although the motifs are oriental, the interpretation is Western in spirit and the border is often definitely English in motif as well as feeling. This difference is readily seen by comparing a piece of Flowing Blue with a piece of English Willow ware which is decidedly oriental in feeling.

Many of the well-known potteries made Flowing Blue. William Turner in his book *William Adams, an Old English Potter*, says, "The flown blue ware of Adams had the reputation of being the best in the trade." Kyber and Tonquin are two patterns in Adams Flowing Blue. The name of the pattern is usually printed on the back of the article and "Adams" is impressed in the ware. Davenport also made excellent Flowing Blue and Brown. The color is dark and the printing good. It is marked with the impressed anchor and "Davenport" impressed. Cypress is a brown Davenport pattern and Amoy is made in Flowing Blue.

E. and J. Mayer of Longport also made fine Flowing Blue, which was imported into America in 1830. Patterns by Mayer include Arabesque, Oregon, and Formosa. The color of Mayer Flowing Blue is strong and clear, the patterns are attractive, and the dark and light well distributed. Fine scroll borders enclose the patterns and the pieces are marked with both the name of the maker and the pattern name.

The best-known Flowing Blue patterns made by Wedgwood are Knight Templar and Chapoo. Chapoo resembles other Flowing Blue designs, the pattern including a temple, a boat and trees, but the trees are flowering in contrast to the palm tree in Adams's Kyber and the bamboo trees in Mayer's Formosa. Chapoo also has a flower border.

Ridgway made several patterns in Flowing Blue, including Oriental and Temple. These are marked with the name of the pattern printed and "Stoneware J.R." or "J.W.R." Ridgway worked between 1814 and 1830.

A pattern called Scinde was made both by J. and J. Alcock and by T. Walker. It is a typical pattern of chinoiserie.

Podmore, Walker & Company also made Flowing Blue. Their best-known designs are Manila, Temple, and Corean. The pieces are marked

"P.W. & Co." and sometimes "Pearl Stone Ware." This firm worked between 1842 and 1862.

Other well-known makers of Flowing Blue were E. Challinor & Company of Fenton, who worked after 1850. They made the patterns Pellew and Kin Shaw. These are marked "E. C. & Co." or "E. Challinor." Babcock made the pattern Chen-Si, and Dixon Phillips manufactured Nonparel in brown. The pattern Troy is marked "C. M.," which may be for the potter Charles Meigh. Barlow was another well-known maker of Flowing Blue.

A group of patterns in Flowing Blue are of Gothic inspiration. These patterns include ruins of old English Gothic buildings and English gardens instead of the usual oriental motifs, and have a graceful border of grapes and grape leaves. Aside from this they are similar to the other patterns of Flowing Blue. The patterns with Gothic motifs are Gothic, Rhine, Rhone, and Coburg, and were made by "J.F. & Co." Rhine is marked "Rhine, Kao-in Ware, J. F. & Co."

Several patterns of Flowing Blue were made by Dillwyn at Swansea in 1838 or later. These include a light-blue print with Chinese scenery—water, rocks, pagodas, sailing boats, a willow tree, and trellis steps. The pattern is called Whampoa and is marked with the name "Dillwyn" impressed over "Swansea," the printed mark "Improved Stoneware, Dillwyn & Co." and a rococo scroll with the name "Whampoa" above. A bold conventional pattern of flowers, foliage, and interlacing stems was also made in Flowing Blue. There is a beaded border, and the plates have a waved edge. Pieces are marked "D" (impressed) and ☉ which is the transferer's mark.

From the list of the many potteries which made Flowing Blue it would seem that Flowing Blue was a popular ware and a great amount of it must have been made. Also the fact that Flowing Blue and Flowing Brown have been found advertised together indicates that the brown, which has always been considered to be of later date, was made at the same time as the blue although it was never so popular even though many of the same patterns were available.

Flowing Blue was popular in 19th-century America, as evidenced by the following advertisement from the *New York Commercial Advertiser*, November 2, 1844: "Flowing Blue toilet sets, also Dining sets of the Flowing Blue."

A late pattern of Flowing Blue, which has no relation to the old Flowing Blue except that it was made by the same process, is called Morning Glory. It is a simple naturalistic floral pattern and does not have the oriental feeling or the depth of color of the older patterns. It is marked "Lancaster."

Flowing Blue was also made in Holland about 1850. This ware is marked "Maastricht China" or "Repout & Co. Maastricht Holland." The patterns are Siam, Timur, and Petrus. There is also a decorative blue flower and leaf pattern similar to the designs on earlier hand-painted earthenware.

FREEHAND-PAINTED EARTHENWARE

I bought my first jug of freehand-painted earthenware in a little cottage on the Gaspé Peninsula years ago. It had the name of the owner's grandmother and the date 1820 and it was painted with splashy pink asters and green leaves. Of course, the day has passed when you can pick up such "finds" and if you do see a dated piece today it will be expensive. Usually only experienced collectors and those with plenty of money go in for such pieces today, but there are still plenty of simple freehand-painted plates and pitchers to be found.

Bold freehand-painted designs of conventional flowers and leaves were painted on 19th-century English earthenware made for the African and North and South American trade as well as for English consumption. The colors most often found on this "gaudyware" are red and green, or blue and yellow, but designs painted in pink and green and blue and purple are also found. The best-known design is now called Adams Rose. The flowers and leaves are usually painted in red and green and the design is found on tea and coffee sets, platters, plates, cup plates, vegetable dishes, and even washbasins and pitchers. The pieces are usually marked "Adams" impressed and were made between 1804 and 1860. Similar patterns were made by Davenport and are found marked "Davenport" impressed, with an impressed anchor or an impressed six-petal flower. A Davenport floral design in blue, yellow, and green was also made in about 1800 or at least before 1830.

Freehand-painted pottery marked "Wood" impressed, or "E. Wood & Sons, Burslem," was also made between 1820 and 1846. This ware was also made by many other English potteries, but the majority of the pieces are unmarked, so that the quality must be judged by the color, design, and shape of the individual piece.

Much of the earliest and finest freehand-painted earthenware is marked with a name and a date. This is true of jugs especially, and such jugs were made at Leeds with festoons and floral designs in green, orange, yellow, blue, and brown. Freehand-painted plates and platters had floral designs in the centers and feather edges of blue or green.

The Cambrian Pottery at Swansea made freehand-painted pottery between 1824 and 1831. Swiftly painted designs of flowers, birds, animals, and cottages were used together with a feather edge of blue or green or embossed shell and acanthus borders. The painting is similar in design to that on lusterware made at the same time and was probably painted and decorated by the same workmen.

In the *New York Commercial Advertiser*, April 25, 1831, Fish, Grinell & Company advertised "100 crates of well assorted painted and edged Ware." Few pieces of this freehand-painted ware were marked, but it was undoubtedly made by all the well-known potters of the period.

VICTORIAN MAJOLICA

One of the popular wares on the present-day market is the majolica made in England and America from about 1850 to the end of the century. Its naturalistic plant and animal motifs molded in relief and splashed with bold color and glaze are especially attractive for informal dining-table use, but figures and small decorative articles were also made in Victorian majolica. There is a great deal of this ware on the market and the prices are comparatively reasonable.

Majolica ware derived its name from the lusterware made on the island of Majorca. The term was later applied to the glazed and enameled wares of Italy, which were also made in the 18th century by Wedgwood and Whieldon and finally imitated and cheapened by European and American potters of the 19th century. Majolica ware is decorated by applying colors mixed with the glaze by means of a brush or dipping. Victorian majolica was influenced by the design of the old Cauliflower and Pineapple wares of Whieldon, Wedgwood, and other 18th-century potters. In fact such patterns as Cauliflower, which has a molded surface pattern, were definitely reproduced by English and American potters as well as other raised fruit, vegetable, leaf, and berry patterns, with green and yellow, pink, brown, and light blue and purple-blue. A teapot of yellow corn and green leaves is especially pleasing in design and similar to the old Whieldon Pineapple teapots.

TOP: Freehand-painted; teapot, King's Rose. CENTER: Freehand-painted Etruscan majolica, seaweed design. BOTTOM LEFT: Plate, Leeds; Pitchers, Adams. RIGHT: Flowing Blue platter, "Gothic"; PLATES, LEFT TO RIGHT: "Coberg," "Rhone," "Rhine."

Many late 19th-century majolica designs followed rustic patterns with backgrounds of basketry and wooden-bound buckets decorated with molded flowers, birds, fish, and even squirrels. Handles were of rustic tree branches or rosebush stems or even flowers or leaves twined together, and sometimes jugs and coffeepots and teapots had covers of hard metal similar to Britannia metal. The wild rose was a popular pattern. Another design was of lily pads and herons, and the begonia leaf plate was also popular. Other patterns included shells, coral, seaweed, corn and bamboo stalks, and certain oriental motifs together with borders of basketry. Especially delicate in motif and coloring is the teapot, pitcher, and sugar bowl of pink coral and green seaweed with accents of brown and blue which is marked "Etruscan Majolica."

Cabbage leaves, strawberries and leaves, fern leaves, and sprays of flowers were also molded on the surface of plates, jugs, teapots, and other articles. Some green plates with leaves and strawberries are marked "Herculaneum." These were not made later than 1841 and are similar to Wedgwood green glaze. In 1850 Minton added the manufacture of majolica to their other art productions and produced useful and ornamental objects, including tiles with designs of naturalistic tulips, violets, hawthorne, bramble, and other flowers in high relief and rich coloring. They also made plates with vine leaves and grapes. Wedgwood "embossed leafage dessert plates and green glazed" continued to be made, and their raised-leaf designs served as inspiration to other potters.

The Trent Pottery, George Jones and Sons, made majolica cupids, shells, dolphins, and coral designs in numerous shapes. Their mark was a monogram of the initials "G.J." joined together. A beehive bread dish with a cover has a design of wild roses against a background of basketwork and has the Trent Pottery mark. Also flowerpots were made in bright colors and with raised designs of natural flowers. T. Furnival & Sons made jugs and plates with raised oriental designs, which had borders of wickerwork in bold color and glaze. Their mark, "Furnival," is impressed in the ware. Majolica was also made by Edward Steele at Hanley, who manufactured both useful and ornamental jugs, flower vases, teapots, dessert services, and centerpieces with fine coloring. Another factory at Hanley in the 1870s was owned by Edward Banks & Thomas Thorley. In majolica they manufactured bread trays, cheese stands, jugs, dessert services, trays, teapots, egg holders, flowerpots, etc. One of their dessert services has a chocolate-colored ground and a raised naturalistic design of ivy, ferns, and anemones.

This has an embossed "key" border. A jug with a chocolate-colored ground has panels of rope enclosing green thistle leaves. This firm also made green dessert plates with raised leaves. The ware is not marked.

Davenport & Banks or Davenport Beck & Company also made all varieties of majolica. The mark used was a castle and the letters "D.B. & Co. Etruria" within an oval garter bearing "Trade Mark."

Other marked majolica includes that of Joseph Holdcroft, Longton, 1870. A Wren Vase with well-modeled birds and flowers is from this pottery and is marked with an impressed monogram in a circle.

Rustic patterned majolica was made by Poole & Unwin and impressed with their initials in a diamond.

Daniel Sutherland & Sons made majolica from 1863. They made a variety of vases; jugs; flowerpots; boxes for cheese, butter, and sardines; bread, cheese, and fruit dishes; tea- and coffeepots; candlesticks; and other articles. Some are marked "S & S."

Majolica made by James Woodward was marked with an anchor and cable forming the initials J.W. John Adams & Co. of Hanley made majolica in 1873. Articles included bread trays, cheese trays, candlesticks, flowerpots, figures, and vases, and the designs included wheat, ferns, and cattails. The marks were "Adams & Co.," "Adams & Bromley," or "A & B."

There were many other English makers of majolica who had no mark. Majolica was also made by several American firms, the best-known of which is Griffin, Smith & Hill of Phoenixville, Pennsylvania, who are known for their Etruscan majolica made from 1880 to 1890. Many pieces were modeled by the Englishman Bourne. These include compotes with dolphin supports and flower, shell, or jewel cups. A design of coral weed and sea shells is one of the most attractive patterns, and tableware was made in designs of leaves and ferns. The mark was an impressed monogram, "G.S.H.," sometimes circled with a band containing the words "Etruscan Majolica" or "Etruscan Majolica" impressed in a horizontal line.

Majolica was also made by Odell & Booth at Tarrytown, New York, and at Greenpoint, Long Island, by the Faïence Manufacturing Company. The mark is an incised "F.M. Co." This pottery was dipped in colored glazes, and the effect was streaked or marbled. Majolica was also made for a time at Evansville, Indiana. Majolica made at the Chesapeake Pottery in Baltimore was called Clifton Ware and was marked "Clifton Decor 'B' " together with the monogram "D.F.H." enclosed in crossed crescents.

As late as 1901 the Arsenal Pottery of Trenton, New Jersey, was making majolica ware and exhibited Toby jugs in imitation of English Tobies at the Chicago Fair. Majolica in many of the old patterns has been reproduced; however, some of the old patterns are still being made on original molds by such factories as Wedgwood.

Without markings, there are no definite rules by which you can distinguish the old majolica from that recently manufactured unless you have that extra sense of feel and touch that tells you that something is old.

From the artistic standpoint much Victorian majolica is harsh in color and poor in design, but such pieces as the green leaf and berry plates, the begonia-leaf condiment dishes, and the delicate coral and seaweed sugar bowl, teapot, and creamer are pleasing in both color and design.

BIBLIOGRAPHY

Ceramic Art of Great Britain, vol. 2, by Llewellynn Jewitt. Virtue & Co., Ltd., London, 1878.

CHAPTER

Children's Mugs

CHILDREN'S MUGS of the 19th century are interesting to present-day collectors. There are many types of mugs, from those with cheap transfer prints and rhymes and jingles, which are collected as a relic of a passing day rather than for any beauty they may possess, to the fine early decorated creamware mugs of Leeds, Bristol, and Liverpool, as well as a variety in lusterware. The subject matter ranges from early scenes to those of the Kate Greenaway period. Of the twelve hundred mugs in the collection of Margaret H. Jewell, which is on display at the Harrison Gray Otis House in Boston, there is hardly a duplicate and there are enough mugs of each type to make the study of the subject complete.

Among the earliest types of children's mugs are the creamware mugs decorated with bands of blue, brown, tan, or olive green together with a name and inscription. Some of them have hand-painted wreaths of light olive-green leaves. On one mug the inscription reads "A Trifle from Yarmouth," and for this reason these mugs have been listed as "Yarmouth type," although, since there was no pottery works in Yarmouth, they were probably made elsewhere. There was, however, a potter at Yarmouth named Absolon who painted creamware made elsewhere and burnt it in his ovens. Since he also painted and sold Bristol glass around 1800, it is likely that he also bought creamware at Bristol to decorate and that the "Yarmouth type" mugs are Bristol pottery. Other inscriptions include "A Gift for Jinny," "A Gift for William," "A Present for Nancy," "A Present for Sarah," and "For My Sweet Girl." These mugs are rare.

Another type of early child's mug was made of canary-color creamware and decorated with a transfer of black or dull orange-red. Some of them have an oak wreath or a garland of roses and an inscription such as

"A Trifle for James"; others have a star enclosing an initial. Still others have a quaint transfer scene such as cows grazing, a Chinese figure, or a scene with mother and children, or a man, boy, and house, and the inscription "For a Good Child." Another group of these early transfers on canary grounds has such inscriptions as "A Carriage for Ann," "A Squirrel for Mary," "A Pony for Edward," "A Harp for Elizabeth," "A New Doll for Margaret," and "A Nightingale for Eliza," together with appropriate and quaint transfer pictures of the animal or object mentioned. Another canary mug has a black transfer with the inscription "Come dear child and let me see how you can do ABC." It has an ABC border around it and is undoubtedly one of the first types of ABC mugs made. Another type of rare and early child's mug was decorated in silver resist on a canary ground. The designs included a bird on a branch, allover geometric patterns, and borders of leaves, scrolls, and bands, in silver resist. One group has bands and a wreath of silver resist on a cream ground and an inscription such as "A Present for Mary," also in silver luster. Classical scenes of mothers and children in red, brown, or black transfer on a canary ground with bands of silver luster form another type. The miniature mugs of silver resist on cream and canary ground are especially rare and attractive. One rare canary creamware mug reads, "To taber and pipe my figures dance Through England, Ireland, Scotland and France." Another group of canary mugs has hand-painted conventional flower borders in greens, pinks, and orange.

Transfer portraits in black upon cream and canary grounds form another small group of mugs. The rarest is the Washington and Lafayette, which was made in about 1824–1825. It is black transfer on a canary ground. The portrait of Adams is also in black transfer on yellow. One rare mug in canary has a transfer in black of an eagle and a laurel wreath. It is attributed to the potter Adams.

The mugs with black transfers and pink luster, or pink-luster decoration alone, seem to be a little later. Besides transfers of scenes of mother and child with pink-luster bands, there were mugs with hand-decorated floral bands in color, and mugs with names and wreaths in black together with pink-luster bands, and mugs with the pink-luster house pattern made in Sunderland. A Sunderland pink-luster mug has the inscription "Forget and Forgive" in a wreath with luster bands. A scene in black transfer of a girl, two men and a dog at a well, and one of "The Gleaners" have pink-luster bands and are marked "Davenport."

There is also a large group of mugs in copper luster. Some of these have transfer patterns and inscriptions, and others have typical copper-luster patterns including colored blue, cream, or tan bands, sanded bands, and flowers in relief, or flowers painted in aster and leaf, and other patterns. There are also mugs with six different patterns of Gaudy Welch pottery with luster. These are of ironstone pottery and date about 1840 or 1850.

An interesting creamware mug marked "Phillips & Co. Sunderland Pottery" has a ship and a garland in black transfer and the following verse:

> Here's to the wind that blows
> And the ship that goes
> And the boy that fears no danger
> A ship in full sail
> And a fine pleasant gale
> And a girl that loves a sailor.

Another group of creamware mugs, made before 1840, have a black transfer laurel wreath of the type used by Enoch Wood and the inscription "A present for Mary," for example, or "A Present for my dear boy." Simple creamware mugs of an early type have the names of children painted in black and a hand-painted band. The names include Maria, Cynthia, Isabella, Anne, Sarah, Martha, Margaret, Frances, Eliza, Ellen, Emma, Sophia, Kate, James, John, Charles, Philip, George, and William. The Union of Odd Fellows mug with a shield and the figures of Justice and Truth printed in brown and red is probably early 19th century.

Another group of creamware mugs were hand decorated with sprays of flowers and borders. One of the earliest of these has bunches of roses and yellow flowers with black foliage and a brown painted band at top and bottom. It is marked "Bristol" on the bottom. A creamware mug with a hand-painted green line and the initial K was made at Leeds or Bristol, and a mug with green and orange flowers is probably Leeds pottery. There is also a group of tiny toy mugs with sprigs of flowers of the same type, but they are heavier than Leeds or Bristol and are probably later Staffordshire. One early creamware mug has a black transfer of a bird's nest and children and is probably Liverpool. The various patterns of Mocha ware including checkered designs, seaweed, rope, and cat's-eye patterns, as well as those with simple bands of color, were made in small children's-size mugs.

Blue-and-white pottery mugs with names and inscriptions form another group of children's mugs. Some of these have blue and white bands and a simple medallion with such inscriptions as "A Present for Sarah" or

TOP: Alphabet plate, Franklin transfer. BOTTOM: Transfer center, Daisy border.

the more unusual "A Trifle shews Respect." Some have a blue-and-white
scene covering the body of the mug, and then there are some mugs with
the same type of blue-and-white scenes without inscriptions. The blue varies
in tone from light to dark, and some mugs are printed in a rich dark blue.
One of the most interesting mugs is a little toy mug with a stippled border
and the old English potter's rhyme:

> No Handycraft can with
> Our art compare
> We make our pots of
> What we are.

Another toy mug worth special mention because of its rarity is the souvenir
mug of the New York fire, with the inscription printed in black:

> Conflagration
> City of New York
> 16th Decr. 1835
> 700 houses burnt
> Amount Property destroyed 25,000,000 Dollars
> Did not affect Public Credit

There are many other toy mugs showing the various activities of children:
playing with hoops, fishing, skipping rope, and playing various games.
There are also toy mugs painted with flowers, as well as those already mentioned with canary glaze and figures and designs in black and red transfer.

The later type of mugs which are most available today had rhymes
and scenes from children's poems, including Dr. Watts's *Poems for Children*, and verses by Jane and Ann Taylor. The scenes were taken from
such books as *The Boys' Treasury of Sports and Pastimes*, which provided
the subjects of the game series, and the "Peacock at Home." Franklin's
maxims from *Poor Richard's Almanack* provided the subject matter for
another series. The Franklin maxim mugs are among those most sought
after today because of their subject matter, although from the costumes in
the pictures they are earlier than other mugs of this later illustrative type.
These Franklin mugs were made by several different factories and the
designs vary as well as the shape of the mugs. Most of them are of a heavy
ironstone, but two are of creamware with a pink-luster band. None of
them are marked, but we know that plates with Franklin maxims were
made at Leeds in 1820 and later by Clews, Meakin, and various other manufacturers. Usually there are two maxims on each mug, but sometimes there
are four. One of the maxims most available on mugs is "Keep thy shop and

thy shop will keep Thee." The earliest scene illustrating this maxim shows a shop with the name "Donothing" and a "To Let" sign.

An early group of mugs with inscriptions is the series called "Flowers that Never Fade" which includes mugs marked Charity, Kindness, Industry, Liberty, Good Humour, Usefulness, and Generosity. Moral maxims such as "Idleness is the Parent of Want and of Misery," "Industry is Fortunes Handmaid," "Never Speak to deceive, nor listen to betray," and "Want of Punctuality is Lying" have a design around the words and a "Holy Bible" on a tasseled cushion at the top. Other religious verses of four to six lines titled "Praise to God," "Evening Song," "Morning Song," and "Early Piety" are enclosed in wreaths of flowers. Some of these have a line of luster.

Another group of mugs is the Reward of Merit series. These have a variety of labels, including: "A Present for Knitting Well," "For Attention to Learning," "Present for Sewing Well," "Present for Going to School," "Present for Writing Well." There is a miniature or toy plate with the inscription "A prize for Sewing Well" and a scene in brown transfer.

One of the prettiest mug series is the Months. Each month has a verse of four lines. The January verse is:

> How the rolling seasons Vary
> Through the years from January
> When the Infant Smile Awakes
> On New Year's gifts and sugared cakes.

There is also a series of months marked "The Seasons," but they are of a later date.

There are several series of mugs with boys playing games. The earliest series includes "Ring Taw," "Whip Top," "Pyramid," "Walk My Lady Walk," "Shuttlecock," "Northern Spell," and "French and English." Later games on mugs included blindman's buff, leap frog, and marbles. These were printed in black, brown, red, or blue with crude splashes of red, yellow, and green daubed on. There is also a series of mugs with children and animals such as "Puss' Breakfast," "Little Playfellow" (dog), "Beggar's Petition" (dog), "Billy Button" (horse), and "Bird Catchers." Another series is entitled "Grandma's Tales." There are mugs with Tam o'shanter, John Gilpin, and several types of alphabet mugs, even the deaf-and-dumb symbols. Most of them have large letters and a picture, and some have a verse with the letter. Of the latter there are at least two series, for one says:

E. was an eagle chained to his perch
F. stands for Fanny returning from church.

and another says:

E. was an Emperor who ruled in fear
F. was a fiddler who fiddled for beer.

There is also a group of mugs with animals including elephants, tigers, goats, dogs, and all sorts of birds. The lion with a palm tree printed in blue is marked "Davenport," and there is a Davenport mug with a zebra, so we assume that Davenport made an animal series. Another series of animals is printed in brown with splashes of green, red, and yellow paint and is marked "Field Sports E. M. & Co." Other animals are shown on the late mugs labeled "New York," "Philadelphia," "Delaware," and "Carolina."

Besides the makers already named, children's mugs were made by Thomas Godwin. One John Gilpin mug in brown transfer with splashes of blue, green, and yellow paint was marked "T. G." and one with a scene of a girl and cats printed in black is marked "Thos Godwin Burslem, Stone China." Several mugs are marked Wedgwood, and mugs with transfer prints were made at Leeds Pottery and Swansea. While a collection of mugs with late transfer scenes may be acquired at a moderate price, early transfers and such types as silver-resist patterns are comparatively scarce and expensive.

CHILDREN'S GIFT PLATES

Children's plates were not made in so many different patterns as mugs. Most of the plates are later in date, and the majority of them illustrate a story or maxim. A few early ones are found with illustrations of mother and child, but the popular plates are the alphabet type which have become increasingly popular with collectors the last few years. These white earthenware plates are decorated with transfer prints which are illuminated with crude splashes of hand coloring. The borders are usually embossed with the letters of the alphabet, hence the popular name of ABC plates.

These plates were made between 1820 and 1860, and reproductions were made even later. The transfers are in black, brown, green, red, or blue, and the hand coloring is usually in red, yellow, green, and orange. Besides the alphabet, dots, scrolls, embossed daisy, lily-of-the-valley, or rose borders are used, as well as the rarer embossed swan and flower bor-

TOP: Yarmouth-type hand-painted mugs, c. 1800–1815. BOTTOM: Franklin maxims and other transfers.

der. These plates have little aesthetic value, and their chief interest for the collector lies in the transfer scenes of American life in Victorian days. One series portrays American sports, including baseball, while another series is called "Our Early Days," and depicts scenes in a child's everyday life, such as "Half Holiday" and "The Playground," which have ABC borders. Another series includes Robinson Crusoe scenes with such subjects as "Crusoe Viewing the Island," "Crusoe at Work," and "Crusoe Milking." This series has ABC embossed borders. One of the most sought-after series is that showing Franklin's maxims from *Poor Richard's Almanack*. The border on this series is embossed wheat and rose, or there may be a raised rosette border which is sometimes colored. All these designs were made by J. & G. Meakin and various other manufacturers. Perhaps the rarest were made by Leeds Pottery in about 1820. They made a series with Franklin's maxims and also made plates with transfer-printed hymns. These are much earlier than those by Meakin, although Meakin and Clews made them originally in the first third of the 19th century. Most of these plates are unmarked. The Meakin mark, when used, was stamped in the ware and also printed in black: "J.&G. Meakin."

Some of the maxims found on these plates are: "Three removes are as bad as a fire. A rolling stone gathers no moss." Wheat and rose on ABC border, or an embossed daisy border on an octagonal plate.

"Keep the shop and the shop will keep thee." ABC border.

"It is easier to suppress the first desire than to satisfy all that follows." Raised scroll border.

"Now I have a sheep and a cow, everyone bids me good morrow." Raised basket-weave border.

Another group of children's ware is printed in dark blue and has borders of raised fruits, flowers, and shells. Among the maxims to be found on these are the following:

"The used key is always bright"; "If you would know the value of money try to borrow some"; "Many a little makes a mickle"; "No pain without pain"; "The eye of the master does more work than both his hands." Different makers used different pictures to illustrate the same maxim.

A rare series was that printed with scenes from *Uncle Tom's Cabin*. These include Uncle Tom at Home, Eva and Topsy, the Death of Uncle Tom, and other familiar episodes. They have embossed daisy borders.

There is a group of children's plates with the center printed with different kinds of animals. These have embossed ABC borders and some are marked "Wm Adams & Co." Still another group with ABC borders has scenes from nursery rhymes such as "Little Boy Blue" and "There was a crooked man." One series of plates has large letters of the alphabet and embossed daisy borders. Examples of these read "B is for ball" and "J is for June." American cities are the subject matter for a series which includes Philadelphia buildings, Manhattan Beach, and Plymouth Rock Monument. These have raised ABC borders.

R. & J. Clews of Cobridge made a series of plates illustrating such moral symbols as Industry, Temperance, and Knowledge. Other plates with alphabet borders include the Village Blacksmith, the Arrival of Gen. McClellan, and a transfer of a Dutch boy and girl with an alphabet in sign language. This last plate is marked "H. Aynsley & Co., Longton," with an English registry mark.

Among the rarer gift plates for children are those made by the Cambrian Pottery at Swansea between 1831 and 1850. These had molded borders of flowers and swans with a line of gilt on the rim. Several plates illustrate the "Ages of Man" and one plate, "The Cruel Boy," shows a boy tying a can to a cat's tail. The plate has an embossed border of roses, and the scene is in pink transfer with hand coloring in pink, green, and yellow. Another Swansea plate has the following religious verse in brown transfer:

> The child that longs to see my face
> Is sure my love to gain
> And those that early seek my face,
> Shall never seek in vain.

Several other plates should be considered here, not perhaps as children's giftware, but because they have the same embossed borders, and their center decoration is transfer with splashes of hand coloring. One of these is the well-known Millenium plate showing Christ Rising from the Dead. This is made with a cauliflower border by J. & G. Meakin who also made a similar plate with the "History of Joseph." The Millenium plate was also made with embossed border of lilies of the valley, wheat, and tulips.

A plate with a portrait of Queen Charlotte printed and colored by hand and an embossed border of flowers was made by Ralph Stevenson at Cobridge in about 1830. He also made a plate with a picture of a woman and child and the inscription "Who ran to help me when I fell, and would some pretty story tell or kiss the place to make it well—my mother." The border is of roses and leaves. Another popular plate shows a transfer portrait of Wesley. The border on this plate is embossed flower sprays of various colors together with luster. A verse called "Grace at Meal" decorates the center of another plate, which has a border similar to the Wesley plate. Other plates have transfers of various colors with such inscriptions as "A reward for diligence." The inscriptions are in black, orange, purple, and other colors, and have gold or silver luster bands. The black transfer of the reclining mother and child and the "Peacock at Home" have similar luster bands. The mother and child plate was made at Leeds Pottery. Plates with "The Sower," "The Plowman," and similar scenes with embossed and colored rose and daisy borders were also made at about the same time. Many of these scenes on children's plates were also made in cup plates as well.

Besides the potteries already mentioned, makers of children's transfer-printed plates were Goodwins & Harris; Elsmore & Forster; Malkin, Edge & Company; H. Aynsley & Company; and various potteries in Scotland.

Pratt Ware and Pot Lids

ONE OF THE oldest Staffordshire pottery works was that of Felix Pratt at Fenton, which was in operation continuously from 1775 to 1885. Of the many different kinds of pottery made by Pratt and his successors two types are especially popular with present-day collectors. The attractive and colorful cream-tinted earthenware jugs and mugs with relief decoration have long been known as Pratt ware, although they were also made elsewhere in Staffordshire, as well as at Leeds, Castleford, and several other potteries. The distinguishing features of this early Pratt ware is the modeled relief decoration and the zigzag and acanthus-leaf borders. The relief designs were painted under the glaze, and brilliant orange, green, cobalt blue, black or brown, and sometimes purple is characteristic of the ware. In its deep, strong, and vibrant color it resembles the finest old Italian majolica. The subject matter on these jugs includes scenes of the sea, hunting scenes, busts of national heroes, genre scenes, and caricatures of the headdresses of the period.

The largest class of subject matter is that which relates to the sailor or the naval hero. The well-known "Sailor's Farewell" and "Return" has the scene of the sailor saying farewell to his sweetheart in a medallion on one side and the return scene on the other. The borders are of zigzag and acanthus leaves. A jug of this type is one of the few pieces known marked "Pratt." The same subject appears on other jugs with varying borders and details. There are also many jugs with portraits of naval heroes. One jug has a relief bust of Admiral Nelson on one side and Captain Berry on the other, and the names of both men inscribed on the neck of the jug. Another jug has a portrait of Duncan with two ships in full sail and his name inscribed, and on the other side a scene of two gleaners in the field. A jug marked "Lord Jervis" has a bust of Jervis rising from the sea holding a trumpet, and the incident refers to the defeat of the Spanish fleet. Another jug shows the Duke of Cumberland on horseback, with Hercules and the Hydra in the panel on the other side. The "Wellington-Hill" jug shows busts of Wellington and General Hill together with flags. There is also a band of silver luster. Another Wellington jug is of later date and celebrates the victory at Waterloo. There is an interesting jug with equestrian figures of the Duke of York in one panel and Coburg in the other. There is also a fluted pear-shaped pitcher with relief portraits of Lafayette and Louis XVI. It is 6 inches in height and has a neckband of ribbon and vines in relief. Relief portrait busts were also made on plates and on plaques to hang on the wall. Plaques were made of Admiral Duncan, Lord Howe, and others.

One of the best Pratt ware jugs is called "Farmer and Fox." It shows the farmer and fox in one medallion and in the other the farmer's wife with dogs. The "Miser and Spendthrift" jug has a bust under the lip marked "Shakespear the Poet." The "Parson and Clerk" jug shows the parson in black with church warden and pipe in one panel, and the clerk in red coat and yellow breeches with a drunken peasant at the table in the panel on the other side. The jug is 8 inches in height. The "Debtor and Creditor" jug has the subject matter in panels and a border of silver luster and is 5 inches in height. A jug with zigzag and acanthus-leaf borders shows a scene of the "Sportsman" with dogs and hares. A jug with children at play in heart-shaped panels is quaint and charming. The scenes are known as "Sportive Innocence" and "Mischevious Sport." The jug is 7¼ inches high and the original dates about 1795. The same jugs are found in 6-inch and 4¾-inch heights. The average height of Pratt jugs is 5 or 6 inches. Another jug with acanthus-leaf borders is inscribed "Success to the Trade." The group of jugs with caricatures of headdresses is especially attractive. These designs are also found on flasks and teapoys. Similar designs as well as other portraits are found on plates and mugs. One mug with figures in relief is called "Midnight Conversation." Teapoys with classic scenes in relief and acanthus-leaf borders dividing the space into panels are often found with pewter tops.

The same type of ware with similar modeling and color was made in figure form. Two figures under an umbrella and called the "Umbrella Courtship" are attributed to Pratt. The "Sailor on Chest" is classed as a figure. It is a jug of a sailor astride a chest and has a kinship to the Toby

TOP: Pratt jugs with leaf borders: Military figure; Farmer and Wife. BOTTOM: Lover's Farewell; Bust of Admiral Duncan. Late 18th century.

jug. The inscription reads: "Hollo, Brother Briton Whoever Thou be Sit down on That chest of Hard dollars by me and drink a health to all sealors Bold." The relief decoration on these articles of Pratt ware either was shaped in separate molds and applied or may have been a part of the general casting process. Although this type of pottery is generally called Pratt ware, it was also made by John Barker of Fenton. Barker, who had been an apprentice of Whieldon's, established his own pottery in 1750 and was a working contemporary of Felix Pratt. In England, Pratt ware is also known as Barker ware. The same type of ware was also made at other potteries in Staffordshire and at Leeds and Castleford, as well as in Sunderland and at the Herculaneum Pottery in Liverpool. Since the ware is seldom marked it is difficult to identify the maker, but some pieces have been found marked "Pratt" and others marked "Herculaneum." Those made in Sunderland have pink luster combined with the designs. The earliest jugs made by Felix Pratt or John Barker are on lightweight cream-color pottery with a bluish glaze. The colors are pure and clear and the relief designs clean cut. Color is the most important factor. These early pieces are comparatively scarce and high in price even though they may be classed as cottage-type pottery.

The Pratt pottery works continued operations for many years and in the middle 19th century, under the name of F. & R. Pratt & Company. (1847–1885), they came into prominence for the excellence of their colored underglaze printing, notably on pot lids and tea ware. Pot lids, originally made as covers for pots holding bear's grease, later fish paste and potted meats, are popular with present-day collectors. With English collectors they hold a place equal to the American collector's craze for pressed glass, and there are check lists and price lists giving up-to-the-minute data for pot-lid collectors. The largest number of pot lids are round in shape but many are oval and some have squared corners. The scenes are painted in deep blues, reds, and buff. The design was printed in four colors: buff, blue, pink or red, and the outline color. Then the glaze was applied and the pot fired again. Lids with gold were fired a third time.

Pot-lid collectors are chiefly interested in subjects which include historic incidents in the life of Victorian times, landscapes, portraits, public buildings, special events such as coronations, and military and naval scenes of the Crimean War. There are also views of the great exhibitions in London, Dublin, Paris, New York, Chicago, and Philadelphia. Portraits include Victoria and Albert, Edward VII and Alexandra, Harriet Beecher Stowe, and Napoleon. A series of scenes has subject matter connected with personal adornment and another series (probably on pots to hold fish) has scenes of the shrimping industry at Pegwell Bay. There is also a group of pot lids with American views, including Washington crossing the Delaware; the State House, Philadelphia; Independence Hall interior; the Administration Building, World's Fair, Chicago; and the Prince of Wales at the Tomb of Washington. The earliest subjects are those including bears and were probably made for pots holding bear's grease. These include the Bear Pit, Bear Hunting, Bear, Lion and Cock, Bears on Rocks, Bears Reading Newspaper, Bears with Valentines, and others. Other scenes show dogs, deer, pheasant shooting, a bullfight, and a boar fight. Sentimental pictures include "Our Pets," "Good Dog," "Gay Dog," "Cottage Children," "Village Wedding," "Grace Before Meals," "The Dentist," and "Blind Fiddler." There are also groups of pot lids with the seasons and floral designs and one with copies of great paintings such as the "Blue Boy." The pictures were often taken from paintings by such artists as Landseer, Gainsborough, Sir David Wilkie, W. Mulready, and C. R. Leslie and from the popular artist of the Baxter prints as well as the water-color drawings of Jesse Austin. Jesse Austin not only made the sketches but also superintended the engraving department at Pratt Pottery except for one year, 1858, when he worked at Cauldon Works in Stoke. Austin went to work for Pratt in 1843 or 1845, and many of the pot lids have his signature, including some of the early bear lids. Other lids were marked with a registration mark, and some are marked "Jesse Austin and Felix Edwards Pratt, Fenton, Staffs 1846."

Pot lids were also made by Brown, Westhead, Moore & Company, Cauldon Works; by T. J. & J. Mayer; and by Ridgway. The following well-known manufacturers used pots with colored scenes on their lids: John Burgess & Son, Crosse & Blackwell, Robert Feast, Totwell & Son, Morrell, John Gosnell & Son, and E. Lazenby & Son. Pot lids have been reproduced from old copper plates which are still in existence. However, the copies which were made between 1880 and 1924 are distinguishable by their light colors. The old pot lids have beautiful deep blues and reds. Hairline work, or "crazing," is often found on old lids and the pottery is heavy, while new lids "ring."

Underglaze-painted scenes are also found on vases, boxes, mugs, loving cups, plaques, trinket sets, teapots, and tea ware. F. & R. Pratt & Company made tea ware pieces for the great exhibition in 1851 for which they won a medal. These exhibition pieces have scenes of Roman ruins, with green and gold borders, and are marked "Pratt Fenton." Other plates have land-scapes and embossed borders and gold filigree borders. F. & R. Pratt & Company was patronized by Prince Albert. Much of their dessert ware was also made for the United States. The works of F. & R. Pratt continued in operation until 1885, making various kinds of pottery including Etruscan ware.

BIBLIOGRAPHY

The Earthenware Collector, by George Wolliscroft Rhead. H. Jenkins Limited, London, 1920.
Color Pictures on Pot-Lids and Other Forms of 19th Century Staffordshire Pottery, by Harold George Clarke. Currier Press, London, 1924.

7

American Stoneware Pots and Jars

THE COLLECTOR interested in quaint and homely American objects will find the fat, sturdy jugs, pots, and crocks of stoneware suited to his taste. There are many available today and the market values are reasonable except for articles made by a few of the early potters, but even these may be located where they may be bought cheap. Stoneware is made from gray and tan clays which vitrify at a strong heat to form a nonporous base, which was glazed by throwing a handful of common salt into the kiln. This gave the ware a pebbly surface. The good old pots were often beautiful in form and proportion, and decorated with cobalt blue and sometimes brown or purple designs painted freehand, etched with a dull point, or ornamented on the lathe. The great variety of shapes is one of the chief joys of the collector.

A certain amount of stoneware was produced in America in the 18th century, but before the Revolution there were only a few stoneware potters in New York; Huntington, Long Island; Norwalk and Litchfield, Connecticut; Boston; and Philadelphia. Remmey operated his stoneware pottery in New York during the Revolution, and a batter jug in the collection of the New York Historical Society is inscribed "Flowered by Clarkson Crolius, New York Feb 17th 1798." According to Barber's *Pottery and Porcelain of the United States*, John Remmey started making stoneware pottery behind the old City Hall in New York City in about 1735. He died in 1762, but the business was carried on for three generations, and a great grandson later established a pottery in South Amboy, New Jersey, Henry Remmey worked in Philadelphia in 1810, while Richard Remmey worked in Philadelphia late in the 19th century. The pottery of William and Peter Crolius of New York City was continued after 1762 by Clarkson Crolius to 1837, and by Clarkson Crolius, Jr., from 1838 to 1850. It therefore is evident that the collector must be careful whether the Remmey or Crolius is of the 18th or the 19th century. However, the collector need not expect to find much stoneware dated in the 18th century, for the bulk of that found today is of the 19th century. Nevertheless, age and rarity have little to do with the excellence of stoneware, for generally speaking American stoneware improved as the industry developed and much of that made as late as 1850 is exceptionally fine. In the 19th century, potters of stoneware were scattered throughout Connecticut, Vermont, New Hampshire, Massachusetts, New York, Pennsylvania, New Jersey, Maryland, West Virginia, and Ohio. Some potteries were small and took care only of local customers, while others were large factories with branches in several towns and considerable shipping business. Thus stoneware potteries were often located on navigable rivers, as waterways were the easiest and cheapest mode of transportation. Some potteries sold their ware by means of peddlers' wagons.

Stoneware pots and jugs are of various types according to their decoration and method of manufacture. The earliest stoneware was incised, and this means of decoration continued between 1790 and 1900. Stoneware figures were modeled by hand in all factories between 1790 and 1900. These articles include Toby pitchers, heads, toys, bird and animal whistles, and banks. These are rare, especially the animals. Between 1825 and 1875 applied relief decoration was used on handles, as borders such as beading, and a classical figure of Diana with a deer was used at Bennington and St. Johnsbury, Vermont, in Massachusetts, and at other Eastern potteries. Applied leaves and fruit and borders of gadrooning are often found on stoneware made after 1825. From 1825 on, stoneware with blue decoration was also pressed in molds, and included pitchers, water coolers, doorstops, vases, and animals such as dogs and lions. Late stoneware had flowers and leaves molded on and then washed with a blue glaze. Stoneware was stenciled between 1840 and the end of the century. Stenciled eagles are often found on stoneware made in Ohio.

Stoneware jars and crocks are heavy and somewhat clumsy in shape, ranging in capacity from 1 quart to 30 gallons. While some shapes are graceful and of slender proportions, generally speaking, the articles made in stoneware are useful rather than ornamental and include jugs for molasses, rum, cider, and vinegar; crocks for butter and apple butter; water coolers, crocks for eggs, bean pots, batter pots, churns, pudding dishes, milk pans, mugs, pitchers, bottles, bowls, churns, money banks, inkwells, and miniature jugs and crocks. Batter pots had wide spouts and a handle, and churns were the kind that operated with a handle. The crocks and preserve jars are usually straight-sided but some are shaped in curves. Jugs were in a wide variety of shapes from common broad-bottomed ones to vase and urn shapes with narrow necks and bottoms.

Although the word stoneware suggests gray, the colors range from light gray and tan to a deep brown. Even the gray varies from blue and lead color to a soft pure tone, and the tans include sand, buff, yellow, orange, reddish brown, and café au lait. The glaze is generally dull, but this varies with the object and the location of the factory. Sometimes there is a lack of uniformity of glaze and sometimes a glaze is iridescent.

The chief interest of stoneware, however, is not in the shape or color, but in decoration. Usually, the decoration was simple and conventional and included flowers, insects, animals, and patriotic symbols, but certain potters used special designs which help us to identify their jugs. For example, the stoneware of the early Remmeys in New York is characterized by the use of the swag and pendant, the chain loop, and the leaf and seed. The holly leaf is characteristic of the wares of Warne and Letts of South Amboy, New Jersey. The earliest technique sketched the design in incised lines and it was filled in with cobalt blue. Later the designs were painted freehand or stenciled. Many pieces are not decorated at all and many have only crude daubs of cobalt blue. The finest pieces, however, have characteristic decorations, including birds, feathers, flowers, foliage, trees, conventional scrolls, and other designs. Birds include robins, bluebirds, cockatoos, and exotic and imaginative birds. The figure of a bird sits on top a jug-shaped money bank made by R. C. Remmey at Philadelphia in 1880. Eagles and roosters are often to be found, but generally animals and human figures are rare. Crudely sketched houses are sometimes seen, and one of more decorative interest than usual was made by A. O. Whittemore, Havana, New York, around 1868. A sailing ship is scratched in a jug marked "G. Goodale, Hartford." This is a rare piece. Inscription pieces, those either inscribed to a friend or with political inscriptions are also rare. One inscription piece is marked "Liberty Forever" and was made by Ware & Letts of South Amboy, New Jersey, in about 1807. It has the typical oak- or holly-leaf decoration used by this potter. Crude incised profiles and Indian heads are found on some jugs made by Joseph Remmey at South Amboy, New Jersey, in about 1823. His pieces are massive and he often

TOP: Stoneware crock, tree design, 1838; gray jug, "J. & E. Norton, Bennington," 1850–1859. CENTER: Early 19th-century pitchers, incised and painted. BOTTOM: Crock, late 19th century. Batter jug, "Cowden & Wilcox, Harrisburg, Penn.," c. 1863.

employs incised loop designs. Three upright stalks of corn ornament a jug probably made for corn whisky. A bee is sketched on a crock made by Israel Seymour at Troy, New York, in the early 19th century. American flags and patriotic symbols often decorate stoneware jugs, but one such jug, made by G. Purdy at Atwater, Ohio, in about 1850 is more elaborate than most stoneware. It has a horn of plenty filled with flowers and a man astride a cannon holding crossed American flags. An unusual design of an angel's head and folded wings is painted on a crock made by William Macquoid & Co., of New York City, in the 1860s.

In addition to the ornamental decoration, a number indicating the capacity of the crock or jug is often incised or painted on the side and sometimes the date is scrawled in large letters. The maker's name, location, and, in rare instances, the date was painted or incised with a sharp-pointed instrument. However, the custom of stamping with the maker's name and address was not general until after 1800, and later makers' names were put on with a die stamp. The inscription not only adds to the attractiveness of the piece but it also helps to locate potteries and thus gives the piece historic value.

In collecting stoneware jugs and crocks it is best for the beginner to look for good shape and pleasing proportions, good color, and decoration. After his collection demands the rarer piece he can seek the unusual design and the pieces by well-known early makers.

Although a list of makers of stoneware might be tiresome here, it is good to know that such lists exist, since they will serve as a means of dating a particular piece. The length of the list gives one an idea of the great number of factories that were making stoneware, particularly in the 19th century. A check list compiled by Carolyn Scoon of the New York Historical Society gives the name of thirty-eight manufacturers located in seventeen different towns and cities in New York State. These include potters in Athens, Albany, Troy, Utica, Rome, Ithaca, Binghamton, Cortland, Lyons, Port Edward, Brooklyn, Kings County, Ellenville, Fort Edward, Havana, Huntington, Suffolk County, Mount Morris, Olean, Penn Yan, Poughkeepsie, and West Troy (Watervliet). The makers listed represent a fair proportion of the stoneware makers of New York State and their geographical location gives us a picture of the early trade. A similar check list of stoneware potters of New England was made by Lura Woodside Watkins. It includes potters located in Bangor, Gardiner, and Portland, Maine; Keene and Nashua, New Hampshire; Bennington, Burlington, Dorset, Fairfax, Poultney, St. Albans, and St. Johnsbury, Vermont; Ashfield, Ballardvale, Boston, Charlestown, Cambridgeport, Chelsea, Dorchester, Medford, Somerset, Taunton, Worcester, and Whateley, Massachusetts; and Bridgeport, Greenwich, Hartford, New Haven, New London, Norwalk, Norwich, and Stonington, Connecticut. Stoneware was also made in South Amboy, Elizabeth, Newark, Flemington, Somerset, Middleton, and New Brunswick, New Jersey; in Pittsburgh and Philadelphia and numerous other Pennsylvania towns; in Baltimore and Hagerstown, Maryland; in Louisville, Kentucky; Strasburg, Virginia; and in Middlebury, Jonathan Creek, Hillsboro, Mt. Sterling, Akron, Springfield, Putnam, Cincinnati, Canton, Cleveland, Zanesville, Crooksville and Atwater, Mogadore, Symmes Creek, Roseville, Athens, and Cuyahoga Falls, Ohio.

BIBLIOGRAPHY

"The Remmey Family," by W. Oakley Raymond. A series of articles in *The Magazine Antiques*, September and June, 1937, and March and July, 1938.

"A Check List of New England Potters," by Lura Woodside Watkins. *The Magazine Antiques*, August, 1942.

"New York State Stoneware in The New York Historical Society," by Carolyn Scoon. *The New York Historical Society Quarterly Bulletin*, vol. xxix, no. 2, April, 1945.

American Rockingham Ware

IF YOU ARE looking for an "antique" interest within your budget start
with a Rockingham "Rebekah at the Well" teapot or an old brown bean
pot of Rockingham ware. Display the stuff in your kitchen and use it
everyday, but when you advance to a marked Bennington pitcher or a
Toby jug, put it in a glass case under lock and key. This one-time utility
kitchenware is fast coming to the attention of collectors.

American Rockingham ware is a soft cream or yellow ware which
is dipped or spattered with a brown glaze before firing. The best-known
Rockingham was made at Bennington, Vermont, but it was also made by
almost every pottery in the eastern part of the United States and in Ohio.
The majority of the Rockingham pieces were made between 1835 and
1900, but Spargo lists potters making Rockingham in America as early as
1812, and a piece in the New York Historical Society is dated 1810. Rockingham was a cheap and durable everyday ware, probably made in imitation of Whieldon's tortoise-shell glazes, although the direct influence
was the English Rockingham made by Brameld and other English
potteries.

More Rockingham has been attributed to Bennington than to any
other pottery. In fact, Rockingham is often wrongly called Bennington
ware. However, the largest assortment of pieces, and indeed almost every
article made in Rockingham was made by Norton & Fenton or United
States Pottery Company in Bennington, Vermont. Among the most
important pieces are the Toby jugs. No less than three of these were made
at Bennington and were probably modeled by Daniel Greatbach, the well-
known English potter. These were the Franklin Toby, the Duke of Wellington Toby, and the quaint so-called Snuff Toby. These Tobies which

are both rare and rather expensive, will be described and discussed in the next chapter.

The most sought-after and most popular article of old Rockingham ware is the hound-handled pitcher. Hunting jugs with hound handles were made by 18th-century English potters, but the hound-handled jug is supposed to have been introduced into America by Daniel Greatbach, the master potter of Staffordshire who came to work for Henderson at Jersey City in 1839. In about 1843 Greatbach designed his hound-handled pitcher there. The pitcher, like most other hound-handled pitchers, has a stag hunt on one side and a boar hunt on the other. A grapevine design decorates the neck and shoulder of the jug. Sometimes a feather border outlines the lip of the pitcher and sometimes a small scalloped border or other variations outline the lip. The hound handle is grotesque and undoglike. Its head rests upon the rim of the pitcher and the feet are hardly discernible in silhouette. This is the type of handle that was copied by most of the other potteries. When marked this pitcher has an impressed "D & J Henderson" in a circle. Another type of hound-handled pitcher was also made at Jersey City. It has a mask on the front under the spout, a hunting scene, and an American eagle pulling the tail of the British lion. The glaze is pale in tint, less mottled, and has less depth than the best Jersey City Rockingham.

Of course, the hound-handled hunting pitcher of greatest interest to collectors is the one made by Daniel Greatbach for the U.S. Pottery Company of Bennington. It is never marked but is easily identified by the chain collar on the dog's neck, the space between the paws and the head of the dog, and the duck's-bill shape of the dog's head. The pitcher was made in three sizes. Its glaze is dark and lustrous. There are several other variations of the hound-handled hunting pitcher that are of special interest to collectors because they are identified with certain potteries and can thus be dated and placed as to locality.

A hound-handled pitcher with similar scenes and a handle similar to the Jersey City pitcher designed by Greatbach but with plain shoulders and a lambrequin border at the top of the shoulders was made at the Salamander Works, Woodbridge, New Jersey, between 1842 and 1850. This is one of the best-designed Rockingham hound-handled pitchers. When marked it bears the scratched mark "Salamander Works / Woodbridge / N.J."

A hound-handled pitcher with stag hunt and boar hunt, grape design

TOP LEFT: Pitcher, "Norton & Fenton, Bennington." RIGHT: Hound-handle pitcher, stag-bear hunt. "J. B. Caire & Co./Po'keepsie/N. Y." BOTTOM: Hound-handled pitchers. RIGHT: "U. S. Pottery, Bennington," 1852–1858.

on the neck, and a hound handle similar to the Jersey City handle is in the collection of the New York Historical Society and marked "J. B. Caire & Co / Po'keepsie / N.Y."

One of the best hound-handled hunting-scene pitchers was made by Harker and Taylor of East Liverpool, Ohio, between 1847 and 1851. The head of the hound is lifted up from the paws, leaving a space similar to the Bennington handle, but while the Bennington head rests on the paws this hound head is free. When marked this pitcher has an impressed "Harker, Taylor & Co." Harker & Taylor exhibited Rockingham ware at the Franklin Institute Fair in Philadelphia in 1846.

In 1852 James Taylor & Henry Speeler from East Liverpool, Ohio, were in business in Trenton, New Jersey, and in 1846 Taylor, Speeler & Bloor, Trenton, New Jersey, exhibited Rockingham ware at the Franklin Institute Fair. They also made a hound-handled pitcher. A. Cadmus of South Amboy made a hound-handled pitcher with a relief of a volunteer fire company. It has a grape design on the neck and the hound's head rests on the rim of the pitcher in the manner of the handles of the Greatbach design at Jersey City. A hunting pitcher with an oak border and rustic handle and a frog in the bottom was also made by Cadmus at Congress Hill Pottery, New Jersey.

A pitcher with a raised boar hunt on one side and a stag hunt on the other was made by Bell at Strasburg, Virginia, and is incised "Bell" on the bottom.

A hound-handled pitcher with game was made at the pottery of Bennett & Brothers at Baltimore, Maryland. It was modeled by Charles Coxon, who also modeled a stag hunt and boar pitcher with a rustic handle. Hound-handled pitchers were made at many other factories, but most of them were of inferior workmanship and while the design was usually a modification of the Greatbach pitchers they fall short of those made at Jersey City or Bennington. As late as 1902–1903 the Vance Pottery Company of Peoria, Illinois, made a hound-handled pitcher in the old Greatbach molds. These pitchers are marked and were not put on the market as forgeries.

Another pitcher of special interest to collectors is the Apostle Pitcher, which was made by Daniel Greatbach for the American Pottery Company at Jersey City. It has embossed figures of the Apostles set within Gothic window frames. An Apostle cuspidor was made at Congress Hill Pottery.

An eight-sided pitcher with a Druid's head beneath the lip was made by

Bennett & Brothers and exhibited in the 1846 Franklin Institute Fair and is still on view at the Institute in Philadelphia. The Heron or Stork pitcher and the Dolphin and Fish pitcher, as well as the Daniel Boone pitcher, were also made by Bennett & Brothers and modeled by Charles Coxon. The figures are in relief and the ware at its best is as good as any made in America. There were four types of pitchers made by the Salamander Works, Woodbridge, New Jersey. Besides the hound-handled pitcher already described, this pottery made a pitcher with a relief decoration of scrolls, fauns' heads, and grapes. Some of these pitchers are marked with an impressed oval stamp holding the maker's name.

A pitcher with an ivy-leaf border and an embossed sidewheel steamer on its body was also made at Salamander Works, as was a pitcher with a similar border and the engine of a volunteer fire company.

A large Rockingham pitcher with an embossed allover floral pattern was made by W. H. P. Benton of Perth Amboy, N.J., in about 1858. They also made a pitcher with an American eagle and shield with thunderbolts and flames in relief and one with *putti* & grapevine. In about 1850 the Congress Hill Pottery of A. Cadmus at South Amboy made a mug-shaped pitcher with a relief decoration of grapes and leaves and a rustic handle. It is marked "A. Cadmus Congress Pottery, South Amboy, N.J." The pitcher with an anchor and rope was also made at Jersey City. It has a beaded border around the rim. Several pitchers of much later shapes have hunting scenes, and these continued to be made until late in the century. Indeed, the shape is usually an indication of when the design was made. Many of the early hunting pitchers had the name of the owner in white block letters on the shoulder.

Two exceptionally fine pitchers of hexagonal form were made at the American Pottery Co. in Jersey City. One has an allover floral design, the other a more formal floral pattern divided into panels. These are attributed to Daniel Greatbach.

A six-paneled pitcher with relief decoration of flowers was made at Bennington, and a fluted pitcher with a spout decoration of beautifully molded scrolls is also worth special attention.

Of special interest to collectors of Rockingham is the "Rebekah at the Well" teapot, because of its price and availability. This teapot was made in several sizes and by many factories. It was originally modeled by Charles Coxon for Bennett & Brothers, Baltimore, Maryland, and was copied from a design of a porcelain jug made by Alcock in England. It was so popular

TOP: Rebekah at the Well teapot made in Ohio. Coachman bottle, "Lyman, Fenton & Co.," 1849–1858. BOTTOM: Eagle flask. Rockingham cake mold, "John Bell, Waynesboro."

that a variation of Coxon's design was made by many factories up to 1893. The teapot shows a relief design of Rebekah with a water jar beside a well and the raised words "Rebekah at the Well." A similar teapot at the New York Historical Society is marked "—Ohio." Rebekah at the Well teapots have also been found marked "J. Mayer, Trenton."

Many tea- and coffeepots were also made in octagonal shapes. The Philadelphia Museum of Art owns a Rockingham coffeepot with eight panels containing eagles in relief. It was made by W. H. P. Benton of Perth Amboy, New Jersey.

The cow creamer was made of Rockingham ware in both America and England from 1845 to 1885, but was originated much earlier, probably by Whieldon. While it was made at many potteries including Jersey City, South Amboy, Trenton, and Baltimore, the one made at Bennington is the most sought after. The Bennington cow is plump; the ribs show but are not ridged to the touch. The eyes are clear and the nostrils are marked with crescent indications. Cow creamers are not marked.

Bennington also made figures of a stag with tree stump, of a recumbent stag and doe, of a poodle dog with a basket, and of a lion with his paw on a ball. A sitting figure of a dog on a pedestal was made in East Liverpool, Ohio. The base has a repeat border of anthemion. A dog doorstop was also made by W. A. H. Schrieber & J. F. Betz at Phoenixville, Pennsylvania, in 1867, and Charles Coxon modeled a figure of a pointer dog which was made by Bennett & Brothers in the 1850s. A Rockingham ware figure of a bull calf was made at Congress Hill Pottery. Various-sized cracker jars with covers were made in octagonal and fluted designs. Inkstands, picture frames, candlesticks, mugs, and vases are also among the interesting articles made at Bennington and at various other factories where Rockingham was made. A shaving mug with a fat man or Toby in relief was made by Bennett & Brothers in about 1853 and also at Brookville Potting Company near Pottsville, Pennsylvania; and the Tam o'shanter mug was made between 1840 and 1850 by Abraham Miller of Philadelphia, a potter whose works date back to 1816. Many plain and undecorated Rockingham mugs were made also. Such mugs were made at East Liverpool and Swan Hill Pottery, South Amboy, New Jersey, and sold through the Norwalk Pottery, Norwalk, Connecticut. Their list of Rockingham included "pressed teapots, fancy jugs, spittoons, soaps, Tobeys, plain jugs and mugs." Sugar bowls, creamers, and bowls and goblets for table use were also made in Rockingham at the various potteries. The goblets are rare.

Flasks in the shape of a book and bottles were made at Bennington, at Phoenixville, Pennsylvania, and at Ohio potteries in East Liverpool and by Joseph Pyatt at Zanesville. A flask with an eagle in relief was made in Ohio. The famous "Coachman"- and "Monk"-figure bottles were made at Bennington between 1849 and 1858. They are often marked "Lyman Fenton & Co., Bennington, Vt." Banks, shoes, flasks, and bottles in shapes such as mermaids and a man on a barrel were among the many miscellaneous articles made.

Among the common household articles made in Rockingham were baking dishes, pudding and jelly molds, pie plates, soap dishes, bedpans, flasks, foot warmers, cuspidors, doorknobs, and tiebacks for curtains. These articles are not to be considered in the same category as the pitchers, figures, and Toby jugs, but nevertheless they are worth collecting, and one often finds such articles with a fine glaze and depth of coloring. Although the Rockingham ware from Bennington is considered the finest, good ware was also made at other potteries. Even that at Bennington varies with the workman, since Rockingham was hand dipped or spattered. A light tone indicates a thinner glaze. Some wares were fired once, and others had two firings. The two-fire process produced more brilliance and depth of color. This variation is noted even in Bennington ware. The earlier Norton & Fenton Rockingham shows no extra gloss on the bottom, while the later U.S. Pottery Rockingham, which had two firings, has more gloss and depth. However, no two pieces are ever the same color because of difference in body and firing as well as the individual dipping process. The best Rockingham, generally speaking, was made at Bennington by Norton & Fenton and U.S. Pottery, at Baltimore, and at East Liverpool and Zanesville, Ohio. However, each individual piece should be judged for its brilliance of glaze, fineness of body texture, and good modeling. The best pieces have good potting and workmanship and there are no defects or "crazings." Judging an article by such standards enables one to choose the best whether the piece is marked or not. Since the marked pieces are rare it is well to keep these facts in mind.

MAKERS OF ROCKINGHAM

1812, Philadelphia, Thos. Haig–Red, black glazed Rockingham

1816, Philadelphia, 1840, Abraham Miller, Queens

1833, Philadelphia, Jos. & Thos. Haig

1837, Philadelphia, Isaac Spiegel

1839, Cincinnati, Uriah Kendall

1840, Cincinnati, Kendall & Sons

1840, East Liverpool, Benj. Harker

1841, East Liverpool, Salt & Mear

1842, Cincinnati, Wm. Bromley

1842, Shenandoah, Strasburg, Va., Solomon & Sam Bell

1844, Pittsburgh, Bennett & Bros.

1844, Philadelphia, R. Bagnall Beech

1844, East Liverpool, Croxall Bros.

1846, East Liverpool, Harker, Taylor & Co.

1846, Cincinnati, Geo. Scott

1846, Baltimore, Edwin Bennett

1848, Baltimore, E. & W. Bennett

1848, Woodbridge, N.J., Salamander Works

1849, Zanesville, Ohio, Geo. Pyaitt

1849, Cincinnati, Geo. Scott & Sons

1850, South Amboy, N.J., Cadmus Congress Hill

1850, West Troy, N.Y., Geo. Walker

1850, South Norwalk, Conn., Asa Hill & L. D. Wheeler, Rockingham buttons

1851, Troy, Ind., John Sanders & Samuel Wilson

1852, Middlebury, Ohio, Enoch Raleigh, Edwin & Herbert Baker & Thos. Johnson

1852, Cincinnati, Peter Lessel

1852, Trenton, N.J., Taylor & Speeler

1852, South Amboy, N.J., Jas. Carr— Swan Hill Pottery

1853, Trenton, N.J., Richard Millington & John Astbury & Poulson— (M.A.P.) mark

1853, Trenton, N.J., Wm. Young & Son

1853, East Liverpool, Ohio, Sm. & Wm. Baggott

1853, South Norwalk, Conn., L. D. Wheeler, Rockingham doorknobs

1853, Burlington, Vt., Nichols & Alford

1854, Cincinnati, Brewer & Tempest

1854, East Liverpool, Isaac ' Knowles & I. Harvey

1854, Boston, Mass., Fred Meagher

1856, South Norwalk, Conn., Wood & Wheeler

1856, Cincinnati, Skinner, Greatbach & Co.

1856, Cincinnati, Tunis Brewer

1856, Kaolin, S. C., Wm. H. Farrar

1857, Philadelphia, Geo. Allen

1857, Akron, Ohio, Johnson, Whitman & Co.

1858, Philadelphia, Isaac Spiegel

1858, Perth Amboy, N.J., W. H. P. Benton, Eagle Pottery

1859, Cincinnati, S. A. Brewer

1864, East Liverpool, Wm. Cartwright & Holland Manley

1865, Perth Amboy, N.J., Enoch Wood, Hall Pottery Co.

1867, Phoenixville, Pa., Phoenixville Pottery Co.

1868, East Liverpool, Ohio, C. C. Thompson & J. T. Herbert

1868, East Liverpool, Ohio, E. McDevitt & Ferd Keffer

1868, Philadelphia, Port Richmond Pottery Co.

1869, Phoenixville, Pa., Schreiber & Betz, 1867

1869, East Liverpool, Ohio, A. J. Marks

1870, East Liverpool, Ohio, Knowles, Taylor & Knowles

1870, East Liverpool, Ohio, Wm. Burton

1871, East Liverpool, Ohio, E. McDevitt & S. Moore

1871, Trenton, N.J., Union Pottery Co.

1871, South Amboy, N.J., J. Mayer— Swan Hill pottery made for Norwalk Pottery

1872, East Liverpool, Ohio, John Goodwin

1872, East Liverpool, Ohio, Manley, Cartwright & Co.

BIBLIOGRAPHY

Early American Pottery and China, by John Spargo. The Century Company, New York and London, 1926.

The Potters and Potteries of Bennington, by John Spargo. Houghton, Mifflin Company, Boston, 1926.

American Tobies

TOBY JUGS WERE first made in England in the 18th century. The Toby jug is a caricature of a fat man with shoulder-length curly hair. The figure is usually seated and wears a three-cornered hat and holds a pipe or ale mug in his hand. Sometimes he is smiling and again he leers or scowls. The name Toby was probably an 18th-century title for those who frequented the alehouse, since Toby jugs were made by Whieldon before Stern created the jovial Uncle Toby in *Tristram Shandy*. At any rate these caricatures of Toby Philipot became popular and were made by many English potteries. The first Toby was made by John Astbury before 1743, and other English potters who made Tobies were Whieldon and Ralph Wood— about 1765—Enoch Wood, Wilson, Voyez, Copeland and Garrett, and Davenport, and from 1832 by Doulton. The English Toby was usually decorated with bright-colored glazes in blue, yellow-green, yellow, tan, black, and rose red. However, the Whieldon Tobies have the typical Whieldon mottling, and several Tobies were made in brown Rockingham, including the "Wellington" and the "Snuff Taker." They range in size from 1 inch to 18 inches in height, but the average is about 10 inches. Miniature Tobies and Toby mustard pots were also made.

The earliest Tobies made no attempt at portraiture, but bore such names as "Night Watchman," "Jolly Good Fellow," "Post Boy," "Falstaff," and "Inn Keeper." However, later, portraiture was introduced as a sales procedure, and a caricature of George II was made. Few portraits were attempted in the 18th century, although one of Lord Rodney was made in 1780 and one of Lord Howe in 1790, but portrait Tobies did not become popular until the 19th century. They were also made full length. English 19th-century Tobies included Mr. Pickwick, Gladstone, Nelson, and

Napoleon. The demand for these early English Tobies has been so great that the price of a really fine one is out of range of the average collector. Moreover there are few to be had and since fake reproductions and late copies flood the market the Toby collector must beware. For these reasons the collector interested in the quaint charm of the Toby would do well to look to another field of interest and consider the American Toby. American Tobies followed the tradition of the English; in fact, some of the oldest American brown Rockingham Tobies seem to be exact reproductions of the English "Snuff Taker" and "Wellington" jugs.

The earliest American Tobies were made of Rockingham ware or stoneware with a Rockingham glaze, and the earliest known American Toby was made at Jersey City in about 1830 and is marked "D & J Henderson Jersey City N. J." It is a large Toby and holds a well-defined jug. A similar Toby was made at Salamander Works, Woodbridge, New Jersey, between 1842 and 1850. In about 1840 Daniel Greenbach made a Rockingham Toby for the American Pottery Company at Jersey City. It has a typical Toby head, but the lower part is divided into panels with floral decoration. It is light in color and is marked "American Pottery Co., Jersey City, N.J." A later owner of the pottery works discovered old molds for four different varieties and sizes of Tobies, but not all of these have been identified or traced to the Jersey City works.

Three types of Rockingham and flint-enamel Tobies were made at Bennington by Lyman Fenton & Co. between 1849 and 1858. The well-known snuff Toby was made at this time. It is a small sitting figure with a wide-brimmed hat and holds a cup and a jug. He sits with one foot crossed under the other. A Toby jug with a bent leg for a handle is often called the Franklin Toby. However, the costume is not contemporary with Franklin and his time, and the jug was probably only a caricature. The other Lyman, Fenton & Co. Toby is a seated figure holding a glass. The Wellington Toby made at Bennington is almost identical to the one made in England. Bennington Tobies have a flat bottom and often a grapevine handle. A later Rockingham Toby represents a full figure of a fat man standing. It may have been made at any of a dozen later factories, for Rockingham Tobies were a part of the stock in trade of W. H. P. Benton of Perth Amboy, New Jersey, in 1858; of Swan Hill Pottery, South Amboy, New Jersey, in 1849 to 1852; of Enoch Wood, Perth Amboy, in 1865; and of Port Richmond Pottery Co., Philadelphia, in 1868, as well as of dozens of other small potteries.

TOP: Rockingham Tobies, "Lyman, Fenton & Co., Bennington." RIGHT: Franklin. CENTER: Lenox Tobies. LEFT: Franklin; RIGHT: Geo. Washington. BOTTOM: Rockingham Tobies. LEFT: Maker unknown. RIGHT: Daniel Greatbach, "American Pottery Co."

In 1848 R. Bagnall Beach of Philadelphia, who had been trained in the Wedgwood potteries in England, made a Rockingham Toby or jug of a head of Daniel O'Connell, the Irish patriot. It was a good likeness and was later copied in 1851 by Thomas Haig of Philadelphia.

In 1848 a large 13-inch Rockingham Toby was made representing the head of Zachary Taylor. Part of the lettering remains which identifies the subject matter, but the maker is unknown. This is a rare jug and is mentioned here only for documental purposes, since the collector has little chance of finding such a jug.

It is a far cry from the ordinary brown chophouse jug made of Rockingham by 19th-century American potters to the late glazed-earthenware portrait Tobies of American heroes. However, although these late Tobies are hardly within the sphere of antiques, they are no farther off the collecting track than much of the glass and china and other Victorian objects which are being collected. There were enough of these portrait Tobies produced to make them available today yet the quantity is sufficiently limited to make diligent search necessary.

The earliest of the American portrait Tobies is the Napoleon made by the Columbian Potteries of Philadelphia in 1876. This is often mistaken and sold for an old Staffordshire Toby, and since it is not marked the mistake is difficult to detect.

In 1892 J. S. W. Starkey, a potter of East Liverpool, Ohio, made glazed-earthenware portrait Tobies of Pope Leo XIII, Washington, and William Penn. The first two were heads, but the William Penn is a full-length figure. They were made at the East Liverpool Art Pottery. There were thirty dozen of Washington made, twenty-five dozen of Pope Leo XIII, but only a few of the William Penn jug, which makes it the rare and scarce item. The Pope Leo XIII is 8½ inches in height and is a good likeness and on the hat is impressed "Leo XIII."

In 1896 the Edwin Bennett Pottery Co., of Baltimore made a crude McKinley Toby with a likeness that can hardly be distinguished.

In 1896 Isaac Broome modeled porcelain Tobies of George Washington for Lenox Potteries in New Jersey. These were made in several sizes. Lenox also made a William Penn Toby which was modeled by W. W. Gallimore. These are easily recognized because they are excellent likenesses. The William Penn Toby is a three-quarter-length figure and has a handle with an Indian head and feathers.

A portrait of Theodore Roosevelt hunting big game was made by

Lenox at the close of Roosevelt's last term in office in 1909. It was designed by Edward Penfield and modeled by Isaac Broome and depicts Roosevelt in hunting costume with a book inscribed "Africa." The handle of the jug is an elephant's head, and the coloring and portraiture are good. Both the Roosevelt and Penn Tobies made at Lenox are well worth collecting for their fine workmanship and design as well as historical interest.

A brown salt-glaze Toby of Roosevelt was also made by Doulton & Watts of England in 1910.

After the First World War a series of portrait Tobies were made of the English, French, and American heroes. They were designed by Sir F. Carruthers Gould, modeled by A. J. Wilkinson, and made at the Royal Staffordshire Pottery. The only American hero represented was Woodrow Wilson, and only five hundred jugs of his head were made. It is not a very attractive jug, but since the molds were destroyed it will some day be valuable.

As late as 1928 the Patriotic Potteries Association of Philadelphia had jugs made with the portraits of Hoover and Alfred Smith. They are white and were made in china by the Onondaga Pottery Company of Syracuse, New York, and in earthernware by the Owen China Company of Minerva, Ohio. The earthenware Tobies are harder to find because only seven thousand were made, while twenty-five thousand china jugs were made. They all have printed autographs along their bases.

BIBLIOGRAPHY

Portraits in Pottery, by Albert Lee. The Stratford Company, Boston, 1931.
Ceramics in Art and Industry, no. 5. Doulton and Company, Ltd., Lambeth, England, 1947.

10

American Chalkware or Plaster-of-Paris Figures

CHALKWARE IS A misnomer for figures made of plaster of Paris. These naïve figures of animals, fruit, men, and women were made and sold throughout the country in the 18th and 19th centuries. More have been found in the Pennsylvania Dutch country than anywhere else and for that reason for some years all chalkware was considered Pennsylvania Dutch. However, history shows that chalkware figures were made in several parts of the country as well as imported from England. Such figures were also made in Italy, Germany, France, and elsewhere. Plaster of Paris was introduced by Ralph Daniel in 1745 and this led to casting from slip, in plaster-of-Paris molds. The figures of English stucco duro ceilings were made in this manner by Italian workmen in England, and the same workmen probably made the plaster-of-Paris figures imported into this country and advertised in New York, Boston, and Philadelphia newspapers in the 1760s. In the *New York Gazette and Weekly Mercury*, October 3, 1768, James Strachan, carver and gilder, from London, and David Davidson, who were in the looking-glass business in New York, advertised: "He has also imported some elegant plaister busts." On February 2, 1769, Bernard & Jugiez, Carvers & Gilders in Philadelphia advertised in the *South Carolina Gazette & Country Journal*: "Have imported from London looking glasses, figures of plaister-of-Paris, brackets, etc." In the *New York Journal or General Advertiser* June 1, 1769, Nicholas Bernard, Carver, "Has for sale . . . Figures of Plaster-of-Paris." The first notice of any plaster-of-Paris figures made in this country appears in the notice of Henry Christian Geyer, stonecutter, of Boston, in January 25, 1770, in the *Boston News Letter*. He advertises "image making or Fuser Simulacrum, Kings and Queens, King George, Queen Charlotte, King and Queen of Sweden, King and Queen

73

of Prussia, King and Queen of Denmark—Busts, Mathew Prior, Homer, Milton—Animals, Parrots, cats, dogs, lions, sheep. All made of Plaster-of-Paris of this Country produce. Country shop keepers supplied." The fact that Geyer was German and used German words in describing his products indicates that he sold to the German trade and may well have sent them to the Pennsylvania Dutch country.

Later, in the early part of the 19th century, peddlers carried trays of plaster-of-Paris figures around the country and sold them on the streets of large cities. As early as 1808 a small book illustrated with quaint engravings, *Cries of New York*, includes the image peddler and his cry: "Images, very fine, very pretty." The text explains that images or representations of animals were made of plaster of Paris, a "kind of stone from Nova Scotia." As late as the mid 1850s there is an illustration in *Godey's Lady's Book* of a peddler with a tray of images and animals. These figures continued in popularity into the 1880s and those found and collected today are, except for a few of them, the products of the last half of the 19th century.

Plaster-of-Paris figures were made in half molds and the two parts cemented together, leaving a hollow center. Some large pieces were cast in a single piece and weighted. In *Select Collection of Valuable and Curious Arts and Interesting Experiments* by Rufus Porter, which was published in 1826, directions are given for casting images in plaster. Sulphate of lime and water the consistency of putty was used. The model, image or fruit, was brushed with olive oil, then covered with plaster 2 inches thick; when dry it was cut in two, the casts were oiled on the inside and bound together with string or tape, and into this two-piece mold the wet plaster to form the image was poured. In *Art Recreations*, published by J. E. Tilton in 1860, similar directions were given for making molds for fruit, lambs, sheep, dogs, and figures. Plaster-of-Paris images may have been made in molds of metal, but I find no mention of any but plaster molds made from the objects themselves and, in the case of fruit, from fresh fruit. The early figures were sized and painted with oil paint, but the later ones were painted with water paint and were not sized before painting. There was never any oven firing and thus no glaze. The figures were, however, hand decorated, and the work, although crude, has a certain folk quality. The artist was in most cases attempting to reproduce likenesses. The shortcomings of the untrained artists gave the pieces a primitive quality. The colors, which are usually pure red, green, black, yellow, and brown, have mellowed with the passing

TOP: Deer, yellow-green with black spots. Bloomer girl. Dog with yellow ears, red-brown spots. BOTTOM: Fruit and leaves. Bird, yellow wing outlined in red. Cat, tan with black spots, red ears and mouth.

of time, so that even though they may have been harsh when they were first applied, they are now attractive.

The subject matter for the most part was drawn from Staffordshire pottery figures. There are pastoral scenes, houses, mantel clocks, and animals, as well as portraits, including Washington, Lincoln, and General von Steuben. The animals include goats, sheep, rabbits, deer, cats, dogs, birds, parrots, squirrels holding nuts, roosters, and lions. A spotted cat reminds one of the early Whieldon figures, and the reclining deer is similar to the Staffordshire deer reproduced in brown Rockingham. There are also sheep, poodle dogs, spaniels, and birds that must have been cast in molds patterned in Staffordshire. Pastoral scenes of shepherds and shepherdesses, and quaint Bloomer girls, firemen, angels, and Kris-Kringles, were also among the figures.

Pairs of stylized fruit and leaves on a vase standard were made for mantel or possibly church-altar decoration. A charming figure of two birds facing each other is typical of peasant design. There is also a vase of fruit with two birds perched on top, one of two roosters facing each other, and one of a cat with a bird in its mouth. Holes for clocks or watches are found in the center of formal groups of fruit and leaves and also in plaster-of-Paris rectangular mantel-clock shapes. Pine cones set on a base and painted yellow or blue were made in pairs for mantel decoration. Fruit pieces are harder to find than animals and birds. They were also cast in two molds, but only the front section was painted. Single oranges pricked with holes, pale and anemic in coloring, were set against a pyramid of green leaves. The pineapple or pine cones are rare. Cathedral pieces with spaces for candles and houses are also found and they too can be traced directly to Staffordshire pottery models. The portrait busts are large and styled similar to the early ones of queens and notables. Large figures of men, women, and angels are also shown sitting in armchairs. Portraits are also made in bas-relief and set in plaster frames, some of which imitate the oval walnut frames of the late 19th century.

Figures of plaster-of-Paris religious subjects were sold in Italy and the Balkan States, as well as the Rhine Valley and the Palatinate. Since the Pennsylvania Dutch came from the Palatinate, the theory has been advanced that the subject matter for plaster-of-Paris figures made in America had a religious background. Figures in the churches of Spain and Mexico which were made in the 19th century are a combination of wood and plaster and often have a symbol, such as a heart or a star, painted on. The conventional star on the plaster-of-Paris dog in the Brooklyn Museum and one in the Museum of Modern Art may thus be traced to an ecclesiastical origin.

These figures were never made in a factory, but were all made by individuals from similar molds. No molds have been found, but the molds themselves were probably made of plaster of Paris, which would account for the fact that none remain. The figures must be judged for their line and color and the naïve and primitive workmanship which gives them their quaint charm. Although these "chalkware" figures have been reproduced, the fakes can easily be recognized, since the plaster cannot be aged.

11

English and American Trivets and Sadiron Holders

TRIVET IS ONE of those words that brings up a picture—a romantic picture of a fireside, burning logs, shining brass firedogs, and a brass trivet on the hearth with perhaps a pot of tea, two armchairs at the hearthside, snow outside the windows. The reader may finish the story to his own liking, and if he is a collector of trivets, I wager he has spun many such tales about these fascinating pieces of iron, brass, or copper. Yet for the uninitiated I will attempt to define or describe a trivet.

A trivet is a metal stand which stood in the fireplace or on the hearth on which a pot or kettle was put to keep hot when off the fire. The usual type of trivet is of wrought iron and is composed of three legs attached to a circular plate or ring with a strengthening stretcher between the legs. Often the trivet has a brass top with a perforated design, which in the early examples may include a date or the owner's initials. "Spider" is another name for trivet. Spiders or frying pans originally had three legs, and when the pan was removed the name "spider" was retained. The "cat" was still another form of 18th-century trivet. It was made up of six spokes and a central body and could be used either side up.

Trivets came into use in the 17th century. A trivet of pierced and engraved brass with a design composed of a baluster device, scrolls, and Atlas holding the globe of the world is dated 1668 and is now in the Victoria and Albert Museum, London. Similar trivets with perforated brass tops, turned wooden handles, and legs of cabriole shape became the typical English trivet of the 18th century. The turnings of the handles are varied and interesting, and the legs and stretchers also differ in construction. Some are of wrought iron and some trivets have brass front legs. These trivets all have three legs with connecting stretchers which vary from simple sup-

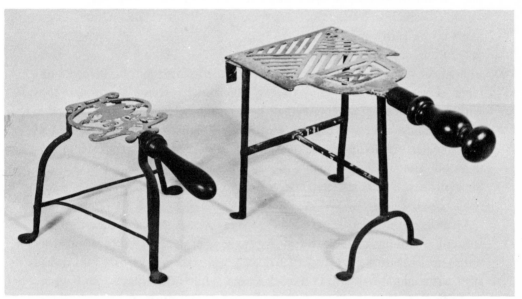

TOP: Crossbar trivet, wooden handle. CENTER: Trivets, pierced brass tops; on Right, Chippendale design. BOTTOM: Crossbar trivet. All English, 18th century.

ports to stretchers which follow the contours of the top plate. However, the most interesting feature of these 18th-century trivets is the pierced or cast-brass top plate. Its design includes human and animal figures, conventional floral and foliated designs, interlaced circles, compass designs, and Chippendale fretwork.

Large tablelike four-legged trivets, with a lifting hole in their brass top, were made to hold the dripping pan under the spit or for parlor use to hold the hot-water kettle. They are called "footmen." They were used in English drawing rooms in the 18th century and also in America. A fine footman of this type is made of copper and brass and has a design of pierced hearts, moon and cross, and the initials "J.S.L." The brass legs are cabriole-shaped and the trivet is probably of Pennsylvania Dutch origin made in the 18th century.

In the second half of the 18th century trivets which hung on fire bars, to hold the teapot or kettle, were a part of the living-room fireplace equipment. These were made of wrought iron and had brass perforated tops with geometrical, guilloche, Greek key, or Chinese designs, and wooden handles. These trivets of brass or steel made to hook on the bars, often had the same perforated designs as the fenders. They not only were used in cottages but also were fashionable in large houses to the end of the century. Some fire-bar trivets also had legs and were made to stand as well as fasten to the fire bar.

In the 19th century, trivets were made of cast brass and they took the form of an oblong table with four legs similar in design to the various furniture styles. Some have turned baluster legs, others legs of Chippendale type with animal feet and lion-mask knees, while others have two baluster supports and resemble a sofa table in contour. These trivets have cast-brass tops with perforated designs of circles, fretwork, or foliation.

Trivets were in use in America as well as in England as early as the 17th century, although according to inventories of the time they were not plentiful. They were of simple wrought-iron construction and probably made by the man of the house or the local blacksmith. I have never been able to find a trivet mentioned in the list of articles made by any of the early iron foundries. I finally turned to a search of old inventories, where I found the few following notices after reading over five hundred inventories of 17th- and 18th-century New York and Salem, Massachusetts. In the inventory of William Paine of Boston made in 1660 a simple iron trivet is listed: "In cellar under ye Hall—1 Iron Trivett and Trampell." Also, in

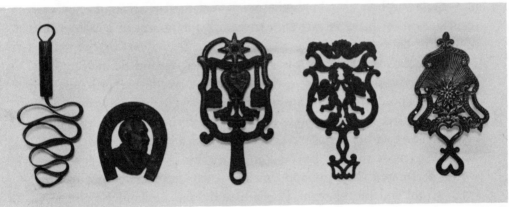

TOP: Iron and pot holders, geometric designs. CENTER LEFT TO RIGHT: Cast-iron trivets: Hand-wrought, Garfield, Love Birds, Cherubs and Hearts, Order of Cincinnati. BOTTOM: Lincoln Drape, Fireman. G.A.R., Serpent, Odd Fellows.

the inventory of Capt. George Corwin of Salem, Massachusetts, are listed "3 grid irons, 1 pr. pot hooks and Trevet." And again in the inventory of Dr. Thomas Braine in 1739 we find "1 iron to set plates on, 1 spit."

In 1753 "1 Triplit" is listed, and in the inventory of D. W. Ditmars, Jamaica, 1755, we find listed "1 Trivet, assorted Pewter plate." In 1767 Mary Hoome owned "2 Hatchets & 1 Trivett" and in the inventory of the estate of James Forbes, a New York merchant, in 1781 we find "1 Trivet." In 1760 Samuel Lawrence owned "4 Trammels, a grid Iron & 1 Trivott." The fact that these early trivets were recorded along with sundry small articles of iron probably accounts for their scarcity today, since most of them probably were put on the junk heap and sold for old iron. These early American trivets were of the spider type with long legs set to a circular band, or with short legs with teeth like projections within the circle. These were made with and without long iron handles. When there is a handle the third leg is placed as a support to the handle. Often a design of circles, crossbars, or honeycomb is found within the iron circle, and often instead of a circle the base that holds the pot is rectangular, triangular, or even semielliptical in shape. A rare iron trivet has a long arm or handle turned upward to hold spoons.

Wrought-iron trivets of these general types were made in New England, Pennsylvania, and other early American states in the 17th and 18th centuries. Those made in Pennsylvania often were heart-shaped or had hearts, swastikas, or barn symbols incorporated in their design. Trivets with cast-iron and cast-brass tops were used in America in the late 18th century. They were made in both England and America. The English-type trivet with a perforated brass top and legs and a wooden handle was imported from Bristol and Birmingham, England, and from Holland. Some had an eagle design. Brass trivets were made in Waterbury, Connecticut, by Benedict and Burnham; the Waterbury Brass Company; Brown and Bros., and Holmes, Booth, & Haydens in the 19th century. They usually copied the English designs.

In the *New York Daily Advertiser*, June 4, 1800, D. Crawley, dealer in "Kitchen Furniture," advertised "Some capital high trivets or footmen with brass tops (much asked for, last winter)." Again on November 19, 1800, Crawley advertised "High trivets with brass tops for parlour grates. Do. with iron tops."

In the *New York Commercial Advertiser*, November 22, 1810, the following advertisement was printed: "Fine Hardware, Cutlery, etc.—Herman Hughes & Co; 298 Pearl St. or Maiden Lane—Copper Coal Scuttles, Brass Footmen, Stair Rods, Chimney Hooks, Bellows, etc."

On January 23, 1823, the *New York Commercial Advertiser* contained the following advertisement: "Drawplates or Tripods—1 case polished Hanging and Draw Plates or sliding Tripods for grates—Also a few elegant trap fenders. Consignment E. Irving."

Stands for smoothing irons, sadirons, or flat irons are now also called trivets. The early iron stands were of hand-wrought iron. They were usually triangular in shape, but similar trivets of round or rectangular shape were used as kettle or plate holders. All of these trivets were made with or without handles. Some handles were of wrought iron and were a continuation of one of the structural lines of the trivet; other handles were of separately attached pieces of wood. Iron stands were made as early as the beginning of the 18th century. One of the earliest iron stands was wrought from a thick piece of bog iron. It was cut lance-shaped with three large spikes riveted through from underneath to act as feet. Another early type consists of three strips of iron forged together in triangular shape, with the three ends bent down at right angles to form feet. Although the general structure of these iron holders was triangular, their contours and lines varied with the whim of the individual maker and no two are alike—circles, horizontal or vertical bands, and hearts are often a part of the design. One especially interesting holder is made of ribbon volutes of thin iron with a wooden handle attached to the base.

In about 1830 trivets began to be made of cast iron, and by 1850 cast iron had taken the place of the earlier wrought iron. However, the shapes and many of the designs were similar. The most interesting of the earlier cast-iron trivets had hearts, eagles, stars, circles, and simple scrolls as motifs, but gradually designs became more elaborate, and naturalistic flower-and-leaf and fruit patterns as well as patriotic and symbolical designs became popular. Designs of Tudor roses, grapes, pineapples, cherubs, and lovebirds are especially decorative.

Designs representing lodges and other societies were made for the Masons, Odd Fellows, Order of the Cincinnati, and G.A.R., while portraits include the fine George Washington trivets, one of President Garfield, and a Jenny Lind trivet made in 1850. Other rare trivets include the Lincoln Drape, a serpent design, the Fireman, one of lovebirds and hearts, and a valentine design of hearts and cherubs.

A design with a cannon, sword, and crest was probably made in the

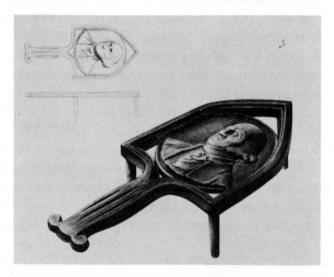

TOP: Cast-iron trivet, late 19th century. CENTER LEFT: Eagle and Heart, leaf border. CENTER RIGHT: Hearts and flowers. BOTTOM: Portrait of Washington.

1860s, while stars of various sizes were often incorporated in the design of cast-iron stands. A design of a star and a cross was made by Colebrookdale Iron Company in 1890.

The late 19th-century iron stands were commercial in every way and many of them had the names or initials of the company that made them as their only motifs of design. Such letters as "E" for Enterprise Company, and "O," "B & D," "H-2H," "R.N.H.," "W," "Less," "Drake," "Harper," all refer to manufacturers' names and have little or no aesthetic interest.

Many late iron holders also contained such mottoes as "Good Luck to all who use this Stand." This motto is set within a horseshoe. A horseshoe with an eagle and clasped hands contains the words "Good Luck." The words "Purity, Truth, and Love" are enclosed in a heart-shaped design which also includes a star in a triangle. Also such trade phrases as "Sensible," "Best on Earth," "Double Point," and "I Want You Comfort Iron" were commonly used in place of decorative motifs.

Makers of cast-iron trivets or sadiron stands include many well-known iron foundries such as Colebrookdale Iron Co., Pottstown, Pennsylvania; Strause Gas Iron Co., Philadelphia; New England Butt Co., Providence, Rhode Island; Less & Drake, Newark, New Jersey; Enterprise Co., Philadelphia; Harper, Rosenbaum Mfg. Co., and Wreedit Gas Iron Co., New York. One trivet commemorates the Centennial at Philadelphia and another says "Richmond, Cal."

These cast-iron stands were even made in the early 20th century. From the collector's standpoint, the early hand-wrought trivets, because of their interesting workmanship, hold a particular interest. The early cast-iron designs are often of decorative or historical value, while the late stands with initials or mottoes are only interesting in rounding out the complete picture of the trivet.

A collection of iron stands is especially appropriate and decorative when hung in the kitchen or pantry. I know of one collector who hangs them on the kitchen fireplace mantel as well as on the walls and above the windows. And I remember a luncheon of fried chicken, homemade biscuits, and oven-cooked rhubarb served in the same kitchen. I left the table from time to time for closer examination of certain iron stands, and we took some of them off the wall and passed them around and discussed their age or the origin of such a design as the hearts and lovebirds. Never does time pass so quickly or food taste so good as when shared with those whose interests match your own. Collecting iron stands or trivets seems such an appropriate hobby for one who likes to spend extra time in the kitchen.

Although iron stands are becoming scarce, they are still within the reach of the collector of average means. However, many cast-iron stand designs are being reproduced today; so the collector should beware of these. Trivets proper are much more difficult to find and their prices are much higher, although they too are among the moderate-priced antiques.

BIBLIOGRAPHY

Dictionary of English Furniture, by Percy MacQuoid and R. Edwards, 3 vols. Charles Scribner's Sons, New York, 1924, 1927.
Index of American Design, National Gallery, Washington, D.C.

CHAPTER

⊷ 12 ⊶

Brass, Iron, and Copper Cooking Utensils

THE EARLIEST American inventories of about 1634 list many of the household articles then in use. Kitchen utensils of metal included brass and iron pots, frying pans, kettles, skillets, baking pans with covers, iron pothooks and hangers, and brass skimmers. Fireplace equipment also included a trivet, firedogs, and shovel and tongs, all of iron. Bellows and warming pans, usually brass, were also listed in the earliest inventories. Other articles included the brass or iron mortar, brass or iron candlesticks, the chafing dish, and the smoothing iron. Copper kettles and pans are not mentioned until about the middle of the 17th century and then they are usually called "coppers" or "a copper" without describing the article. However, in a Salem, Massachusetts, inventory of 1647 we found "1 small copper kettle."

The inventories listed about as many brass as iron pots and more candlesticks and mortars of brass than of iron, but the metal used in warming pans was not designated. However, since copper seems to have been scarce, the early ones were probably of brass. There were also more brass than wooden mortars. Snuffers were scarce. In an inventory of 1646 "snuffers with bras chayne"—to keep light fingers from carrying them off—are listed.

Although most of these early utensils were imported from England, and the blacksmiths who came in the first ships to America made many wrought-iron trivets, pothooks, forks, shovels, tongs, and andirons, the man of the house probably made many of his own utensils. However, before 1650 there were iron furnaces in Lynn and Braintree, Massachusetts, which made stoves, pots, skillets, and mortars, and in 1658 a furnace in New Haven, Connecticut, was making iron pots. Braziers and coppersmiths do not seem to have worked to any great extent in America until the first

87

TOP: Copper kettle and brazier, 18th century. Copper measure "W.H.T., 1871." CENTER: Copper cup, ring handle, Copper brazier, 18th century. BOTTOM: Copper jug and pitcher.

quarter of the 18th century, and copper articles still continued to be scarce until the end of the 18th century.

The hand-wrought trammel or pothook to hold the pot over the open fire was an important item in the early American home. It varies from about 6 to 15 inches in length and is in two pieces so that it could be lengthened or shortened to suit the size of the pot and the flame of the fire. Trammels often had as many as five hooks. Long-handled meat forks with two prongs, long-handled spoons, ladles, and spatulas, and brass strainers with wrought-iron handles were in common usage in the 17th and 18th centuries. The handles of these were usually flattened into an outline of rectangles, elongated diamonds, or ovals, with a hole in the end for hanging. Some handles are decorated with hand-punched designs or perhaps a date or name or initials is traced on the rare ones.

The early iron pots and kettles—even the early skillet—usually had three legs. Baking pots had an iron cover. There was a long-handled frying pan and a short-handled frying pan or spider. A chafing dish is listed in a Massachusetts inventory of 1641. It may have been brass but more likely was iron or at least on an iron stand. Pots and kettles were of many sizes and shapes. Those made to swing from the crane had flat bottoms, while late kettles may be recognized by the extension made to fit in the stove hole. Kettles had straight sides and pots usually had bulging sides. The early iron pots and kettles were made on molds. The earliest are said to have been made at the Lynn, Massachusetts, furnace. Later double boilers and charcoal braziers were made of iron. The early hand-wrought iron pots and kettles were irregular in form and had simple top edges, while the later factory articles were more true in shape. The first cast-iron teakettle was said to have been made in 1760. Cast-iron pots and kettles show a joining line and they also often have several raised lines about their circumference. The hook for the handle is usually cast in the utensil and is rounded, in contrast to the handles of the wrought-iron pots, which are a projection of the pot itself. Sometimes extra handles or rings are found down the sides of the pot. The handles of later pots were of heavy cast iron. Square and round gridirons were stands with gratings and legs. The long-legged ones, or trivets, are discussed in Chapter XI.

Several early-17th-century furnaces in Massachusetts and Connecticut made hollowware, pots, skillets, kettles, and mortars of iron. By the 18th century there were also furnaces in New York, New Jersey, Pennsylvania, and Delaware, and late in the century in New Hampshire and Vermont. Some of the best-known furnaces that made hollowware as well as other articles were Kings Furnace, 1724, and Six Furnaces, 1731, Massachusetts; Hope Furnace, 1735, and Three Furnaces, 1735, Rhode Island. The Salisbury Furnace advertised in the *Connecticut Courant* for April 16, 1770: "Five Potash Kettles, Tea, of Pig Iron, 3 large iron kettles, a no. of cast boxes—all manufactured at Salisbury Furnace." This furnace made cannon and camp kettles in 1776. In 1771 the New York Air Furnace advertised "Iron pots, kettles, pye pans, chimney backs cast iron according to customers pattern.—Peter T. Curtenius." In Rivington's *New York Gazette,* November 18, 1773, the following advertisement appeared:

Vesuvius Furnace—At Laight & Ogden Air Furnace, are made Iron Castings of every kind, equal in quality to any imported from Europe. They now have for sale at the store of Edward and Wm. Laight, Pot—Ash Kettles, Coolers, cauldrons of forty gallons; iron pots and kettles from 28 to 1 gallon, lighter than Holland or English: iron stoves of various sizes; plates for chimney backs and jambs; iron sash weights . . . ox-cart and waggon boxes; iron tea kettles and pye pans; griddles, etc. Any or every of the above enumerated articles are made at the shortest notice agreeable to any pattern or dimensions to be left . . . at the furnace in Newark.

In the *New Jersey Journal,* November 8, 1779, the Mt. Hope Furnace advertised "Nails, Hollow Ware and other casting to be exchanged in the old way for country produce."

In 1796 Leshers Furnace in Reading, Pennsylvania, shortly to dissolve, advertised "Hollow Ware patterns for stoves and Hollow Ware." This furnace established in 1738 had manufactured much hollowware.

New Jersey furnaces which are known to have made cooking utensils are Hanover Furnace, 1793; Hibernia, 1764–1778—pans, kettles, stoves; Martha Furnace, 1793–1834—hollowware, kettles, spiders, sugar kettles, stoves, firebacks; Mt. Holly, 1730–1778—camp kettles for the army (paid $249 for 187 kettles in 1775); Mt. Hope, 1773–1825—Pots, kettles, griddles, andirons, smoothing irons, mortars; Taunton Furnace, 1765–1830; Batsto Furnace, 1766–1842—iron pots, kettles, oval fish kettles, skillets, and large kettles 30 to 125 gal. Mortars marked "B" have been found. Trenton Forge, 1729–1784 (?), made frying pans, dripping pans, ladles, etc., from 1745. Furnaces in Pennsylvania known to have made hollowware were Mt. Pleasant Furnace (1738–1783), Mt. Holly Furnace, and Murray, Griffin & Bullard. The last two furnished Revolutionary War camp kettles. In Virginia the Massaponax Furnace (1732), made pots and skillets.

In 1795 the Shakers at Shirley, New York, had a furnace which cast iron and brass for their own use. The Reverend William Bentley describes it in his diary:

We visited their furnace which had been employed casting stoves, andirons, boxes for wheels and such like purposes. From the Blacksmith we purchased one of their brass candlesticks which was very plain and neat. We saw iron candlesticks of the same form. They make all their own ironwork.

As late as 1767 imports from England to America included "Iron pots, kettles, tea kettles, skillets, spiders, stew pans, mortars, pudding pans, chimney backs, dogs." However, by 1806 the American furnaces were making enough household articles to furnish the needs of all. A list of American-manufactured goods appears in *Poulson's American Daily Advertiser*, May 18, 1807: "Iron pots, ovens, spiders, skillets and bake plates, gridirons, ladles, skimmers, flesh forks."

Although brass and copper household articles continued to be imported from England until the 19th century, there were braziers in New York and Philadelphia as early as 1717. In 1725 Caspar Wistar hammered brass and copper kettles and made some cast brass. Henry Shrimton is said to have worked as early as 1665. In 1735 Jonathan Jackson made plates, spoons, andirons, warming irons, skillets, kettles, and candlesticks. But the first Boston brazier who appears in the early advertisements is William Coffin, who in 1736 made and sold knockers for doors, brass dogs, candlesticks, shovels, tongs, small bells. In 1736 Mary Jackson and her son William, of Boston, advertise "Hearths, Fenders, Shovels and Tongs, Hand Irons, Candlesticks, Polishes Braziers Ware." In 1750 "Said Mary makes and sells teakettles, coffee pots, copper pans stew pans and baking pans, kettle pots and fish kettles." Thomas Russell, brazier, of Boston, made and mended "tea kettles, warming pans, and coffee pots, skillets, frying pans, kettle pots, sauce pans, wash basins, skimmers, ladles, copper pots copper funnels brass scales."

As early as 1737 William Linthwaite advertised in the *South Carolina Gazette*: "Sells only such goods as he makes himself viz. Brass, Copper, Tin Wares."

In 1757 Philip Syng, brass founder from Philadelphia, made and repaired candlesticks, heads or knobs for shovels, dogs, plate warmers, bells, knockers for doors, in Annapolis, Maryland.

In 1763 Richard Collier and Daniel Jackson, two braziers from Boston, moved to Providence, Rhode Island. Collier advertised in the *Providence*

William Bailey,

COPPERSMITH,

Of the BOROUGH *of* YORK,

TAKES this method to inform the public in general and his numerous customers in particular, that he carries on the COPPERSMITH BUSINESS, in all its various branches, as usual, at his dwelling house opposite Mr. Andrew Johnston's Tavern, sign of the Bear and Cub.—At CHAMBERSBURGH, under the direction of his son WILLIAM.—At HAGER'S-TOWN, next door to Mr. Jacob Harry, Hatter, in Partnership with his son-in-law Mr. WILLIAM REYNOLDS—and at FREDERICK-TOWN, near the Poor-House, in Partnership with his brother-in-law Mr. ROBERT M'CULLEY.

Notwithstanding the scarcity, these four shops are completely supplied with Copper, suitable for all kinds of Copper Work; and in particular STILLS of all sizes, BREWING COPPERS, WASH, FISH, and TEA KETTLES, SAUCE-PANS, COFFEE and CHOCOLATE POTTS. — He has Complete Workmen in each shop, regularly bred to the business, many of them having been taught by himself. He also carries on the TIN-PLATE BUSINESS, in all its various branches, at each of the above mentioned places. He will also attend on Wednesday and Thursday in every quarterly Court week, at Mr. Thomas Foster's in the Borough of Carlisle, in order to save his customers trouble and expence, who wish to agree for Copper or Tin Ware to be made at any of the above mentioned places.——The highest price will be given for OLD COPPER, BRASS, PEWTER, and LEAD, at each shop.

He returns his sincere thanks to all his former customers, and hopes the continuance of their favours.

York Borough, July 23, 1792.

LEFT: *The Carlisle Gazette*, Carlisle, Penn., July 25, 1792. RIGHT TOP: Copper and brass tea kettle. RIGHT CENTER: Tea kettle, 18th century. RIGHT BOTTOM: Copper cake mold

Gazette and Country Journal: "Tea kettles, kettle pots, skillets, warming pans, stew and bake pans, frying pans, skimmers, ladles, etc." Jackson advertised "Brass hand irons, fire shovels, tongs, candlesticks, snuffers, knockers of all sorts, furniture trimmings for cabinet makers, saddlers and chaise makers."

In 1744 John Halden, of London, made "brass and copper kettles, tea kettles, coffee potts, pye pans, warming pans, chaffing dishes and candle sticks" at his shop in New York. Other braziers working in New York at about this date were John Genter; Nicholas Vandyck; Moses Taylor, who made brass and copper kettles in 1751; James Byers, who made "andirons, tongs & shovels, fenders, candle sticks, buckles, etc."; William Scandrett, who made brass and iron hand irons; and Jacob Wilkins, at the "Sign of the Brass Andiron and Candlestick," who made all kinds of brasswork. Thomas Pugh made brass bells and Henry Witeman made brass buttons. John Graham and John Taylor also advertised brasswork at about this time. Needless to say, these articles of American braziers followed the styles of English brass goods. Indeed as late as 1775, Richard Skellorn, brass founder from London, "makes the following articles from the newest patterns now in vogue in London. Namely all sorts of fine and common candlesticks, brass and iron, fret fenders, coach and cabinetwork—all sorts brass weights, mortars and millwork. Bells cast." In the same year in New York handsome brass candlesticks were advertised at 22s., 20s., 18s. 16d., and 16s. a pair. In 1794 Peter Van Norden was operating a brass foundry in Bound Brook, New Jersey, and making such articles as brass and iron andirons, candlesticks, and shoe and knee buckles. Braziers, tobacco boxes, jugs, sugar bowls, milk cans, pitchers, measures, pipkins or coal skuttles, whale-oil lamps, thimbles, buttons, and eagle ornaments were also made by American braziers from the middle of the 18th century. Brass kettles "from a barrel to a quart" were sold in nests in 1775.

The early articles were made from sheet brass, which was hammered over a mold with handles riveted on. The handle was flattened where it joined the body of the pot or pan. Sometimes these flattened ends took the form of hearts, squares, rectangles. They were fastened to the body of the utensil with two or three rivets. Sometimes the handles were of hand-wrought iron, or they might be a hollow tube of brass with a wooden extension handle. Such articles as andirons, candlesticks, and door knockers were usually cast. From 1832 brass kettles were cast, but as late as 1834 they were often hammered into shape by hand. Often iron and brass casting was carried on in the same foundry, as in the case of the Revere foundry established in 1793.

By the 19th century the brass business had centered in New England to a great extent, and large foundries were established in Waterbury, Connecticut. Andirons and tongs and other articles were made in Berlin, Connecticut, and brass kettles in Torrington, Connecticut. There were brass foundries in and near Boston.

It is rare to find brass marked with a maker's name, but enough exists to give evidence that brass household utensils were sometimes marked and enough names of early braziers are now recorded to make a search for more marks one of the chief interests of the collector. We know that Paul Revere & Son marked some of their brass, including andirons now in the Metropolitan Museum of Art. William C. Hunneman (1769–1856), an apprentice of Paul Revere, operated foundries in Boston and Roxbury, Massachusetts. He made andirons, skillets, brass kettles, candlesticks, warm-.ing pans, copper teakettles, and large copper kettles with covers. His stamp (below, right) has been found on andirons and on the handle of a kettle. Richard Lee of Massachusetts (1747–1821?) marked the handles of brass skimmers (below, left). Skimmers were also a specialty of Amos Purrington at Weare, New Hampshire, in 1815.

Except where the maker's mark can be identified, it is almost useless to try to distinguish between English and American articles of brass. Generally speaking, American brass is heavier than English, and English brass is usually more elaborate and refined in design.

Utensils of copper do not appear in American inventories until the middle of the 18th century, and not until the end of the century do we find more than one or two stray articles listed. These facts, together with the fact that advertisements of coppersmiths seldom appear until about 1750, lead us to believe that there were few coppersmiths in America until that time and that few copper articles were made here—because of the scarcity of copper. However, from 1744 to 1746 the advertisements of John Halden, brazier from London, read: "Makes and sells all sorts of copper and brass kettles, Tea Kettles, Coffee Pots, pye pans, Warming Pans, and all other sorts of Copper and Brass Ware.★★ Makes and mends copper stills."

Moses Taylor made copper kettles in New York in 1751, Richard Kip in 1758, and John Smith did both the work of a brazier and coppersmith at the sign of the Brass-Kettle, Tea Kettle and Coffee Pot from 1769 to 1774. In 1752 Joseph Leddel advertises that he engraves copper and brass. In 1767 Joseph Wicks made copper utensils at Huntington, Long Island. In the account book of a general store in Schenectady, New York, in 1752 we find "nest copper kittles." The following year, payment of "John Halding (Halden), Brasher" is listed as follows:

> To 4 copper kittles 2/9   12:4:9
> To 1 copper kittle 12 to 10 oz.   1:14:9
> To 6 copper kittles 9 oz. to ¾ pound   12:14:3¾

In 1779 the *New Jersey Journal* advertised "Copper tea kettle bottoms" to be sold at Chatham. A few months later, "a large copper kettle which holds 250 gallons" was offered for sale at Morristown and also "a brew kettle 300 lbs weight [which] will contain near nine barrels."

In the inventory of Jonathan Holmes of New York in 1774 the following household articles of metal were listed, which include enough copper to indicate that by then it had come into general use: "Brass chimney hooks, andirons, shovels & tongs, Warming pan, Pestle & mortar, brass coffee pot, pr. smoothing irons, iron fender, brass candlesticks, snuffers, copper kettle, brass tea kettle, pye pan, copper sauce pan, copper chaffing dish, copper skimmer." An inventory of 1781 includes: "4 copper kittles, 2 copper pots, 2 copper sauce pans, 1 copper stew pan."

By 1787 there were about an equal number of braziers and coppersmiths working in New York City. Coppersmiths in New York at this time included Thomas Thomas, James Bennett, John Grill, Robert Burnham (who lists himself as a coppersmith and brazier), Jeremiah Jessop, John Sewind, John Taylor, and C. Pell. At present no more is known about these men, but they are listed to aid the collector who may have a marked piece.

There were a large group of coppersmiths in Pennsylvania in the 18th century. As early as 1737 Peacock Bigger advertised in the *Pennsylvania Gazette* that he made teakettles, coffeepots, warming pans, copper pots, saucepans, kettle pots, Dutch ovens, and brass kettles. William Bailey and his sons carried on the business of "Coppersmith, Brazier, and Tin

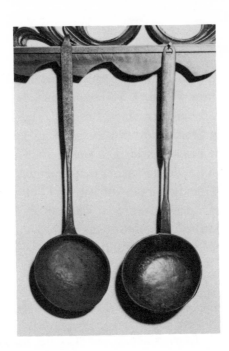

TOP: Copper ladles. CENTER: Copper dippers. BOTTOM: Brass kettle, 19th century. Iron pot.

Plate Worker" from 1783 in York, Pennsylvania, and in 1792 also opened shops in Baltimore, Hagerstown, and Frederick, Maryland, and Chambersburg, Pennsylvania. He manufactured brewing kettles, fish and washing kettles, saucepans, and coffee and chocolate pots. One of Bailey's advertisements mentioned that he "stamped with his name," but to date no articles have been found thus marked. Jacob Heyser (1796–1842) marked his wares with his name and city, Chambersburg. This mark has been found on a teakettle. Israel Roberts of Philadelphia marked his ware "Isral Roberts—Phil." John Morrison, also of Philadelphia, marked his articles "J. Morrison" inclosed in a scalloped rectangle. "W. Heiss—Phila." is the mark on a pot in the Salem Historical Society. Copper has also been found with a two-eagle mark which is certainly early, although not identified. A list of Pennsylvania coppersmiths which may be of assistance in identifying marks has been compiled by George Kauffman and is taken from his article on Pennsylvania coppersmiths in volume II, 1946, *Pennsylvania German Folklore Society*.

PENNSYLVANIA COPPERSMITHS, 18TH CENTURY

Wm. P. Atlee, Lancaster
Wm. Bailey, York, Baltimore, etc.
Mathias Babb, Reading
John Babb, Reading
Peacock Bigger, Philadelphia
Victor Blanc, Philadelphia
S. S. Bradley, Philadelphia
Gerald Cotton, Philadelphia
William Cumins, Philadelphia
James Curry, Philadelphia
Rumford & Abyah Daves
Robt. Doughty, Philadelphia
Jacob Durr, Philadelphia
Andrew Eisenhart, Philadelphia
Jacob Eicholtz, Lancaster
Wm. Forster, Philadelphia
Gilbert Gaw, Philadelphia
Francis Graham, Philadelphia
Lewis Grant, Philadelphia
Jas. Haldane, Philadelphia
Benj. Harbeson, Philadelphia and Lancaster
Joseph Harbeson, Philadelphia
Alex Henry, Philadelphia
Wm. Henry, Philadelphia

Fred Hubley, Philadelphia
Alex Helmuth, Philadelphia
Jas. Jobson, Philadelphia
Robt. Lyne, Philadelphia
Geo. Lefrentz, Philadelphia
Marvereau, Philadelphia
John McCauley, Philadelphia
Jas. McCalmond, Philadelphia
Jeffe Oat, Philadelphia
Oat & Cook, Philadelphia
Geo. Orr, Philadelphia
Jas. Potter, Philadelphia
Israel Roberts, Philadelphia
Frances Sanderson, Philadelphia
Geo. Sefferon, Philadelphia
Fred C. Steiman, Lancaster
Peter Steel, Philadelphia
Reuben Topham, Philadelphia
Benj. Town, Philadelphia
Jas. Trueman, Philadelphia
Jas. Winstanby, Philadelphia
Caspar Wistar, Philadelphia
Malcolm Wright, Philadelphia
G. Yousse, Philadelphia

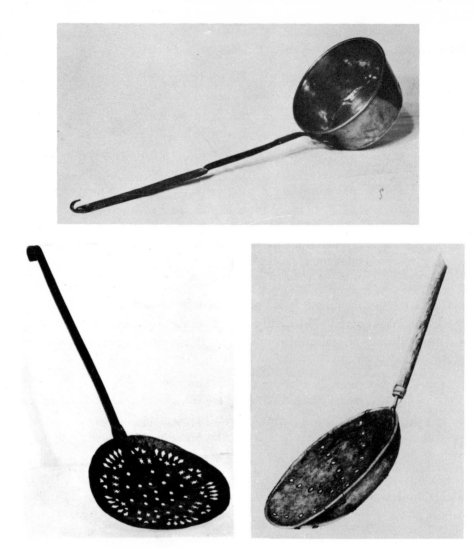

TOP: Brass dipper, iron handle, 1780. CENTER: Copper strainer, etched design, iron handle. Copper strainer, wooden handle. BOTTOM: Set of copper measures, 19th century.

To this list may be added the name of David Lindsay of Carlisle, who made copper stills of various sizes in 1792, and Henry Grottman, who is certainly from Pennsylvania, although I have not been able to place him as to date or city.

In 1796 Matthias Babb opened his coppersmith shop in Reading, Pennsylvania, at his house, where he made and repaired "stills, wash kettles, tea kettles, and all sorts of copperware. Kopper tea kettles for store keepers."

From 1800, the coppersmiths are too numerous to list. There were twenty-five in Philadelphia alone, and as many in other large cities. As their business grew along 19th-century commercial lines, it became the common practice to mark much of their goods. J. P. Schaum and Samuel Diller of Lancaster, Pennsylvania, worked late in the 19th century and stamped their wares. Wash kettles and large apple-butter kettles were much in demand among the Pennsylvania Dutch farmers.

The most common copper articles to be found are pots, kettles, teakettles, stills, measures, and ladles and skimmers. Urns, braziers, chocolate pots, and warming pans are rarer and thus bring higher prices.

Utensils of copper are both hammered and cast. The early utensils were hammered out of sheet copper with a wooden hammer over an iron mold. Spouts and handles were riveted on by hand. Pans and kettles and ladles, dippers, and skimmers, usually had a handle of hand-wrought iron riveted on the body of the utensil. The blacksmith usually made the handle. Sometimes the handles are of copper tubing, or a short hollow copper handle may hold a longer handle of wood. The bottoms of old kettles were separate from the sides and were cut in a pattern of tooth edges that joined to the sides of the utensil. Bottoms of kettles wore out sooner than the sides and were often replaced. Although not many early articles of copper are marked, there are enough to make the search rewarding. Marks are stamped on the handles of teakettles, ladles, and pots and on the sides of large wash kettles or apple-butter kettles. A large copper apple-butter kettle in the collection of the Landis Valley Museum is marked "P. Schaum."

Old copper may be identified by its workmanship, which not only includes hand riveting but hammer marks and irregularities of shape. Hand-wrought iron handles are also found on old pieces.

13

Iron, Brass, and Copper Andirons, Door Knockers, Candlesticks, Warming Pans, and Bellows

FOR THE COLLECTOR of iron, brass, and copper there are many different household articles available, including door knockers and andirons of iron and brass, candlesticks and snuffers, and warming pans as well as bellows made of brass, wood, and leather. All of these articles are available and most of them reasonable in price.

Although andirons are too large to be of interest to the average collector, those who have houses with several fireplaces may be interested in collecting several types. The earliest andirons, or "dogs" as they were called, were of wrought iron. They were made by a blacksmith or hand-hammered by the man of the house. These andirons had simple curved legs and feet and usually a straight flattened shaft and an enlarged top or head. Sometimes the head was looped to hold a roasting spit or it might be a colonial pigtail or a flattened scroll, heart shape, or ogee type. Other hand-wrought heads were gooseneck with a ball top or goose head with a bill; sometimes the shaft was twisted and ended in a ring top. In the last half of the 18th century hand-wrought andirons often had a brass head in the shape of a ball or a sunflower face. The earliest andirons usually had hooks to hold a spit for roasting meat, and some had a basket top to hold a grease cup. Early cast-iron dogs were made with a straight shaft, which was often decorated with a geometric pattern. Such andirons made in England often had a date cast in the shaft. About the middle of the 18th century andirons were cast in designs especially suited to American tastes. These cast-iron andirons often actually had primitive dog, owl, or eagle heads. Other early designs were of Adam and Eve or busts of women.

About 1780 the Hessian soldier, smokers, and the figure of George Washington were especially popular as were, later, ships and houses. Some of these designs were also made much later, and such andirons as the ship, owl, and eagle have been copied today. "Brass andirons, tongs, and fender" were listed in a New York inventory of 1740, in 1767 "brass knobed andirons," and in 1783 "brass headed andirons." By 1780 the English brass founders of Sheffield and Birmingham were issuing trade catalogues, so it was easy for American braziers and brass founders to follow the English models. Thus it is difficult today to distinguish American from English cast brass. As early as 1744 copper and brass pipkins or coal buckets were also made. English pipkins followed the styles of Chippendale, Hepplewhite, and Sheraton, and many of these were imported to America. However, there were brass founders in America in the latter part of the 18th century, and in 1794 Peter Van Norden, brass founder of Bound Brook, New Jersey, advertised "brass and iron andirons, candlesticks, shoe and knee buckles," in the *Guardian* or *New Brunswick Advertiser*. Cities as large as New York, Boston, Philadelphia, Baltimore, and Charleston had as many as a half-dozen brass founders at this date.

Wrought-iron andirons with brass knobs with facet cuttings and a flame top date late in the 18th century. Andirons with spiral knobbed turnings and a similar top were made entirely of brass, and similar brass andirons with claw-and-ball feet were made by Paul Revere & Son in about 1800. Such a pair is in the collection of the Metropolitan Museum of Art. The classic influence of Adam influenced the shape of andirons, and vase-shaped shafts were made in the second quarter of the 18th century. At first the vases were large and were a part of the shaft itself, but later the vase moved up the shaft and the shaft finally became a narrow column with a vase finial. Similar andirons also had steeple tops and others had round ball tops or flame tops, while still others had lemon tops. All of these various styles had pad feet or claw-and-ball feet and pillar or turned shafts. In the 19th century the shaft was made up of heavy turnings and often ended with a ball top, but many of the earlier styles also continued to be made.

Andirons are seldom marked, but the Metropolitan Museum of Art owns not only the marked andirons made by Paul Revere but also a pair made by J. Davis of Boston that date from the early 19th century. These have slipper feet, a straight base shaft, and a ball with a steeple top. T. De Coudres, a worker in copper, brass, and tin in Newark, New Jersey, from 1825 to 1840 often marked his brass andirons. William C. Hunneman of

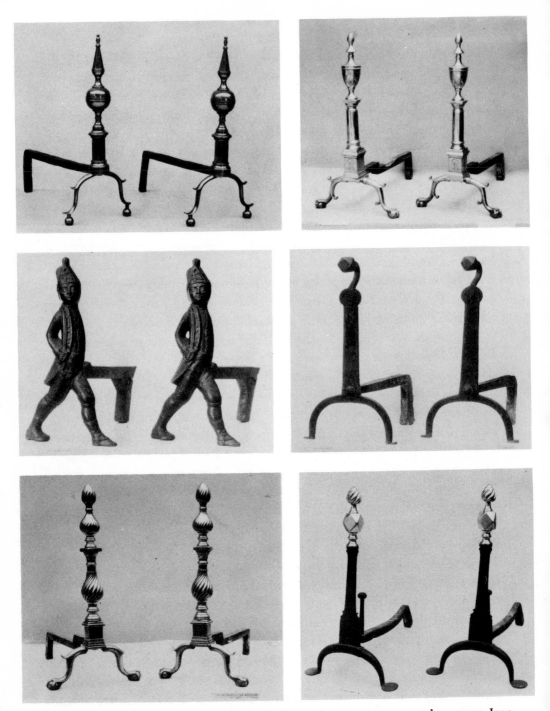

TOP: Brass andirons, steeple tops, "J. Davis, Boston"; vase top, engraved. CENTER: Iron Hessians, 1780. RIGHT: Wrought-iron, faceted knob. BOTTOM: Revere & Son, 1789–1803. RIGHT: Brass faceted knob, flame finial, 1767–1783.

Boston and Roxbury, Massachusetts, made and marked some brass andirons as well as kettles, skillets, candlesticks, and warming pans.

IRON AND BRASS DOOR KNOCKERS

Another article of interest to the collector of metal household articles is the door knocker of iron or brass. Simple hand-wrought iron knockers with a ring and plate were used in the 17th and 18th centuries in America, England and in the various countries of continental Europe. Cast-iron door knockers came later. In America the eagle was the favorite motif for the cast-iron knocker. Other cast-iron knockers of the 19th century had leaf decorations, Egyptian heads, the head of the goddess Diana, a hand grasping the knocker, or a woman's profile on the plate, and a wreath of flowers and leaves as the ring knocker. English knockers were cast in the form of a lion's head. However, since there are no marks it is difficult to distinguish the American from the English product. Most of the brass door knockers date from the 18th century. The two most popular motifs were the shell and vase designs. Shells are usually the earliest. Sometimes the shell forms the plate and again it is only a small motif on the ring of the knocker itself. The vase motif usually forms the plate against which the handle knocks. Early vases are simple and slender, while late in the 18th century the vase forms have a broader shape. The influence of Adam brought in details such as fluting, swags, laurel leaves, and floral motifs. Brass door knockers are seldom marked, but the collector should look for marks. Indeed the question of markings on articles of antique brass has not been explored, and diligent search may reveal makers' names with as much interest as those of other metalworkers.

CANDLESTICKS

The brass candlesticks used to have a place of honor on the candlestand by a comfortable armchair or at the four corners of a game table. They vary enough in design, following the influence of the various periods of decoration, so that a group makes an attractive display. English and American brass candlesticks are so similar in appearance that it is difficult to tell which is which except in the case of a rare marked one. Candlesticks were used in churches from the earliest times, and domestic candlesticks also date back to the use of the early spricket type. However, the earliest brass candlestick that the present-day collector is likely to find is the 17th-cen-

tury column type with a small socket and no lip and a bell-shaped base with
a drip pan low on the base. A few years later the base flattened out and the
grease pan was moved about halfway up the column, but the small lipless
socket remained. This candlestick is usually made of solid metal and is quite
heavy. There is no removable nozzle, but often a bolt to adjust or expel the
candle. These early candlesticks have a turned baluster stem which is plain
or in simple knots. The large grease tray at the base or up the stem was a feature of many brass candlesticks late in the century, but candlesticks were
also cast with an octagonal baluster stem embellished with narrow moldings
and a large octagon-shaped base which held a small concave circle for drip-
pings. They still did not have a socket lip. A little later, in the early 18th-
century pictures of Hogarth, we see baluster candlesticks with knobs and a
wide saucer drip pan at the base. By the middle of the 18th century, under
the influence of Chippendale, the grease pan has moved to its place at the
socket lip. The baluster stems are cast into various ridges and the base is
octagonal and often shaped into curves or petals with many narrow moldings. A few years later the Adam influence brought in candlesticks with urn-
shaped sockets, plain or fluted. Stems were sometimes fluted, and sometimes
the baluster took the form of an elongated urn. Bases were square and often
had a border of beading. These designs were delicate and refined and show
the influence of silver-candlestick design more than at any other period.
By the 19th century brass candlesticks again were larger and heavier. The
stems had heavy knobs, which were both round and cone-shaped; sometimes the cone is upright and sometimes inverted. The bases were square or
rectangular and often the corners are cut to make them octagonal. These
candlesticks are hollow and lighter in weight than those of the century
before.

It is rare to find an exact pair of old brass candlesticks, so when a pair
is offered, one should be sure that the candlesticks are old. Here are a few
things to consider. The weight is important, since old brass is usually
heavier. It also has a peculiar silky surface that you are able to distinguish
only after you have handled many pieces and compared them with reproductions. The detail on old brass is more refined in workmanship than on
new work. Marks are rare but worth looking for. Sometimes one candlestick is marked and the mate of the pair is not. The Metropolitan Museum
of Art owns two pairs of candlesticks with a baluster stem and an eight-lobe
base (1750–1760), one of which is marked "E. D. Durnall" in a semicircle

TOP: Brass knockers, shell, vase, and lyre, 18th century. SECOND: Vase types, 18th century. Masonic and Egyptian, 19th century. THIRD: Vase and eagle, 18th century. Cast-iron eagle (center), 19th century. BOTTOM: 18th-century brass on the ends. Classical vase types, brass, 18th century. Diana and bust of woman, cast iron, 19th century.

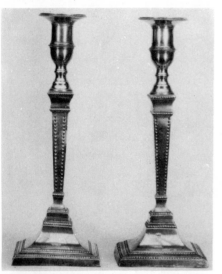

TOP LEFT: English brass, 17th century. RIGHT: American brass saucer base, 18th century. CENTER LEFT: English brass, Georgian. RIGHT: Chippendale style, "E. D. Durnall." BOTTOM LEFT: Victorian brass. RIGHT: Chamber candlestick, 19th century.

on the underside of the base. Candlesticks were made in America in the early 18th century in Boston by Jonathan Jackson, who also made door knockers, firedogs, warming pans, and skillets. In 1763 Daniel Jackson of Boston moved to Providence, Rhode Island, where he made "brass hand irons, fire shovels, tongs, candlesticks, snuffers and knockers," according to his advertisement in the *Providence Gazette and Country Journal*, October 26, 1763. Richard Collier, brazier from Boston, also moved to Providence in 1763. There were braziers in New York as early as 1744 who made candlesticks, andirons, tongs, shovels, fenders, and warming pans, as well as kettles of various sorts. Jacob Wilkins in 1765 worked at the "Sign of the Brass Andiron and Candlestick." In 1775 brass candlesticks were advertised at 22s., 18s., 6d., and 16s. a pair. Candlesticks also continued to be imported from England.

The candlestick collector is also interested in snuffers and trays, which were necessary accessories. The trays were usually at least 6 inches long, and narrow, with a flanged border. The edges were plain or might have a scalloped or Chippendale shape and may have a border of lines, beading, or leaf decoration. While we are particularly interested in brass trays, there were also snuffer trays of tin, plain or painted, and also trays of silver. Snuffers are of various forms, and their evolution from the 16th-century double-heart-shaped box type of brass or iron down to the late 18th-century patented types offers many interesting and different designs for the collector. In the 17th century the familiar rectangular box came into use. The point at the end of the snuffer seldom varies, but the design of the box and particularly the handle design is different on each pair of snuffers, and this is the collector's delight. In the 18th century snuffers were mostly made of steel, but there were some in iron and brass. Late in the century they were made of Pinchbeck metal, and the first patent mechanical snuffers came into use. Many patents on snuffers followed, and for the collector interested in this phase of the antique this offers a field in itself. There are many 18th- and 19th-century snuffers available of both English and American make.

WARMING PANS

One of the most interesting articles for the collector of brass and copper is the warming pan. Warming pans are quite plentiful and reasonable in price. English, Dutch, and American warming pans are to be seen in shops today and except for the rare marked piece it is hard to distinguish one from another. Early Elizabethan and early American warming pans had wrought-iron handles. Warming pans are listed in old New York inventories as early as 1730, but the material is not designated. However, the early ones were probably of brass rather than copper because copper was more scarce. However, in 1744 John Halden, brazier from London, advertised in the *New York Weekly Post-Boy*: "Makes and sells all sorts of Copper and Brass Kettles, Tea Kettles, Coffee Pots, Pye Pans, Warming Pans and all other sorts of Copper and Brass Ware." An early American warming pan of chased brass with a hand-wrought iron handle is in the Metropolitan Museum of Art; and there is also a brass warming pan with a handle of turned applewood, made by Revere & Son. Other early turned handles on brass and copper warming pans were of ash or oak. While most warming pans were either of copper or brass, some were made with a combination of the two metals, such as a brass bottom with a copper lid, and some crude warming pans were made of tin. The most interesting feature of the warming pan was the chased and pierced pattern on the cover. The designs included flowers, leaves, birds, and geometric patterns. A favorite design was the tulip, which is found on both the Dutch and the Pennsylvania Dutch. Another design was a conventional flower made up of circles, scrolls, and rayed lines; leaves and dots are also arranged in patterns. The open perforations are usually arranged in a geometric pattern. While few warming pans were marked those found marked include such makers as Revere & Son, Boston; Hunneman, Boston; and A. D. Richmond, New Bedford. Old warming pans show smoke marks inside, and the joint between the handle and pan is usually loose and the engraving worn. When the handles are turned the knobs are often light-colored from wear.

BELLOWS

Fireplace bellows made of wood, leather, and brass and decorated with painting, turning, and carving are available in antique shops today. Bellows of some kind date several centuries back, but any bellows found today date no earlier than the 18th century and most of them were made in the 19th century. Paul Revere sold bellows made of turned wood, leather, and brass, but he probably did not make them but imported them from England. A similar pair of bellows with sides of turned wood is in the collection of the Metropolitan Museum of Art. Samuel McIntire, the wood carver of Salem, Massachusetts, carved bellows, and a bill dated November 6, 1808, shows

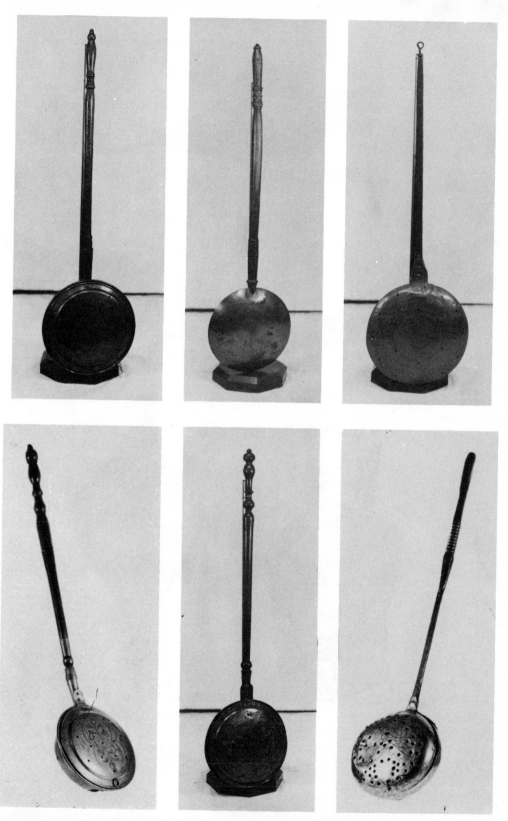

TOP RIGHT: Brass warming pan. CENTER: Copper, "A. D. Richmond, New Bedford." LEFT: Brass with copper cover, iron handle, 18th century. BOTTOM LEFT: Brass, etched design. CENTER: Copper, tulip design. RIGHT: Copper, etched design.

TOP: Bellows, turned wood, 18th century. CENTER: Wooden and leather bellows. RIGHT: Painted daisies. RIGHT: Turned wood and brass. LEFT: Country bellows.

that Jacob Sanderson the cabinetmaker paid McIntire 24s. for carving bellows. A pair of mahogany bellows carved by Samuel McIntire is in the collection of Mrs. J. Insley Blair. The design includes a basket of flowers, swags, and a wreath of roses. In 1815 McIntire's son Samuel Field McIntire carved bellows tops as well as cake and butter stamps, chimney pieces, eagles, and ships' heads. In 1811 there was a brush and bellows manufacturing company in Albany, New York; Charles McMurtry's patented bellows were sold in Connecticut and Massachusetts; and Eckstein & Richardson of Philadelphia made bellows in about 1820 for which they owned a patent. These were stamped "Eckstein & Richardson Patent No. 36/ Philadelphia." One pair of bellows made by them had a painted landscape with a woman on one side and flowers in a basket painted on the other side. The flower-and-basket motif was typical bellows decoration. Sometimes the painting combined gold with the color and some later designs were stenciled.

Early country-type bellows had no decoration. They are of various shapes, round and rectangular, as well as the more sophisticated heart shape which is more often seen. These simple bellows combined cowhide, wood, and nailheads but did not have a brass end and also did not have the braided- or woven-leather decoration. On some bellows the brass stem and nailheads are particularly decorative, but it is the combination of materials that makes even the simplest bellows interesting. If you find a pair with painting or carving or even turned-wood decoration, you are fortunate, for although many bellows were made in America as well as in England and other countries, they have been handled carelessly and most of those found today are not in very good condition. However, bellows are interesting and worth collecting and moderate in price.

~14~

Britannia Ware

FOR MANY YEARS our corner cupboard has held a decorative old pewter teapot with incised decoration and acanthus-leaf feet. On the bottom is the stamp "1669." Of course we knew that it wasn't the date, but Mother always said, "That is an old pewter teapot that I got from your father's family in Scotland." She also had a pewter pitcher which came from the same relatives, and it is marked "James Dixon & Sons 4868P½" on its base. These pieces seemed of different weight and harder and even of a slightly different color and had more sheen than some of the pewter plates which we had, but it was many years before we found out that they were Britannia and not pewter proper.

Now, Britannia ware not only has a different appearance from pewter but it is made by a different process. Pewter is cast and Britannia is spun. The chemical make-up of Britannia has little variance from that of pewter. In fact, it is a superfine grade of pewter, and the name Britannia was invented to dramatize and revive the declining public demand for pewter. But the process of rolling the pewter into sheets and the stamping and spinning required less skill of the craftsman and thus less handwork. Also the spinning process changed the metal, making it harder, thinner, and lighter in weight. With the introduction of mass production in about 1825, the shapes became poorer in design and less individual.

Britannia can usually be identified by the small catalogue numbers which are stamped on it. Also much of it is stamped with the maker's name. The shapes of the Britannia period differ from the old pewter shapes. The tall coffeepot, the pigeon-breasted teapot, the water pitcher, and the whale-oil lamp are typical of the period. Edges are sharp and lines of structure broken. Handles terminate in blunt stubs soldered flush against the body.

Forms were simple at first but with Victorian times fluting and decoration such as molded gadroon borders, acanthus-leaf feet, spout decorations, and even etched designs became common, and the shapes were
distorted with concave and convex bulges. Some tea sets were octagonal.
Black wooden handles and finials were usually hand carved, and bottles
for the popular caster frames of the 1830s were usually made at Sandwich
and the New England Glass Co.

Britannia was first made in England in about 1780 by Nathaniel Gower
and James Vickers and after 1804 by James Dixon & Sons. Dixon was the
best-known maker. Dixon made no pewter, but only Britannia, and thus
anything marked Dixon is Britannia. Other English makers were Wolsten-
holme, I. Vickers, Ashberry, Broadhead & Akin.

Any piece of pewter marked Sheffield is probably Britannia, as is a
piece with the mark "Colsmans Improved Compost," and of course the
small numbers which accompany the name of the maker are catalogue
numbers.

A great deal of English Britannia was exported to America, especially
that made by James Dixon & Sons, and this was for sale by New York
merchants as early as 1821: "Britannia teapots—J. B. Skillman." The following enlarged advertisement appeared in the *New York Commercial
Advertiser* for June 12, 1822: "Britannia Teapots—The subscriber has just
received and has for sale at auction prices a good assortment of Britannia
Teapots with sugar Basins and cream Ewers to match—J. B. Skillman."
Several other New York merchants advertised Britannia ware in the year
1823: "Britannia Ware—Table and teaspoons, Tea & Coffee pots, tea sets,
Flaggons, Cups, Platters and Plates of Church service.—Pelletreau &
Upson" (*New York Commercial Advertiser* May 6, 1823). In September
the same firm ran the following advertisement: "Britannia Ware—Tea Sets,
Coffee pots, plain and engraved." In December, 1823, the well-known merchant E. Irving inserted the following advertisement: "Britannia & Brass
goods. Best double mounted Britannia Tea Pots, 4, 5, & 8 gills—Extra
quality & in sets."

As late as 1840 "Dixon's Victoria Patterns" were for sale in New York
and Dixon's Britannia continued to serve as models for Britannia ware
made by American pewterers.

Pewter collectors have scorned Britannia, and it is alluded to with a
feeling of contempt because of its generally poor craftsmanship and shapes,
which have no individuality but were the same at all factories. However, a

TOP: Ladle, James Weekes, 1822–1845. CENTER: Flagon, T. D. Boardman. Lemon bowl lamp, 1825–1850. Coffeepot, Samuel Simpson, 1833–1852. BOTTOM: Shaving mug, George Richardson, 1782–1848. Two-handle beaker, T. D. & S. Boardman, 1810–1854.

few early American pewterers made fine Britannia, and any articles made by them have gladly been accepted by the most discriminating collectors even though they side-step calling them Britannia. At first so little Britannia was made that it passed for pewter, and it was not until about 1825 that American Britannia was manufactured in any quantity, so that this date really marks the beginning of its popularity.

Britannia was first made in America in about 1810, but we cannot be sure of its first American maker. Ashbil Griswold of Meriden, Connecticut, (1807–1835), was one pewterer who made early Britannia, according to a letter in the *Diary of William Bentley D.D.*, now in the Essex Institute. Isreal Trask and Eben Smith of Beverley, Massachusetts, were making Britannia in 1814. But even as late as 1824, when Babbitt & Crossman of Taunton, Massachusetts, began the manufacture of pewter and Britannia, the business was on a very limited scale. Roswell Gleason of Dorchester, Massachusetts, may have made Britannia this early, but he did not make many pieces before 1830, when he became one of the largest manufacturers of Britannia in America. Gleason made lamps, candlesticks, pitchers, tea- and coffeepots, and communion plate.

H. Yale made Britannia from 1824 to 1835, while William Calder made Britannia lamps as early as 1826. Among the items listed in William Calder's daybook from 1826 to 1838 appear "Britannia best and no 2 tumblers; teaspoons and tablespoons of both pewter and Britannia; handled Britannia church and molasses cups; plain nurse and Britannia lamps." The term "Britannia" was used sparingly until 1828, but after 1830 distinctions between pewter and Britannia were seldom made, for the entire product of the shop was then probably Britannia. The Calder name-in-rectangle mark was used after 1825, and the "Providence" mark is found on late forms. Although both of these marks indicate Britannia, they may also have been used on pewter.

George Richardson (1818–1848) made teapots, sugar bowls, pitchers, washbowls, ewers, tumblers, and lamps, but he is famed for his fine sugar bowls.

Early pieces of Britannia made by Babbitt & Crossman include inkstands, shaving boxes, cups, and looking-glass frames. Britannia tea ware was not made until 1827, when a set was exhibited in the factory show window. Wm. W. Porter, foreman and overseer of the factory, stated that the next batch which was made consisted of eighteen teapots and that they were the first American Britannia teapots ever on the market. At any rate the design for these teapots was excellent. It copied the English fluted style, was footed, and had a decorative gadroon border and black wooden handle and finial. Urns, coffeepots, and teapots are also mentioned among the first products, but by 1829 Babbitt & Crossman were making door plates, latches, and mountings for harness as well as cream and sugar sets, lamps in pairs, lather boxes, tumblers, slop bowls, goblets, and pitchers. Babbitt & Crossman later became the present firm of Reed & Barton. In the 1829 fair of the American Institute, Crossman, West & Leonard, as the firm was then called, was awarded a discretionary premium for "superior Brittany Ware." At the same fair the following year the company also received a prize "for an assortment of very handsome Britannia Ware."

In regard to the Britannia industry in Meriden, Connecticut, in 1833, Leander Bishop in *A History of American Manufacturers*, volume 2, makes the following statement:

> One company employed two hundred and fifty hands in the manufacture of Britannia Ware such as coffee pots and mills, spoons, waffle irons, signal lanterns, etc. to the value of $200,000 per annum and another made to the amount of $25,000.

One of the best-known names among makers of American Britannia was Boardman. As early as 1821 Timothy Boardman was advertising in the *New York Commercial Advertiser*. A review of the advertisements of this firm from this date through 1850 gives the best picture possible of the Britannia industry in America. The notices are full and give detailed lists of the articles made and even descriptions and sizes of several of them. The first advertisement appeared June 11, 1821:

> Block Tin & Pewter Ware Mfg—178 Water St. 2 doors west of Burling Slip. Timothy Boardman & Co. have on hand and are constantly manufacturing Teapots, Cups, Porringers, Basins, plates, Platters of various sizes, Bed & close stool pans; sucking bottles, Ladles, Spoons, Tumblers—Block Tin Flaggons, Tankards, Goblets, Baptismal Founts, etc. which will be sold at reasonable prices at wholesale and retail. Orders in the above line thankfully received and faithfully executed.

This advertisement ran daily throughout the month of June. The same advertisement, with a few additions — "Music plates, syringes, etc." — appeared in July, 1823, together with an illustration showing a flagon and two styles of teapots. Laughlin records that the firm's name changed to Boardman & Co. in 1825 after the death of Timothy Boardman. The next notice does not appear until March, 1827, when Britannia is mentioned for the first time. It reads as follows:

Boardman & Co., Manufacturers of Britannia Metal, Block Tin and Pewter Ware. 78 Water St., have on hand and are manufacturing a large assortment of the above ware consisting in part Flaggons, Goblets, Tankards, Pottery, Plates & Baptismal bowls for churches, Coffee urns, tea and coffee pots, Porter cups, liquor measurers, Bed and chair pans, Nursery bottles, tumblers, ladles, spoons, syringes, inkstands, basins, plates, porringers, etc. which are sold on lowest terms wholesale & retail.

Besides the record of the change of the firm name to Boardman & Co. we also have an indication of the importance of Britannia ware in the output of the company, since it is listed first from this date on.

By May, 1828, the firm name had been changed to Boardman & Hart, and an advertisement states they "continue to manufacture and keep constantly on hand" not only the usual stocks of articles but a few additional items such as "sugars, creams, slop bowls and Church Furniture." A similar advertisement ran from then on throughout the year 1828. In addition, several small advertisements stated "Britannia Teapots carefully repaired"; "An apprentice wanted at the manufactory of Britannia, Block Tin and Pewter Ware—None need apply without best recommendation." In June the advertisement carried an illustration of a coffee urn and read, "Coffee Urns, Boardman & Hart, 178 Water St., manufacture and keep on hand a good supply of Britannia Tea and Coffee Urns suitable for steamboats, hotels, and boarding houses; also Tea and Coffee Pots, etc. etc., together with a general assortment of articles of Britannia, Block Tin and Pewter Ware, wholesale and retail."

Children's plates and cups of Britannia metal were advertised as New Year's presents in 1829, and the firm continued to advertise extensively throughout that year and 1830, when coffee pots and teapots "of various sizes and patterns" were listed.

In the *New York Commercial Advertiser*, May 2, 1831, the change of address is announced as follows: "Boardman & Hart have removed their manufactory of Britannia, Block Tin & Pewter Ware to No. 6 Burlingslip between Pearl & Water Sts. Near their former stand."

According to the advertisements between 1831 and 1834 business increased and orders were solicited "from the city and country," and to the long list of articles, oyster plates, Britannia casters, and "spittoons suitable for parlors" were added. In 1835 Britannia tumblers and pewter syringes for druggists appeared. The revolving casters in 1835 were supplied "with neat bottles, a new article." But the most interesting new articles were "lamps and candlesticks," which appeared for the first time on September

TOP: Inkwell, H. Boardman. CENTER: Pitcher, McQuilkin. Covered pitcher, Boardman & Co. BOTTOM: Acorn whale-oil lamp, 1825–1850. Teapot, George Richardson. Lamp, Allen Porter, 1830–1838.

29, 1835, and "uniform companies furnished to order with a new pattern. Canteen & cups for target excursions."

On November 2, 1835, the following advertisement appeared, listing several interesting items: "Britannia Ware—Britannia metal urns, coffee pots & tea pots, pitchers, castor frames, lamps & candlesticks, water plates, venison dishes, cups, tumblers, spittoons, etc. Boardman & Hart—6 Burlingslip."

Just when it seems that pewter has dropped from the list, an advertisement such as the following appears October 10, 1835: "Pewter candle-moulds—Manufactured of good metal. Boardman & Hart." By June, 1836, the demand for lamps had increased and we find the following: "Britannia Lamps. A fine assortment of Britannia metal lamps of various patterns, just received from the manufactory, for sale at our warehouse—Boardman & Hart." Again, in August, 1836, there is "Britannia Metal lamps and candlesticks—new patterns" and in September this interesting advertisement appears: "Britannia Metal Ware. Urns, Coffee & Tea pots, Pitchers, lamps, candlesticks, etc. A few specimens of which are exhibited at the Fair in Castle Garden."

The advertisements in 1837 give us the following detailed information: July 3—"Covered Pitchers—A new supply of 3 qt. Britannia pitchers with covers." August 11—"Britannia Bowls—Quart & pt. Britannia bowls very neat pattern." August 4—"Oval Tea Pots—A few sets of oval Britannia Tea pots, sugar & cream cups." August 7—"Lamps—Britannia metal lamps, a great variety of patterns and sizes. . . . Britannia Lamps & Candlesticks by pair, doz. or gross." September 9—"We have just finished a lot of beautiful Britannia lamps equal to any ever before offered in the market. . . . Bacon's Suspending Lamps." March 18—"Acorn Pattern Lamps."

Block tin and pewter ware continued to be made in 1837 and 1838. November 22, 1837: "Pewter Plates—Pewter plates for the Southern and Western markets." May 4, 1838: "Block Tin Urns—Just finished a supply of Block Tin Urns of various sizes with lamps attached. Also a good assortment of Britannia & Bronze urns with iron heaters." March 28, 1838: "Pewter Plates—A supply of pewter plates & basins."

Not only did Boardman & Hart sell their own goods but they also sold tea sets made by James Dixon and Sons, Sheffield plate, and even German silver goods. In addition to selling wholesale to the army, steamship companies, hotels, druggists, and "inkwells for counting houses," they furnished undertakers with "coffin plates of assorted sizes" and made pewter and block-tin faucets for plumbers.

After a fire in the locality of their shop Boardman & Hart took the opportunity to advertise on October 9, 1838: "Britannia Ware. The subscribers having escaped the conflagration are prepared to furnish orders to patrons on short notice—Boardman & Hart."

The year 1840 brought forth advertisements of several new products as well as a call for pewter: "Old Pewter Wanted—Wanted a few thousand pounds of old pewter." The next month we find: "Pewter Plates—An assortment of pewter plates warranted to be not the latest fashion" and "Old fashioned pewter plates" and on August 1, 1840: "Bells for academies, factories, steamboats & locomotives." Lamps and candlesticks continued to be advertised along with other articles, including teapots, pitchers, and revolving casters. The next few years brought interesting advertisements regarding lamps:

November 23, 1844: "Britannia Lamps—A fine assortment of Britannia Lamps with both flat & round tubes for burning, oil, gas, or lard. Britannia Lard Lamps—Neal's patent lard lamps, a very superior invention." May 6, 1845: "Pewter Measurers."

In 1846 Boardman & Hart still manufactured the following articles of Britannia: caster frames—all sizes, coffin plates, a variety of patterns, Britannia pitchers, coffee urns, nursing bottles, teapots, communion furniture, lamps and candlesticks, a great variety of patterns, Hall's patented spoons, as well as pewter plates—"Old fashioned pewter plates, dishes, & basins."

The firm continued as Boardman & Hart through January, 1847, but on February 1 there appeared in the *New York Commercial Advertiser*:

Dissolution—The co-partnership hither to existing between the subscribers under the firm of Boardman & Hart is this day dissolved by mutual consent. The business of the late firm will be settled and all claims paid by Lucius Hart.

   Thomas D. Boardman
   Sherman Boardman
   Lucius Hart.

The undersigned having purchased the entire stock of the late firm Boardman & Hart will continue the business as manufactory & importer of Britannia Ware & Dealer in metals at the old stand.—Lucius Hart.

The New York directories confirm this dissolution, since Boardman & Hart, Britannia Ware Mfg., is listed in the directory of 1846–1847 but not in 1847–1848, while in the later directory Lucius Hart, Merchant, 6 Burling-Slip, is listed.

In the *New York Commercial Advertiser* for March 18, 1847, the following advertisement appeared:

> Britannia Ware, etc. The subscriber having purchased the entire stock of goods in the store No. 6 Burling-Slip—consisting of Britannia Metal ware in all its varieties, Block Tin ware, Plated goods, Blanca tin, strait's tin, Regulus of antimony, metallic Bismuth etc. and having had the sole charge of the business for the last fifteen years, invites his friends and patrons to continue to deal with him as with the former firm. He hopes by attention to business to give satisfaction to the numerous customers both wholesale and retail who have for many years dealt at the old and well known stand between Pearl & Water Sts.—Lucius Hart—successor to Boardman & Hart.

Lucius Hart continued to use the parenthetical expression "late Boardman & Hart" in his advertisements to 1850. In the *New York Commercial Advertiser* for November 8, 1848: "Fluted Candlesticks. Britannia fluted mantel candlesticks, new and beautiful patterns. Lucius Hart (late Boardman & Hart)."

January 3, 1849: "California Pewter. A new supply of Pewter plates, dishes and wash bowls just received. In future a good assortment will be constantly on hand & orders filled at a moment's notice.—Lucius Hart (Late Boardman & Hart)." Thus the story of pewter is associated with the California Gold Rush!

Other members of the Boardman family who made pewter and Britannia include J. D. Boardman and Luther, Sherman, and Thomas Boardman of Hartford, Connecticut. Laughlin believes that all of the New York Boardman pewter and Britannia was made in Connecticut at the Boardman factory there, but, while there was a definite connection, newspaper sources indicate that there was also manufacturing done on the New York premises. Henry S. Boardman and Boardman & Hall of Philadelphia also made Britannia.

Perhaps the most interesting single article of Britannia from the standpoint of the collector is the whale-oil or "fat" lamp. It is definitely American in origin. Most of these lamps date after 1830, although a few were made before. In shape, the whale-oil lamp is particularly interesting. There are several distinct types, distinguished by the shape of the bowl. The best-known are the acorn bowl, the lemon bowl, the cylinder bowl—plain or hexagonal—the lozenge bowl, the truncated bowl, and the urn bowl. Some of these lamps have round or hexagonal bases and others have saucers. There is also the skirt lamp and the small nursing lamps, as well as the miniature or sparking lamps and the swinging or ship lamps. Lamps range in size from about 4½ inches in height to 14 inches high. They are seldom marked, but many were made by well-known pewterers.

Such well-known Britannia makers as Roswell Gleason, Isreal Trask, Taunton Britannia Manufacturing Company, William Calder, Boardman & Hart, Reed & Barton, Henry Hopper, Eben Smith, and Allen Porter made and marked lamps. Others, such as Brook Farm (1841–1847), Capen & Molineux (1848–1853), Morey & Ober (1852–1854), Morey & Smith (1857), Leonard and Samuel Rust (1837–1844), Thomas Wildes (1832–1840), Yale & Curtis (1858–1867), were known only as makers of lamps.

Lamps and candlesticks were also made by Marstow, J. H. Palethrop (1820–1845), Sickle & Shaw, and by J. B. Woodbury (1837) of New York. John and Joseph Bonis of Baltimore made lamps also, as did Browe & Dougherty of Newark, New Jersey, in 1845 and Houghton & Wallace; Endicott & Sumner; Bailey & Putnam and Archer & Janey of St. Louis; T. M. Buckley of Troy; and Homan & Company and Sellew & Company of Cincinnati, Ohio.

Candlesticks of various types and sizes have been found with the names of Lewis & Cowles, Henry Hopper, Taunton Britannia Manufacturing Company, Boardman & Hart, Roswell Gleason, Charles Ostrander, Wm. Bartholdt, and many others. A complete list of makers of lamps and candlesticks can be found by checking the list of Britannia makers in volume 2 of Ledlie Laughlin's *Pewter in America*.

Many of the whale-oil lamps had patented lighting units, some invented by Britannia makers, others by makers of lamps of other materials. The following list of patented lamps from 1830 to 1880 will be of interest to collectors.

Wm. Lawrence, pat. Mar. 23, 1831; Mar. 10, 1834
E. S. Archer, June 18, 1842 (lard)
Southworth, July 2, 1842
Tomlinson, Sept. 1, 1843 (lard)
Samuel Rust, 1837–1854
John Newell, Oct. 2, 1853
Adams Fountain Lamp, June 30, 1857
Endicott & Summer, 1850
John Love
Wm. Howe, 1812
John W. Schulz & Wm. Trull, 1831

Winslow Lewis, 1818 (lard)
Cornelius, Apr. 6, 1843
Kinnears, Sept. 1851
Geo. Carr (W. H. Parmenter)
Houghton & Wallace, 1843 (lard lamp)
Neal, 1842 (lard)
E. W. Perry, 1842 (lard)
Whitaker's miniature solar
J. P. & E. Kenyon, 1858 (lard)
Butler, Hosford & Smith, 1860 (fluid vapor)

Britannia continued in favor with the American public until electroplating came in and replaced it in about 1850. However, many Britannia makers were working a few years later, and thus you will find designs and shapes with ornate Victorian patterns. These late pieces include covered dishes, cake baskets, tumblers, molasses cups, cups for children, and Hall's patented tablespoons and teaspoons. Any Britannia made before 1830 is worth including in a pewter collection. Britannia made by makers of earlier pewter is also of interest to the discriminating collector. Any piece well executed and of fine design, such as the Richardson sugar bowls, the Boardman & Hart communion flagons, the Taunton Manufacturing Co. tall candlesticks, or the ladle by James Weekes, would form a nucleus for a collection of pieces dating from 1825 to 1850. If the prices of pewter proper are beyond your reach, why not start with your grandmother's old pigeonbreasted coffee or tea set, made by Dixon or Reed & Barton, and assemble a Britannia collection?

BIBLIOGRAPHY

Pewter in America, by Ledlie L. Laughlin. Houghton Mifflin Company, Boston, 1940.
American Pewter, by J. B. Kerfoot. Houghton Mifflin Company, Boston, 1924.
Bulletin of the Pewter Collectors Club.
New York Commercial Advertiser, 1820–1850.
The Whitesmiths of Taunton, by George Sweet Gibb. Harvard University Press, Cambridge, Mass., 1943.

❧ 15 ❧

American Woodenware

THE WOODEN BOWL in which you mix your green salad today is a direct descendant of the wooden bowls used by the 17th-century American colonists. The first woodenware in America was made by the Indians, and later by the individual settler who whittled out a spoon, ladle, or bowl to add to the small supply of household articles which he had brought over from England. However, the making of these small articles soon centered in the tradesmen.

Commercially, woodenware was made by coopers and turners. Plates and bowls and other articles made on the lathe were called "turner's ware." Edward Hazen in his *Panorama of Professions and Trades* gives a description of how such articles are made. "In case the wood is to be turned on the inside as in making a bowl, cup or mortar, the piece is supported by means of a hollow cylinder of wood, brass, or iron called a chuck." There were individual turners and there were also woodworking mills where these household articles of wood were made. The early articles were, however, finished by hand. Kegs, barrels, tubs, churns, and buckets were made by coopers. There were coopers in America from the earliest days. There were tight coopers and dry or slack coopers. Tight coopers made the barrels for liquids, usually out of white oak, and were often known as "oak coopers." Slack coopers made buckets, tubs, and boxes to hold dry materials. They used maple, elm, ash, red oak, chestnut, and hickory. The "white" cooper made small tubs, buckets, churns, and boxes out of maple, pine, birch, hickory, and beech. Cedar coopers made buckets, tubs, churns, and various other small articles of cedar.

However, there were few of these tradesmen until the 18th century, and woodenware was listed among the articles brought over from England by the early colonists. In Governor Endicott's report in 1629, he advises that a planter should provide himself with "wooden platters, dishes, spoons, and trenchers." As late as 1690 an invoice of goods to Boston from England included: "9 doz. best maple trenchers @ 30/doz., 1 doz. porridge dishes at 11/4, carved spoons, beer taps, hair sieves, sucking bottles and milk trays." A few years later, however, woodenware made in America was advertised. The first workmen to produce articles in any quantity were probably craftsmen from England, as evidenced by the following advertisement from the *Pennsylvania Gazette*, October 26, 1732. "Wood Turner from London—All sorts of turning in Hard Wood—Coffee Mills, Pepper boxes, Punch bowls, mortars, sugar boxes—at the shop of Wm. Morgan." In the *South Carolina Gazette*, January 25, 1739, the following advertisement lists woodenware: "George Bridge—Turner in Brass, iron or ivory— makes and sells screws of all sizes, presses of any sort, teaboards of all sizes, pestils and mortars, billiard balls, ninepins and bowls—mends coffee mills." In May, 1739, this interesting note appeared in the *Boston Gazette*: "Whoever has got any curious maple tree knotts to sell may hear of a purchaser from the Publisher." Although by this time turner's ware as well as cooper's ware was being made in many parts of the country, the industry centered in Massachusetts and New Hampshire, and woodenware was being shipped from Boston to the Carolinas as early as 1732. Woodenware, especially buckets, was also shipped south from Philadelphia. In 1730 in a Schenectady general-store account book, the following item appears: "To a wooden bowl 2/." In 1751 John Henry Dyer of Boston advertised: "Cooperware— Rum hogsheads, barrels, caggs, little tubs and trays." In 1768 Joseph Roper, turner, made "Plain and scalloped teaboards, spice mortars, etc., etc"; and Thomas Elfe, cabinetmaker in Charleston, also made "scallop teaboards"; while in 1775 Thomas Tuft, "Joyner" of Philadelphia, advertised: "Rolling Pins, bread tray, Pye board, Mahogany Knifebox, tea board-Ironing board. Walnut butlers tray."

The earliest American inventories of the 17th century list many pieces of "woodenware," and I find no mention in 17th-, 18th-, or 19th-century inventories of any other name for wooden household articles, except the terms "turner's ware" or "cooper's ware," which related the articles to the men who made them. In *New England Plantation* the inventory of Francis Higginson, 1630, contains "wooden platters, dishes, spoons and trenchers." In *Two Voyages to New England* an inventory of 1638 lists "platters,

TOP: Measures, cups, tankard with hand-carved handles. BOTTOM: Turned trenchers. Burl bowls.

dishes and spoons of wood." The name "treen ware" is of foreign usage and was not used here until the 20th century.

The woodenware mentioned in several mid-17th-century inventories of Essex County, Massachusetts, gives an idea of the articles in use at that time: 1675—John Davis, Newbury "a powdering tub, 2 barrels, 2 boxes, meale tub and trough, baking tub, keeler, 4 trays, 2 buckets, 4 sieves, wooden mortar, 2 churns"; 1676, Thaddeus Brand, Lynn, Massachusetts, "3 trays, 8 Wooden vessels, 6 trenchers, wooden ladle, 8 wooden vessels, and ye platters, dishes and wooden strainer."

Many interesting items are also listed in New York inventories of the 18th century and undoubtedly most of them were made in America, since by the 18th century there were both coopers' and turners' and woodworking mills making these articles. A list of the most interesting items with their dates follows:

1726
1 cedar tub
58 butter firkins
one dozen wooden tranchers

1727
a churn and 4 tubs
5 keelers
milk vessels, churn, keelers, pails

1728
wooden dishes

1730
4 trays
ladle
9 trenchers
mortar
cedar bols

1733
wooden mortar
3 wooden bowls
pepper mill

1734
cealors, pales, 4 butter tubs
cheese press, Dolphin cheese mold

1737
wooden trays
a spoon case

1739
one cedar tub
lye tub
5 wooden bowls

1740
wooden dishes and bottles

1741
2 wooden mills
spoon and butter mold

1742
4 wooden bowls

1745
Powdering tub
Trays, pails, and piggin

1747
Rundlet and a ladle
Pails, tubs, churn
Piggin

1752
sider rundlets

1753
1 knot bowl

1755
Sedor tubs
(cuppors tools)
3 pales

1755 (cont.)
2 churns
6 calors and 3 butter tubs
washing tub and lye tub

1757
strainer
cedar tub

1760
3 cedar washing tubs and 2 old piggins

1766
ladles
9 saucers, 7 cups with wooden bowl
barrels, cagg, firkins
Tubb, cyder funnel, butter tub and firkin
3 keelers and churns, 5 milk tubs
5 pails, milk pan and trays and firkin and
    ladles

1767
wooden bools

1768
"not morter"

1769
wooden troff
tubs, barrels, boxes, sieves
wooden plates

1771
6 knot, 2 root bowls
suet tubs
candle box

1772
a wooden bottle
a wooden bowl

1774
seeder iron bound wash tub
seeder wooden bound tub
tray and wooden boles ·

1776
2 knot bowls
7 old bowls, bread tray
scoop

1781
wooden bottle

1784
2 wooden soap ladles
1 butter ladle
cedar churn

1785
11 wooden dishes and 1 trencher
2 trays and 1 wooden bowl
rolling pin
2 molds
knot bowls
white bowls
9 wooden bools

1795: Van Varick, Albany
painted wooden rack to set china in
3 wooden dishes painted
a wooden tray with feet.

Although trenchers are not listed in the later inventories, they were advertised for sale as late as 1775 by William Beadle at Wethersfield, Connecticut, and sold in his general store. In the *Connecticut Courant*, May 1, 1775, appeared the following: "1 doz. of wooden trenchers and some home-made wool cards." Both wooden platters and trenchers were imported from England for some years and although trenchers were made in America, plates or wooden dishes began to take their place in mid-18th-century inventories. Knot bowls were always a rare item and seldom did a household own more than one. In the inventories of John Arms, Westchester, New York, 1771, root bowls are distinguished from knot bowls, but the term "burl" was not used, at least until the 19th century.

In his diary, the Rev. William Bentley gives a description of an Indian bowl or pan. Dated August, 1793, at Dartmouth, Oxford, New Hampshire, an entry reads: "Some Indians do appear at the colleges of whom Capt. Pratt purchased a birch milk pan. The bottom is square and sewed to four pieces of the bark which are formed so as to appear round when the bottom of the pan is covered."

James Pitcher, who owned several farms near New Rochelle and whose account book from 1760 to 1790 is in the New York Historical Society, gives some interesting data on woods and their use as follows:

Red oak, of a porous nature and good for dry casks
Black ash, hoops for coopers
White ash, for chairs and coach wheels
Hickery, for hoops
Maple, turner's ware and chairs
White wood (basswood or popular), trays, bowls, trenchers
Wild cherry, joiners work, desks
Gum wood, joiners work
Chestnut, pales
Dogwood, weavers shuttles
Witch elm, turners, for bowls, ladles
White cedar, tubs, rails

Lignum vitae, which is the hardest and heaviest wood, was often used for mortars. The sapwood is light and the heart is dark. It was imported from the Bahamas, and New York merchants, Lawrence & Whiting, list "Lignum Vitae from Bahamas" in 1808. At about the same time they paid 15s. each for two dozen wooden bowls, which they included along with a dozen green Windsor chairs made by Charles Marsh, in their cargo to the Bahamas.

Collectors today have found articles of woodenware made of various kinds of wood. The following list of woods and the articles most often found will be of help to the collector of American woodenware.

Ash. White and hard; used by turners and for barrel and keg hoops. The Shakers made dippers of ash. White-ash knots are used for bowls.
Beech. Hard, heavy, dark reddish in color. Used for scoops, rolling pins, and boxes, plates, and trenchers.
Birch. Hard, light, close grained. Washboards, clothespins, boxes, plates, and mortars. Curly birch.
Chestnut. Light weight, used for boxes, bowls, mortars.
Cedar. White cedar, light in weight; coopers for pails, washtubs, churns, firkins, keelers, piggins. Red cedar, strong for cooperage.
Lignum Vitae. Dark and light wood, heavy, for mortars, bowls, rolling pins.
Mahogany. Dark, strong, for boxes. *Boston Gazette*, 1740: "John Waghorne—Turnery Ware of Mahogany."

Maple. Hard, light color. Curly and bird's-eye used more than any other wood for
   woodenware: bowls, ladles, spoons, mashers, stirrers, rolling pins, butter prints
   and molds, mortars, boxes, tubs, pails, sieves, dippers, trenchers. Burl for mortars
   and pestles, salts, bowls, platters.
Pine. Soft, light in color: cheese and butter boxes, pipe boxes, salt bowls, platters,
   spice mortars, wall boxes, spoon racks.
Poplar or Whitewood, Basswood. Soft, white, even texture: bowls, spoons, plates, and
   scoops.

Woodenware may be classified as to its use, and collectors will want
to specialize rather than pick at random. An interesting collection would
consist of tableware and eating utensils. This would include trenchers,
platters, various sizes of plates, bowls, drinking cups, sugar bowls with
covers, salts, the tankard and sirup jug, the wooden pitcher or noggin, as
well as spoons, forks, and ladles.

Pantry utensils would include the rolling pin, mashers, spatulas, scoops,
apple parers, pie crimpers, spice boxes, and mortar and pestles, as well as
the spoon rack, salt box and other small wall boxes, butter molds, and cake
and cooky molds.

Buttermaking has its own list of woodenware, which includes milking
buckets, tubs, keelers or half-tubs, butter workers, scoops, butter paddles,
churns, butter molds, and butter prints. Butter molds are of two types—cup-
shaped and boxed. Butter prints with their round turned handles were
factory-made and usually date from the beginning of the 19th century,
although a few were made as early as 1750. The old prints are hand cut
and the patterns are of many designs, including the pineapple, acorn, wheat,
leaf, grape, swan, hen, cow, dove, eagle, tulip star, crisscross allover, and
later a scene with a woman and a churn.

These carved articles of woodenware have a Continental background
and many of them, especially the large mahogany cake boards with their
elaborate scenes, may have been made abroad. Spoons with carved handles,
carved spoon racks, and small carved boxes were made by the Pennsylvania
Dutch and also by settlers of Swiss-peasant or other peasant origin.

Cheese making required special sieves, tubs, boards, paddles, knives,
presses, and molds. These too form an interesting collection.

Spatulas such as the soap stick, the dye stick, the maple-sugar stirrer,
the feather-bed smoother, the butter paddle, the dough paddle and knife,
the hasty-pudding stick, and the toddy stick with its knob end are also of
interest.

Scoops were of various shapes and sizes. The largest scoop is the box-

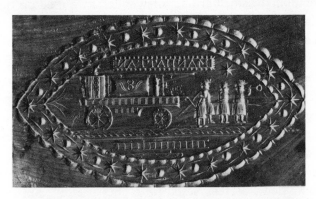

TOP: Butter molds, early 19th century. CENTER: Butter mold, tulip design. RIGHT: Plunger type, pineapple design. BOTTOM: Mahogany cake board with fire engines "Superior 17" and "Manhattan 8."

like soap scoop. The apple-butter scoop and the maple-sugar ladle are also large. Other scoops include cream scoops and skimmers, and scoops for flour, meal, and sugar. The Swiss made their cream scoops with curved handles so that they could hang on the edge of the cream bowl, and bowls are pictured with as many as six scoops hanging about their rims.

A collection of mortars would include large grain and corn mortars as well as the small salt, sugar, spice, and herb mortars. Many mortars are made of burl and fine lignum vitae as well as Quassia wood, maple, and birch. Mortars and pestles were turned on the lathe and decorated with lines spaced to form borders around their circumference. Mortars are of various vase shapes, some having feet or bases, and some are funnel-shaped. Knot and root mortars, curly birch, and bird's-eye maple are rare. Often the pestle is made from a piece of root.

An interesting group of wooden articles was used in spinning and weaving. These include the stick shuttles, the boat shuttles, the bobbin, and the dye mortar.

Unusual small articles in woodenware include the cobbler's forms for shoes, forms for gloves, felt smoothers, and forms for hats.

Hobbles, yokes, stakings, collars, and even wooden stencils to mark sheep are some of the small articles of woodenware used on the farm.

The maple-sugar industry produced interesting articles, such as the long-handled scoop and the shoulder yoke, and the making of apple butter produced two-way scoops and the large loop-handled scoop of the Shakers.

Woodenware was a thriving business in early New England, especially in New Hampshire, Vermont, and Massachusetts, beginning in the 18th century. Ash, maple, beech, and birch were so commonly used to make cups, bowls, and trenchers that these woods were known as "dish timber." White-ash knots also were made into bowls, a knot making a nest of bowls. As early as the 18th century there were several sawmills which made "tuggs, collers, sleds, corfeus, leach tubs, ches presses" and also did wood turning. As early as 1779 Thomas Clark was making wooden dishes, bowls, spoons, and mortars on a foot lathe and coloring them red or blue. And in 1817 Timothy Gillete made ash bowls, plates, cups and saucers, and skimmers on a lathe and peddled them on horseback. In Sutton, New Hampshire, trays, plates, bowls, noggins, ladles, platters, and piggins were made.

By 1825 Rindge, New Hampshire, was a woodenware center for clothespins made of white birch, wooden bandboxes, and veneer spice boxes. Berlin, Wentworth, and Jaffrey were also woodenware centers. At

Jaffrey mortars and pestles and chopping bowls were made, and at Weare, New Hampshire, dishes, spoons, forks and cooper's ware were made of red oak. Bread boards, mugs, trays, and mortars were also made at Weare.

In Massachusetts the town of Winchendon became the 19th-century woodenware center of the world and from 1800 on, Hingham, Massachusetts, was known for cooperage, especially the Hingham bucket. In 1815, in the *Connecticut Courant*, (a newspaper) the following advertisement appeared: "Hhds, pipes, barrels, half bbl., kegs, painted tubs, pails, dry measures and about 50,000 white pine boards." Woodenware was made by B. Leavitt in Chicopee, Massachusetts, from 1830 to 1850.

The large woodenware manufactory of Gideon Cox operated in Philadelphia from 1825 to 1840. This firm made bowls, churns, sieves, butter prints, bathtubs, buckets, and cedar wares as well as "curly bowls" and baskets. Indeed from 1825 on there were many woodenware factories throughout America. After the Civil War and until 1902 butter prints and rolling pins were manufactured at the Kimball Mills in Rindge, New Hampshire. Butter paddles were made of cherry. Much of this woodenware was peddled, first on horseback and then in the peddler's well-known red wagon.

The woodenware of the Shakers in New Hampshire and New York is of special interest. As early as 1789 cooper's ware is mentioned in the account books, and keelers, pails, tubs, churns, casks, barrels, and firkins were sold until 1830 or 1832. On January 31, 1790, the following item appears: "To 6 wooden bottles 2/8—0:16:0." Wooden dippers were made of ash and maple as early as 1789. In 1835 they were making "Root dippers" at 22s. and 2-quart ash and 1-quart maple dippers at 20s. Nests of dippers (3) sold for 20s. The Shakers were also noted for their hair sieves and for their pantry and herb boxes.

Round and oval boxes with pine tops and bottoms and maple bands cut in fingers and secured by hand-made copper or wrought-iron rivets were stained red, yellow, or blue-green. The Shakers also made wooden bowls, spoons, rolling pins, trenchers, and mortars and pestles for their own use. The bowls were usually painted on the outside. The large Shaker apple-butter scoop is of fine design. Small boxes for candles, knives, and pipe boxes and pipe racks were also made of pine. Shaker articles are simple in design and excellent in proportion and workmanship. They have no carving or decoration except for the use of mellow yellow, orange, blue, or blue-green on their boxes, bowls, and buckets.

TOP: <u>Pine salt box.</u> CENTER: Cedar tub, Painted piggin, 18th century. BOTTOM: Burl scoops and ladle.

Shakers used walnut and curly maple for bowls and ash for sieves and cooper's ware. They also used apple, cherry, and pear. They used lignum vitae for an occasional article. Except for the few still owned by descendants of the original families the majority of the Shaker articles are in museums or private collections, so it would be a rare find for the collector to come across any of the early pieces.

The woodenware of the Pennsylvania Dutch also deserves special mention. It included many carved pieces such as the spoon racks painted red and blue and with decoration of stars, spirals, tulips, heart, and "hex" signs. Spoon racks with similar carving were also made in the Delaware and Hudson valleys, and the swastikas, hearts, and tulips are also found on Swiss carved spoons, spoon racks, and small boxes. The spoon racks usually date from the 18th century and some are marked with initials, names, and dates. Carved embroidery-yarn holders, spindles, pie markers, and spoons with carved handles as well as knife and fork boxes with hearts and tulips and many other small wall boxes, both with and without drawers, are of Pennsylvania origin. The carved Pennsylvania Dutch butter molds usually have tulips or hearts, but the strawberry, the cow, and the three-feather designs are also found. The tulip is used as a single flower and leaf, or sometimes as many as three tulips are grouped in the small circle. Again, the tulip may be arranged in a conventional basket or designs may be made of the tulip and geometrical figures. Initials are often incorporated in the oldest butter prints. One such mold has two hearts and the letters "H.R." The Pennsylvania Dutch also used various eagle motifs. These molds were lathe-turned and then carved by hand until about the middle of the 19th century, when the factory took over.

Cooky molds, known as "springerle" molds for decorating flat cakes, are also from Pennsylvania. These usually consist of sections with six, eight, or as many as two dozen patterns, all carved in detail with a border around each design. The patterns include flowers, a kingfisher, cherries, a goat, birds flying, a carrot, a fish, a rabbit, a Turkish mosque, and allover designs, scenes of a summerhouse, and a girl with a basket. Some springerle designs are carved on cylinders that look like rolling pins. Springerle molds are 19th-century products, as are most of the butter molds, although rare ones are found dated as early as 1793. Carved cabbage cutters and linen pressers with heart motifs were also made. Pennsylvania Dutch toys were carved out of red cedar, and the carved eagles and toys of Wilhelm Schimmel date from the second half of the 19th century, as do the turned and painted egg-cups, salt boxes, saffron boxes, and bowls and buckets and tubs made by Joseph Lehn.

Marzipan molds are square and oblong. They were made out of pear, apple, cherry, box, pine, maple, and walnut. Their subjects are religious, historic, military, and commemorative. They were later made in tin and iron.

Woodenware is still being made, and bowls and spoons with a few years' usage often look old, so that the collector must be careful. Certain earmarks identify the genuine old pieces of woodenware. The marks of the old tools are uneven and worn. Wooden pegs, hand-forged nails, and hand-threaded screws distinguish the genuine antique. In cooper's ware the old staves are smooth and well finished, while the new product is sharp and unfinished. Old wood is light in weight, and to the trained eye there is a certain patina. The sides of old bowls are often uneven and they show the stain and scratches of wear. Old dippers are worn at the ends. And finally, if you have trained your eye to recognize fine line and form, the old object always has the finer proportion and the old carved designs are superior in spacing to the later products. Of course, certain articles are rare; among them, knot or burl bowls, especially those with handles, burl plates, mortars, or, in fact, any article of burl. Curly and bird's-eye maple articles are few and desirable. Ladles or spoons with carved handles and carved spoon racks are scarce items. Small mortars, cups, platters, wooden sieves or drainers, the large apple-butter scoop, smoothing boards with carved handles, salt bowls, and all dated pieces are rare and desirable for your collection.

BIBLIOGRAPHY

18th- and 19th-century newspapers.

17th- and 18th-century Inventories, New York Historical Society.

18th-century account books, household and merchants, New York Historical Society.

Early American Wooden Ware, by Mary Earle Gould. The Pond-Ekberg Company, Springfield, Mass., 1942.

American Glass

WISTAR OR SOUTH JERSEY TYPE

GLASSHOUSES were started in colonial days at Jamestown, Salem, and New Amsterdam, and in Pennsylvania and New Jersey, but except for a few glass beads thought to have been made at Jamestown, little is known today of their output. The real history of American glass begins in 1739 with Caspar Wistar in southern New Jersey. Wistar was not a glass man but he brought skilled workmen from Germany who made glass for him. Indeed, from the beginning, American glass has been guided and influenced by foreign craftsmen from Germany, Holland, France, England, and other countries. Wistar has been given such a prominent place in American glass history that until the last decade all American free-blown glass was called "Wistarberg." Actually only a few pieces of glass are known to have been made at the Wistar glassworks, but free-blown glass similar to that made by the early workmen whom Wistar brought over continued to be made in the same technique, forms, color, and decoration in small glasshouses in New York, New England, Pennsylvania, and Ohio as late as the 1870s. And 90 per cent of the glass known as Wistar or South Jersey type was made in the late 18th and 19th centuries.

South Jersey-type glass is made of "green" or bottle glass. The natural colors are greens—from light olive to dark green; aquamarine; and amber—from golden brown to honey. Artificial colors, which are less common, are blue, both light and cobalt, and amethyst. South Jersey-type glass is free-blown. The ornamentation is governed by the process and, except for the occasional use of the pattern mold, it is shaped and decorated by blowing and by hand manipulation. The decoration includes (*a*) prunts and seals, which are applied blobs of glass; (*b*) quilling or trailing, which consists of applied wavy ribbons; (*c*) rigaree, which consists of ribbon in parallel lines; (*d*) threading, which consists of rows of superimposed glass on necks or rims; (*e*) crimping, which is a dent or flute in the foot of an article; (*f*) superimposed or tooled gathers of glass into a swirl or drape in the lily-pad design. The most characteristic type of decoration on South Jersey-type glass is the lily-pad. There are three varieties of lily-pad: the earliest is a stem and a bead, the second has a broader stem and oval pad, and the third type really resembles a lily-pad. Some articles are decorated with several types of decoration, such as a threaded neck, lily-pad on the body, and a crimped foot. Handles and finials are particularly decorative, and pieces are often threated with contrasting colors, such as red threading on the neck of an aquamarine pitcher.

Sugar bowls, creamers, pitchers of various sizes, vases, bowls and compotes, salts, and inkwells were made in free-blown glass. Besides these articles there were workmen's whimseys such as glass hats, slippers and shoes, canes, rolling pins, toys, and witch balls. There is a similarity between the pieces of South Jersey-type glass made in the different sections of the country, not only because of the use of the same technique and the same type of glass, but also because the workmen are the descendants or apprentices of the original foreign-trained craftsmen. Of course, there are differences between the glass of the various sections of the country, and, generally speaking, Middle Western glass is less sophisticated in shape and has less decoration. Cobalt blue is typical of New Jersey, while aquamarine is more often found in New York, and blood-amber glass pieces are associated with Stoddard, New Hampshire, and Connecticut. Indeed, there are many variations which the collector will wish to study elsewhere in detail, for this reference is only for orientation and general information.

STIEGEL-TYPE GLASS

The next well-known type of American glass was that made by the German William Henry Stiegel in Manheim, Pennsylvania. Stiegel operated his glassworks from 1763 to May, 1774, and employed over 130 foreign workmen. Although thousands of articles were made here in the almost ten years of operation, other glasshouses in New York, Boston, Philadelphia, and a little later in Maryland, made glass of the same type, which was similar to the glass being imported from England and the Continent. Indeed Stiegel and other American glassmakers made such excellent imitations that it is hard to distinguish between much of the American and the foreign glass made at the same time. Stiegel glass generally was of three types, all of it blown: (*a*) pattern-molded; (*b*) cut and engraved; (*c*) enameled. The pattern-molded glass is the largest class and also the most distinctive. The glass was given its pattern by blowing the gather of metal into a mold which had a design cut on its inner surface. After the gather of glass was impressed with the design, it was withdrawn and the article was blown into shape. Pattern-mold designs include vertical and spiral ribbing, fluting, paneling, and variations of the Venetian Diamond such as the Checkered Diamond, ogival, or Daisy Diamond. All of these designs except the Daisy Diamond were made at other glasshouses in different parts of the country and the same type was made even a century later. However, the Daisy Diamond design has not been found elsewhere and is considered to be original with Stiegel. It is found on perfume bottles, small vases, and salts in clear glass, amethyst, sapphire blue, and rare emerald. Other pattern-molded designs are found on sugar bowls, salts, creamers, condiment bottles, small bowls, and drinking glasses. A great deal of Stiegel-type pattern-molded glass with expanded swirled and vertical ribbing and diamond allover designs was made in Ohio in the 19th century. Bottles, flasks, compotes, sugar bowls, pitchers, and creamers, as well as salts, were blown in amber, green, amethyst, and blue, and pattern-molded. Vertical ribbed and popcorn-design bottles are typical of Middle Western pattern-molded glass. Bottles or flasks were also pattern-molded in the Pitkin Glass Works in Connecticut. The so-called "Pitkin" flasks have an extra gather of glass on the neck of the flask and are usually found in olive green and ambers. They were also made in other Connecticut and New Hampshire glasshouses. Clear-glass mugs, decanters, flip glasses, wines, and other drinking glasses made by Stiegel often have designs of shallow-cut copper-wheel engraving. The motifs include various types of tulip decoration, heart and bird motifs, baskets of flowers, vines, garlands, wreaths, and latticework, and often names, initials, or inscriptions are added. The work is usually a little careless and naïve and is similar to European peasant decoration. Stiegel enameled decoration was painted on clear and colored glass, mostly blue. The designs were peasant in spirit and the motifs included birds, flowers, human figures, steeples, and inscriptions. Dove and floral designs with inscriptions, parrots, rooster, and a design of a woman in a boat are well known. Borders on these enameled pieces includes lines and scallops in white, dull red, and mustard yellow. The designs themselves are enameled in blue, yellow, red, green, and black and white. Cordial bottles and drink-

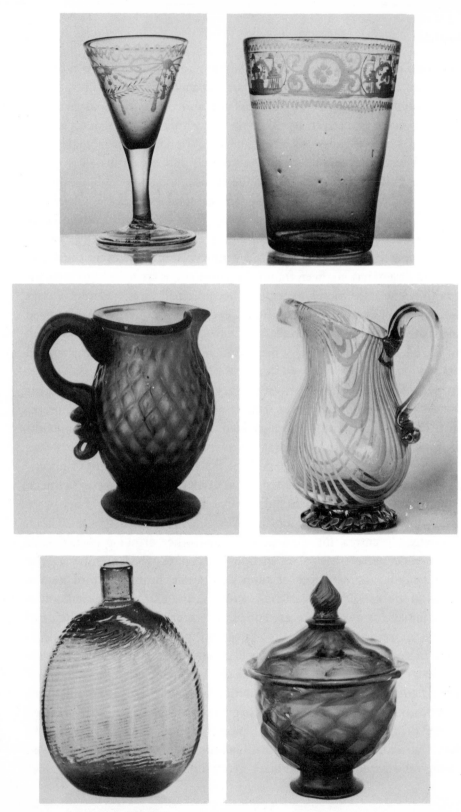

TOP: Engraved wineglass, 19th century. Stiegel-type glass, 18th century. CENTER: Emerald-green molded pitcher. South Jersey type, green with white looping. BOTTOM: Ohio "Pitkin" flask. Blue-flint Stiegel sugar bowl.

ing glasses of various types are the articles most often found with enamel decoration but Stiegel's own records list enameled salts.

Pattern-molded and engraved Stiegel-type glass was also made by Amelung at the New Bremen Glass Manufactory in Frederick, Maryland. This factory was established in 1784 and skilled German craftsmen were brought over. They excelled in engraving, and marked and dated pieces which they made for the state of Pennsylvania, the mayor of Boston, and the city of Bremen, Germany, are equal to some of the finest pieces of engraved foreign glass. The regular output of the factory included window glass, bottles, decanters, wine glasses, and "every other sort of Table Glass." Coat of arms, devices, ciphers, and fancy figures, including sprays of leaves, birds, daisylike flowers, festoons, and names and inscriptions, are typical of the engraving on clear glass. After the factory shut down in 1796, these skilled workmen were employed in Baltimore and at the New Geneva Glass Works in Pennsylvania.

BLOWN THREE-MOLD GLASS

Blown three-mold glass in imitation of cut glass was made at American glassworks in different parts of the country from 1820 to 1830. Blown three-mold glass is made in full-sized hinged metal molds in several sections. One way to distinguish blown three-mold glass is to locate the mold marks. Blown three-mold glass was made of both bottle glass and flint glass in a combination of the mold and hand-manipulation methods. Many pieces such as pitchers are blown into the mold for shape and pattern, but their handles and rims are finished by hand. Blown three-mold glass is divided into three types according to its design. Designs with fluting, ribbing, diamonds, or sunburst are classed as Geometric. High-relief designs of scrolls, hearts, and palmettes are called Baroque, while patterns with Gothic or Roman arch are called Arch. Geometric designs are found on decanters of various sizes, toilet bottles, salts, flip glasses, goblets, cruets, pitchers, inkwells, hats, and other articles. The rare early square decanters blown in two-piece quart- and pint-size molds are found only with wide diamond diaper bands together with vertical fluting. The stoppers are blown mushroom type or pressed wheel shape. Decanters were usually blown of clear flint glass, but some are of aquamarine, olive-green, or amber bottle glass. They usually had one or more applied collars, and stoppers were of molded mushroom type or pressed wheel shape. Pitchers, salt cellars, and perfume bottles were made in a wide variety of colors, patterns, and sizes. The best-known articles in Baroque patterns are pitchers and decanters. The patterns include Shell and Ribbing, Shell with Diamond, Star, Heart and Chain, Horn of Plenty, and Horizontal Palm Leaf. Arch patterns include Arch and Fern with Snake, and Gothic and Roman Arches, alone or together with sprays of leaves. Some of these patterns were made at Sandwich. Blown three-mold glass was made in New England, New York, Virginia, and at several glassworks in Ohio. Ohio pitchers, bowls, and decanters were usually blown in greens and ambers, but some clear three-mold Ohio glass is found. Blown three-mold glass has the mark of the individual workman and the charm and irregularities of early glass.

CUT AND ENGRAVED GLASS

Cut and engraved glass was made in America from the middle of the 18th century. The cutting consisted of knobbing on stems of glasses and flutings on the bottoms of decanters. The "devices, cyphers, coats-of-arms or other Fancy Figures" were engraved rather than cut. By the end of the century, however, there were many men employed in cutting blanks which were made at the factories. Many bowls, pitchers, and wine- and celery glasses were cut from about this time until 1820, when cutting became a commercial production in many American factories, including Bakewell & Company of Pittsburgh, the New England Glass Company at Cambridge, and Boston and Sandwich Glass Company. Some of the finest early American cut glass was made by Bakewell & Company before 1817. The output included chandeliers, decanters, wineglasses, tumblers, and punch bowls. In 1817 President Monroe visited the factory and ordered a set of decanters, wineglasses, and tumblers. Cut glass was also made at Bakewell's for Lafayette, President Jackson, and President McKinley.

The early motifs included fans, strawberry cut, and rayed circles similar to those in old German glass. A little later large cut circles and concave ovals were used. Among later Bakewell patterns were Argus, Thistle, Prism, Flute, Cherry, Arabesque, Heart, Etruscan, and Saxon. The Boston Glass Manufacturing Company in 1816 advertised best double-flint tumblers engraved and goblets and salts "common and cut" as well as "wines, different patterns some elegant—Decanters plain and ring necks; Sugar bowls plain and cut—Sweetmeat baskets, pitchers, castors, travelling bottles, Fish globes, Finger Bowls—Jelly—Lemonades plain and cut." The

TOP: Blown three-mold wineglass and pitcher. CENTER LEFT: Sunburst, blown three-mold. RIGHT: Creamer, baroque design. BOTTOM: Pressed glass, Lyre and Eagle salts.

New England Glass Company in 1818 set up a cutting department with "twenty-four cutting mills operated by steam." Cutting experts were brought over from Ireland, and the decanters, wines, and tumblers they made can hardly be distinguished from Waterford Glass. Chandeliers, lamps, and dessert services were cut to order. The "Splendid bowl 26" x 14" diameter-cut in strawberry diamonds, and in color and brilliancy equal to any ever imported" advertised in the *Niles Weekly Register*, July 7, 1821, may have been cut there. The early cutting was combined with engraving, which was also deep cut on heavy glass. Pictorial scenes, wreaths, and flowers were the motifs. Later the engraving became more delicate. In a pattern book used after 1850 the designs included Hobnail, Diamond and Block, and such Victorian motifs as grape, ivy, rose, wheat, strawberry, thistle, stars, fans, Greek key, birds, and hunting scenes. By 1825 the Boston and Sandwich Glass Company was established and "flint diamond cut" glass was advertised. Salts bottles, bowls of whale-oil lamps, and stems of elaborate overlay lamps were cut. The early patterns were Diamond and Strawberry. Later patterns included Diamond and Punty, Rosette and Octagon, Fan and Strawcut. From this time on there were numerous glass manufactories making cut glass in all parts of the East and as far west as St. Louis. Individual cutters were also cutting articles to order. However, late in the century a great deal of poorly cut and badly designed glass was made and for this reason cut glass came to be synonymous with poor taste. Cut-glass pattern motifs are the same on late pieces as those on early pieces, since the patterns are geometric and are determined by the process of cutting. A study of representative pieces of early cut glass will show that clean cutting, a simple design, and heavy clear glass are the characteristics of really fine cut glass.

PRESSED GLASS

Pressed glass in imitation of cut glass was made in nearly all the American glassworks in the late 1820s. Pressed glass with delicate sparkling patterns is called lacy glass. Characteristic motifs of design include scrolls, hearts, acanthus leaf, sunbursts, peacock, feather, fleur-de-lis, roses, and other leaves and flowers. Historical patterns, including the American eagle, were also popular. Many articles of tableware were made in lacy glass, but the cup plates and salts are the most interesting for the collector because of the diversity of patterns. Historical cup plates include such subjects as George

Washington, Henry Clay, and Major Ringold as well as center motifs of ships, log cabins, steam coaches, plows, and the Bunker Hill Monument. The greatest number of cup plates are made in clear glass, but some were also made in amber, blue, green, amethyst, yellow, and opaque colors, including opal. Designs on salts also vary from lacy designs, and those imitating cut glass to historical motifs. Early lacy-glass salts were rectangular with feet and pilasters at the corners and a single motif, such as a rose or basket of flowers, on the ends and sides. Other salts were round or oval and had lacy patterns such as scrolls, rosettes, shells, and leaves. Historical salts include the Washington-Lafayette; the "Lafayet" boat-shaped salt; eagle salts; "Providence"; and "H. Clay" salt with an engine and car.

PRESSED PATTERN GLASS

In the 1840s pressed glass began to be made in complete table settings. Thousands of patterns were made. The earliest were simple ovals and loops and included such patterns as Ashburton, Flute, Loop, Excelsior, Argus, Colonial, Pillar, Diamond Thumbprint, Bigler, Huber, and Victoria. A little later more detail was used in such patterns as Comet, Horn of Plenty, New England Pineapple, Gothic, Hamilton, and Sandwich Star. Another group of designs are called the Ribbed Group and include such patterns as Bellflower, Ribbed Grape, Ivy, Acorn, Fine Rib, Ribbed Palm, and Inverted Fern. These patterns are delicate and are characterized by a fine vertical ribbing. In the 1860s one of the best-known patterns was the Lincoln Drape. Other patterns of this era include Cable, Tulip, Thumbprint, Frosted Roman Key, Honeycomb, and Philadelphia. More elaborate and more naturalistic patterns, such as grape and flower, were made later. In the late 1870s a group of clear-glass patterns, with frosted figures on the lids and in the stems and bases, were popular. These patterns included Westward-Ho, which has the figure of an Indian on the lid and a scene with a log cabin on the bowl. Lion, Three Faces, Baby Face, Polar Bear, Dog and Deer, and Jumbo patterns also had frosted figures on lids of dishes and stems of compotes and glasses. A group of conventional patterns such as the Daisy and Button, Hobnail, and Stipple were made in the 1880s. Pattern Glass designs were made in clear glass, yellow, blue, green, and in opaque glass of various colors. The articles readily available to the collector are goblets, tumblers, and pitchers.

PATTERN MILK GLASS

In milk or opaque glass the patterns most available include Strawberry, Sawtooth, Wheat, Blackberry, Grape, Princess Feather, Waffle, Daisy, Scroll, Basket Weave, Cosmos, Shell, Swan, Cameo and Beaded Jewel. Many patterns with openwork design are beautiful and plates with borders of these patterns, which include Arch, Lattice, Gothic, Wicket, Scroll and Leaf, Diamond and Shell, Fan and Circle, and S and Backward C, are popular with collectors of milk glass. They are found both in black and white glass and occasionally in blue. Milk-glass plates were also made in sentimental patterns such as Three Kittens, Owl, and Chickens. Compotes, bowls, dishes, and platters, including the well-known "Retriever" platter and "Give Us This Day Our Daily Bread," are also available to the collector. Bottles include a fluted flask, a duck bottle, and bear bottles. Historical bottles, including Grant's Tomb, Statue of Liberty, Bunker Hill Monument, and Columbus Column, are rare. Covered dishes include ducks, turkeys, hens, swans, rabbits, fish, dogs, cats, eagles, deer, lions, birds, and other animals as well as battleships. The best-known covered dishes were made by McKee Brothers of Pittsburgh, Pennsylvania, and by the Atterbury Company. Opaque caramel, custard, and purple slag or marble glass was made in less quantity and in only a few patterns. For this reason it is harder to find.

FANCY GLASS

In the 1880s many fine pieces of fancy glass were blown in America. The shapes were Victorian and not very good in design, but the color and technique make it worth collecting. The most important glasswares made at this time were Peachblow, Burmese, Amberina, Pomona, Agata, Satin, Spangled and Hobnail. Peachblow shades from ivory or yellow to deep rose-red. Articles made in Peachblow include vases, rose bowls, finger bowls, baskets, tumblers, salts, peppers, pitchers, decanters, and sherbet cups. Agata glass was a variation of Peachblow with a mottled effect. Amberina glass shaded from amber to ruby and was blown and patterned in molds in designs of Expanded Diamonds, Swirled Ribbing, and Inverted Thumbprint. Amberina was made in fancy vases, pitcher and berry sets, celery holders, and finger bowls. Burmese glass shades from lemon yellow and pink. Pomona was a clear blown glass treated with etching, tinting, or staining. Satin glass was made in a variety of plain and shaded hues of blue, green, rose, brown, yellow, amber and gold, as well as stripes of yellow and white, blue and white, and blue and pink. Often a pattern of herringbone, polka dot, or diamond quilt is pattern-molded on a vase. Satin glass was made in vases, rose bowls, sugar and creamers, and pitcher and tumbler sets. In the 1890s Tiffany's Favrile glass was made by exposing various-colored glass rods to the fumes of vaporized metals. The designs were blown and are imaginative and fanciful and include leaves and peacock feathers in blues, greens, reds, golds, and light mother-of-pearl. Tiffany glass is often marked "Favrile" and besides "Louis C. Tiffany" (or "L.C.T.").

PAPERWEIGHTS

Paperweights were made after 1850 at Sandwich and several other American glass factories. Sandwich paperweights were of the millefiori and candy-cane type; and also with fruit and flowers on a lattice background. Among the well-known Sandwich weights are a pink poinsettia, or a purple or blue dahlia or a pansy on a white lattice background. Some paperweights have tiny pears, apples, or cherries, and green leaves on a white lattice background and one of the loveliest Sandwich weights has five strawberries with leaves and dew bubbles on a fine lacy ground. The Mt. Washington Glass Company made a paperweight with a salmon-pink rose held by a hand with a gold ring on one finger. Cameo weights with heads of Washington, Lincoln, and Victoria and Albert were also made. New England Glass Works made a blown pear and apple set on a crystal base. They are distinctive in that they are not encased in glass. One of the most distinctive American paperweights is the Milleville Rose. The rose is usually pink, white, or yellow, and stands upright on a heavy circular foot with a cylinder or baluster stem. Other paperweights include a hunting scene and sentimental subjects with inscriptions such as "Friendship," "Home Sweet Home," "Hope," and "Remember Me" set within a wreath, anchors, butterflies, or patriotic or Masonic emblems.

HISTORICAL FLASKS

American history is written on whisky flasks blown in two-piece molds in American glass factories between 1816 and 1860. In size these flasks range from ½ pint to 1 quart, and amber, green, aquamarine, emerald, blue, and

TOP: American paperweight, aster. CENTER: Blown three-mold decanter, shell and ribbing. Bottles with encased ship and with star design, Sandwich glass. BOTTOM LEFT: Tree design. RIGHT: Flask, Eagle & Shield, reverse, Gen. Washington.

purple flasks are available. However, the real interest in these flasks is the subject matter molded on them, which includes the portraits of presidents, the American eagle, Masonic emblems, Jenny Lind, Lafayette, and ships, railroads, and other subjects of American life. Some flasks are blown in violin shape and others are house or log-cabin form. The most valuable flasks commemorate events and people in American history. All of the Washington flasks are desirable. Some of them have reverse sides with eagles, others have the Baltimore Monument, and others have a ship or a bust of President Clay, Taylor, or Jackson on the reverse side. The bust of John Quincy Adams is found on one flask that has an eagle on the reverse side. The bust of William H. Harrison is also found on one rare pint flask. However, several flasks with inscriptions such as "Hard Cider" and two flasks in the shape of log cabins are also connected with the Harrison presidential campaign. Another flask in the shape of a house or cabin was the popular Booz bottle made in 1840. The portrait of Zachary Taylor is found on no less than twenty-eight different flasks, and the reverse sides of these flasks carry such Taylor campaign slogans as "Rough and Ready," "A little more Grape Capt. Bragg," the Baltimore Monument, or the bust of Major Ringold. Other flasks have the bust of Benjamin Franklin, and Lafayette's bust is on fourteen different flasks. Several flasks have the bust of Louis Kossuth, and there is also a group with the bust of Jenny Lind. Masonic flasks make up one of the most interesting groups; there are at least forty of them. Other subjects include ships, railroad subjects, Pike's Peak, and even popular songs. Historical flasks usually have the name of the subject molded on the flask and often the name of the glass factory as well. Although many flasks are rare and expensive, there are also a great many attractive and interesting flasks of each type available at a small cost.

BIBLIOGRAPHY

American Glass, by George S. and Helen McKearin. Crown Publishers, New York, 1946.

Two Hundred Years of American Blown Glass, by George S. and Helen McKearin. Doubleday & Company, Inc., New York, 1950.

American Glass, by Katharine Morrison McClinton. World Publishing Company, Cleveland, 1950.

17

Bristol and Other European and American Opaque White and Colored Glass

BRISTOL, LIKE BATTERSEA is one of those magic words to the collector. Everyone wants his opaque glass to be Bristol, and every dealer thus puts the Bristol tag on certain type of opaque white and colored glass, knowing full well that it probably came from Germany, France, or Bohemia or at best Birmingham or Stourbridge and not Bristol. However, much of this glass is decorative and attractive even if it isn't Bristol, but in order to avoid paying Bristol prices for less valuable wares it is well to be able to distinguish the difference between the various types.

Opaque white glass was common to every European country. It was made as early as 1470 in Venice, in Orleans, France, in 1662, and continued being made down into the 19th century. Collectors have been interested in it from the time of Lady Charlotte Schreiber, whose collection is now in Victoria and Albert Museum, down to the present day. This glass is decorated with enamel or oil painting and often with transfer designs. A collector may run the gamut from the rare and expensive Bristol glass vases to the decorative mugs of Bohemia, the quaint "Remember Me" mugs of the 19th century from Yarmouth or Sunderland, or the fluted Victorian vases from Stourbridge or Birmingham.

Fine old opaque white glass was made at Bristol as early as 1745, but their finest glass was made between 1762 and 1787. There were fifteen glass-houses at that time. Deep blue, pale green, and clear glass was also manufactured, but the opaque white glass made Bristol famous. It was made to imitate fine porcelain and was decorated by the same men who decorated Bristol china. The designs are similar to that on Bristol Delft of an earlier date.

Authorities disagree on the exact appearance of Bristol white glass. That it should have a dense appearance similar to porcelain is positive; whether or not it should have any opalescence is a question. The finest pieces do not have any glow but are creamy white. There are no streaks or marbling. The surface is fine, smooth, and soft in texture, and white Bristol glass is thin although it has the appearance of being thick and heavy. The pontil mark resembles porcelain and is solid white and creamy, not bluish.

The decoration on the finest Bristol pieces is enameled and fired, but some ordinary articles were painted with oil color and were not baked. Bristol opaque white glass is thin and brittle. It was known as enamel glass, and the name referred to the process, not the decoration.

However, the shapes and the type of decoration are the surest means of identifying authentic old Bristol glass. Almost without exception the shapes are those of fine Chinese porcelain. There are vases of ovoid shape, beakers, pear-shaped vases with cylindrical necks, and covered and open inverted baluster-shaped mantle vases. There are bowls, decanters, bottles, and bowls and jugs. Tea caddies are rectangular with beveled angles, round shoulders, and short, circular necks. They have metal tops and are painted with birds and the name of the tea, such as Bohea, Hyson, and Green, in rococo puce-color cartouches. Candlesticks had tapered and writhen ribbed stems and adorned base.

Michael Edkins left records of some of the articles which he painted. They include beakers, canisters, "blue cornicopias," hyacinth glasses, a wineglass with "Pitt and Liberty," "Liberty and No Excise," "cans and milk jugs," and "enamel and blue glass." Edkins painted both white and blue glass, and his records show that he worked for the following firms:

1762–1767, Little & Longman
1767–1787, Longman & Vigor
1765, Wm. Dunbar & Company
1775–1787, Vigor and Stevens
1785–1787, Lazarus Jacobs

Designs on old opaque white Bristol glass are of both Chinese and English inspiration. The Chinese designs include Chinese figures, buildings, rockery and birds and are very similar to those on Chinese porcelain and English china of Chinese inspiration. English-inspired designs include native English birds, such as the goldfinch and bullfinch; sprays or sprigs of such English flowers as tiger lilies, tulips, roses, honeysuckle; and insects and butterflies. Some rare pieces are dated, such as the finger bowl with "J.F. 1757" and the scent bottle with "Mi-Alfer 1781" and a basket of flowers. Brilliant enamel colors were used, including viridian and malachite greens, lemon yellow, light red, ultramarine blue, mauve, and violet. Faces of Chinese figures are outlined in red, and the eyes are black dots. The hands have a characteristic long first finger. The legs, beaks, crests, and tails of birds are in red and the landscape foreground is green with black and brown dots. The rococo frames are often lavender. Gilding is used both alone and together with enamel decoration.

Pieces of Bristol glass are comparatively small. The beakers are usually 6 to 8 inches high, the candlesticks and vases 6 to 9. Plain white or fluted vases are 8 inches high, and tea caddies about 6 inches in height.

At Sotheby's sale in London, November, 1937, a collection of Bristol opaque white glass was sold which included a cream jug with sprigs and sprays of flowers; candlesticks with sprays and bouquets of flowers; a vase with tiger lilies; a plain white mantel garniture consisting of a covered vase and a pair of beakers; a beaker with sprays of tulips, roses, and a butterfly; a vase with roses tied with a blue ribbon, butterflies, insects, honeysuckle, and curled green leaves; and finger bowls decorated in "famille rose" style with sprays of peony flowers and birds.

While Bristol glassware was imported into America in huge quantities in the latter half of the 18th century, there is no mention of white glass and we can well imagine that it was too fragile for shipment.

In the *New York Daily Advertiser* in 1799 the following items appear, which, however, do not refer to white glass.

13 crates Bristol glassware consisting of decanters, tumblers, wine glasses, phials, etc.

15 cases containing a very elegant assortment of glassware such as cut decanters, tumblers, wine glasses in light blue and pale green colors.

Now, the above notes refer to a very definite type of decoration and shape and should cause collectors and dealers to have caution in the use of the word "Bristol" in connection with carelessly painted floral decoration or souvenir mugs with endearing phrases or Rubens cupids. While these are all desirable pieces of opaque white glass the majority of them are not Bristol or are Bristol of a much later date. Mugs with "Bristol 1812" have been found. Benjamin Edwards, a glassmaker from Bristol, went to Belfast and there manufactured opaque white enamel glass in 1781.

Glass similar to Bristol was also made at other factories in England,

TOP: Opaque white glass mugs, 19th century, English. CENTER: Bristol opaque glass. German milch glass coffeepot. Dutch opaque white glass teapot. BOTTOM: Dutch opaque white glass mug. Scent bottle, 18th century, German. Bristol opaque Chinese figures.

including Newcastle, where cream jugs, sugar bowls, and rolling pins were made in opaque white and blue and often labeled "A Present from Newcastle." It was also made in Gateshead, Birmingham, Stourbridge, and Sunderland in the late 18th century and in the 19th century. There was also one factory in Bristol as late as 1851, but this factory made inferior glass. The glass at Stourbridge and the North Country (namely Sunderland and Tyneside) was opalescent and the painting was inferior to that done in Bristol in the 18th century. Most of the 19th-century mugs with Masonic decorations were made at Newcastle or Yarmouth. Some read "A Trifle from Yarmouth" or "For My Dear Emily." Barrel-shaped mugs of opaque white glass were decorated with gilding and black paint by Absolon of Yarmouth around 1800. Absolon was a dealer who bought pieces of china and glassware and decorated them. He did not manufacture any glassware. A mug with gold stars and link border and a coat of arms painted in black is marked "Absolon Yarm. No —." Footed bread and butter bowls with initials or "Peace and Plenty" were made at Stourbridge and Tyneside. These are interesting items.

Much of the "Bristol glass" sold today is "milch glass" made in Bohemia and South Germany. Mugs and beakers with Watteau scenes of figures around a tea table painted in black with gold or silver rococo decoration were made in Bohemia in the late 18th and the 19th centuries.

Milch-glass cups, jugs, plates, and snuffboxes were also enameled with figures of saints, flowers, rococo scenes, allegorical pictures of the months and the four continents, childhood scenes, pastoral scenes, and religious scenes such as David and Goliath. Many of these scenes are taken from well-known engravings and paintings. German Empire and Biedermeier opaque white glass included subjects similar to that on Bohemian glass. Copies of Rubens paintings of cupids in terra cotta are of German origin. Contemporary scenes and portraits in medallions framed in gold and allegorical and mythological figures of Venus and Adonis and Venus and Psyche after Boucher were painted in about 1816 and signed by such artists as Friedrich Egermann, Ignaz Fritsche, and R. Martin. Mugs with flowers and inscriptions date from about 1830, and Victorian vases with roses and scenes are of about the same date.

German and Bohemian opaque milch glass is much coarser and more watery than Bristol opaque glass. The opacity and coloration are irregular, sometimes blue or yellowish. The workmanship is rough and the shapes have no distinction. The painting is usually poor.

In the late 18th century, tea ware consisting of teapots, sugar basins, cream jugs, and handleless cups was made in opaque white glass. It was decorated in floral designs, with blue or purple predominating, and was of either German or Dutch workmanship. Although the following advertisement from the *New England Journal*, July 31, 1731, seems to suggest an earlier date, it may refer to English or Venetian glass: "Tea setts of White, Blew, and Japann'd glass."

Tall mugs or steins with naïve portraits of George III surrounded by floral decorations and crude line borders were also painted in the Netherlands. The painting is in oil and was not baked, so that it wears off easily. Similarly decorated mugs were made in the Tyrol and Switzerland. These are interesting and desirable for the white glass collector.

The Royal Glass Manufactory in the Palace of La Granja, San Ildefonso, Spain, was a notable center for the manufacture of Spanish opaque glass in the late 18th and the first half of the 19th century. They imitated oriental floral designs on Chinese porcelain, and some decanters with floral sprays and cartouches with inscriptions are closely related to Bristol opaque glass. Cups or mugs were also made with typical French decoration of enamel and gold, and large chandeliers in opaque blue or white glass found a ready European market in the mid-19th century.

In the 19th century Italy again made opaque white glass and evidently sought the American trade with a crudely shaped mug with a poorly painted eagle and the inscription "Liberty." These are on the market today represented as old Bristol glass. Victorian vases with fluted tops and crudely painted roses and other flowers and hand-shaped vases and lusters with crystal drops were also made at Tyneside, Stourbridge, and Birmingham from 1830 and at some factories as late as the 1880s. Some were made at Bristol as late as the 1850s. Although these vases are charming on a Victorian mantelpiece or made into bedroom lamps, they are not in my opinion rare enough to be collected in great quantity. Attractive dressing-table sets of two or three bottles were also made in opaque white, pink, green, and blue glass, with fluted rims and tuliplike stoppers. You can find them in all the shops today, but remember that they were made as late as 1880 and their decoration though quaint and colorful was of department-store quality. I have a pair of lamps in that elusive blue that was also copied in the later American milk glass, and together with a pair of dresser bottles and a blue pin tray they contrast with the yellow wallpaper of my bedroom and set the color scheme for the room.

American milk glass can easily be distinguished from the European types since it was usually made in different shapes and most of it was made in table sets of plates, goblets and such pieces, or in covered-box shapes. These have all been classified and listed and have a value and individuality of their own so that they are not confused with Bristol-type glass.

Although milk glass was made in America at the Sandwich Glass Company, the later available milk glass popular today was not made until the close of the century. Milk glass is an opaque glass made in white, black, blue, and green. Lamps, animal dishes, compotes, and table sets, including plates, creamers and sugars, spoon holders, salts, pitchers, and goblets were made.

Patterns are either pressed or plain with openwork edges. Pressed patterns include Sawtooth or Pineapple, Thumbprint, Sheaf-of-wheat, Blackberry, Strawberry, Cherry, Grape, Gooseberry, Rose, Princess Feather, Icicle, Lincoln Drape, Bellflower, and Waffle.

Openwork plates are square, round, and heart-shaped and are made with an openwork border design of S, C, Loop, Interlacing Heart, Leaf, Forget-me-not, Gothic lattice, Arch, Wicket, Pinwheel, Beaded or Peg and Circle border. Plates were also made with a molded decoration in the center, including a ship, Indian head, three bears, three kittens, owls, Easter ducks, chicks and rabbits, "Cupid and Psyche," "Lady at the Well," "Down on the Farm," and an ancient castle. Other designs include Columbus, Lincoln, Taft, and Bryan. Fish-shaped and double-handle dishes were also made.

Covered animal dishes are in great demand, especially those made at Sandwich between 1870 and 1880. They include covers with chicken, swan, bird, rabbit, duck, dog, as well as battleships and eagle and flag.

Milk glass was also made in Ohio, Indiana, and Pennsylvania. Well-known makers include: McKee Bros., Indiana Tumbler & Goblet Company, Challinor, Taylor & Company, The Atterbury Company, The Canton Glass Company, Richards & Hartley, Bryce Bros., and the Flaccus Company.

There is very little fine old Bristol opaque white glass in the American market today, so the collector should beware. Judge a piece from the distinction of its shape, the quality and finish, and the workmanship of its painting. No one will dispute the charm of Victorian mugs with names and sentimental inscription, of small rosy-wreathed scent bottles, or of the black and white "tea party" decorated Bohemian mugs, but banish the idea that you are buying Bristol. There are no signatures or marks to guide, and you must choose each piece for its aesthetic values; however, if you have ever seen and handled an old piece I think that you will be able to recognize a later product.

BIBLIOGRAPHY

Gläser der Empire und Biedermeierzeit, by Gustav Edmund Pazaurek. Klinkhardt & Bierman, Leipzig, 1923.

A History of English and Irish Glass, by William Arnold Thorpe, 2 vols. The Medici Society, London, 1929.

Catalogue of the Museum of Industrial Art, Prague. Glass Collection.

The Magazine Antiques, March, 1924.

Two Centuries of Ceramic Art in Bristol, by Hugh Owen. F. S. A. Bell & Daldy, London, 1873.

Opaque Glass Book, by S. T. Millard. Crown Publishers, New York, 1949.

18

American Historical Kerchiefs

IF YOU ATTENDED the World's Fair in New York or San Francisco in 1939 you may have a printed souvenir handkerchief with scenes of the buildings. In a few years this kerchief will be old enough to add to a museum or private collection of historical-event kerchiefs. These kerchiefs printed on cotton or silk with events of history—wars, political campaigns, expositions, and such happenings as balloon ascensions and horse races— have been made in many countries since about 1760. Historical kerchiefs are popular antiques since their commercial origin made them available to everyone. They are of interest to us today because of their association with American history and as such they are valuable not only because of the stories they portray, but because the early ones are the products of an early American industry. Through a study of those made by early textile printers we also learn the story of the beginnings of the industry in America, so that a collection of historical kerchiefs has a twofold interest. However, the earliest kerchiefs with American historical subject matter were not printed in America. Although there were calico printers in Boston before the Revolution—George Leason & Thomas Webber in 1812 and Francis Gray from Holland (*Boston Gazette*, 1735)—it was the isolation caused by the war that really started calico and linen printing in America.

There were quite a group of linen and calico works in and near Philadelphia in the late 18th and early 19th centuries, and from newspapers of the time we have gathered the following list:

1774, John Hewson, Philadelphia
1775, John Walters & Thomas Bedwell, Philadelphia
1777, Nathaniel Norgrove, Philadelphia
1784, Henry Royl & Co., Philadelphia

1786, Robert Taylor, Merion Township
1791, Nicholas Mayer, Philadelphia
1792, Stephen Addington, Springfield, N.J.
1796, G. Mountcastle, Philadelphia

1797, Oakford & La Collay, Philadelphia
1798, Davy Roberts & Co., Germantown, Pa.
1803, Stewart, Germantown, Pa.
1811, Francis Labbe, Philadelphia

1824, Germantown Print Works
1825, Matthias Baldwin & D. H. Mason, Philadelphia
1829, Thomas Hunter, Philadelphia.

The best-known, and probably the man who produced the finest printed goods, was John Hewson. He is the only early calico printer whose work is preserved and identified today. However, all of these men printed cottons for curtains, handkerchiefs, men's waistcoats, and other wearing apparel. In 1786 Robert Taylor even advertised that he had pattern books. Yet the fact that none of these early textiles were marked makes their identification uncertain today, and just which ones of these early calico printers made printed kerchiefs with historical scenes we do not know, with two exceptions: we know that Hewson made a kerchief at Martha Washington's request, and we can identify the later kerchiefs stamped "Germantown Print Works."

The subject matter of the earliest group of American historical kerchiefs centers about Washington and the Revolution and the early federation of states. In 1775 Martha Washington when driving through Philadelphia is said to have stopped at the calico-printing factory of John Hewson and ordered a kerchief showing Washington on horseback. Hewson, who had an apprenticeship at Bromley Hall printworks near London, started business in Philadelphia in 1774 under the patronage of Benjamin Franklin. Many interesting advertisements of this factory appear in the Philadelphia newspapers between this time and 1810, when Hewson retired. His son continued the business until 1823. Hewson's advertisement of 1774 includes "calicoes and linens for gowns, etc., coverlets, handkerchiefs, nankeens." The kerchief that Hewson made for Mrs. Washington has not been definitely authenticated. There are several kerchiefs with equestrian portraits of Washington, but none seem to have the quality of Hewson's work as shown in the bed coverlets owned and authenticated by Joseph B. Hodgson, Jr., and Miss Ella Hodgson.

The Washington equestrian kerchief owned by Mrs. J. Insley Blair and considered by many to be the Hewson kerchief is printed in pink on white linen. In the center is a portrait of Washington on horseback, based on the print from Alexander Campbell's portrait of George Washington by C. Shepherd, 1775. In a circle about the figure of Washington are the words "George Washington Esq. Foundator and Protector of America's

Liberty and Independency." The use of floral motifs suggesting oriental influence was typical of Hewson, but the wording suggests a foreign source
and the design seems to have a Dutch influence. It is, however, excellent
both in design and coloring and is a very scarce item, so do not whet your
collector's appetite for this particular kerchief.

An even rarer kerchief is the one printed in red on white linen with the
name of the makers, "Talwin and Foster / Bromley Hall, Midde." The
central medallion depicts Washington on horseback, with a rolled scroll in
his left hand. Above his head is the trumpeting figure of Fame. The Con-
tinental troops are in the background and at the right are the figures of
Justice, Peace, and Plenty and the inscription "Gen. Washington directing
Peace to restore to Justice the Sword which had gained Independence to
America." Portraits in medallions are of H. Laurens, Esq.; Hon. T. Miffin;
Benj. Franklin, Esq., W. H. Drayton, Esq., Baron Steuben, Hon. J.
Adams, Hon. J. Jay, J. Dickinson, Esq., Gen. Green, Gen. Washington,
C. Thompson, Esq., Gov. Morris, Esq. The outside border is of flowers and
lacework. The medallion portraits after Du Simitière date the kerchief after
1783.

One of the oldest Washington kerchiefs shows a bust portrait of Washington in its center, labeled "General Washington," and four smaller flag-
and trumpet-draped medallions with portraits of Benjamin Franklin, General Lincoln, John Adams, and General Green. The background is an allover of small red dots, and a simple line border edges the kerchief. There
is no date or maker's name but it can be dated by the engravings, especially
the Cochin portrait of Franklin, which was done in 1777. The kerchief is
of English manufacture and dates 1777–1778.

A kerchief with a center medallion of Washington and Franklin under
a palm tree and profile portraits of Hancock, Laurens, General Lincoln,
and General Green has a background sprinkled with small trefoils and a
border of bunches of grapes. It is marked "Henry Gardiner / Wandsworth
Surey" and was probably made in 1784. Since the signing of the Treaty of
Paris in 1783 is included in one of the inscriptions printed on the kerchief,
it could not be before that date. A kerchief with a central medallion of
Washington holding a scroll with his farewell address and portions of the
address in side medallions was printed in 1796–1797. The central medallion
is sometimes printed in red and sometimes in sepia, while the extracts from
the speech are printed in black. The kerchief was printed by W. G. & Company, Anderston, N. Britain (W. Gillespie, Scotland). Also printed in red

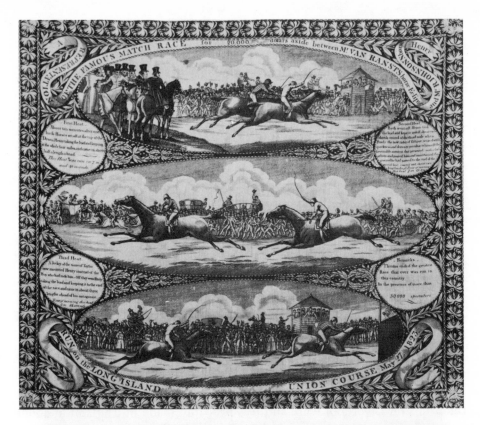

TOP: Race between Eclipse and Henry. Kerchief, red on yellow ground, c. 1823. BOTTOM: Britannia presenting Washington with olive branch. Kerchief, pink on white ground, printed by B. Warren, London.

or sepia on white linen with the text in black is the kerchief showing "Genl. Washington addressing the People of the United States of America on his Resignation of the Presidency." This, too, was probably printed in Scotland in about 1797. Another Washington kerchief has a central medallion showing Britannia presenting Washington with an olive branch and a figure of Fame blowing a trumpet with the words "Independence to America." A soldier holds a striped flag surmounted by a Liberty Cap. This kerchief is printed in pink on a white ground and has the stamp: "Drawn and Engraved by B. Warren No 6 / Vine Street Adjoining Mutten lane & Clerkemuell / London." It was made about 1800.

Several kerchiefs were printed upon the death of Washington. The designs were taken from engravings, some of which were made in Philadelphia. One showing Washington on his deathbed with two doctors and two women in attendance has the inscription "The Death of General Washington" and also extravagant printed eulogies. This kerchief was made in America about 1800. It is printed in sepia on white. A kerchief with a center scene of a monument to Washington with figures and a willow tree and a scroll border with names of states and various inscriptions suggests the prints on Liverpool ware and was probably made in England in about 1800. It is printed in sepia on white linen. Another kerchief with a memorial urn, the figures of two women and palm trees, and box inscriptions was probably printed in Philadelphia in 1800. Still another mourning scene about the tomb of Washington was printed in purplish brown on a white ground in about 1800 by "Jno Maclie & Co., Glascow." In 1819 a memorial based on the Bowling Green portrait of Washington, from a drawing by Charles Buxton, engraved by Cornelius Tiebout, was "Printed and Published at Glascow by C. G. 1819." The kerchief depicts the standing Washington with a background of a fort and a statue of George III. Above is the inscription "Sic Transit Gloria Mundi" and in a wreath the names of states and verses in praise of Washington. This kerchief is also printed in sepia on white.

In 1819 a kerchief was also made with a portrait of Washington after the "Dorchester Heights" portrait by Gilbert Stuart. It has a border of twenty-one squares with stars and is printed in sepia on a white ground. Two American-made kerchiefs relating to Washington were printed in the early 19th century. One depicts Washington and the cherry tree and has verses and the inscription "The Love of Truth Mark the Boy"; the other has the inscription "The Effect of Principle Behold the Man" and a full-length portrait of Washington under a tasseled drapery with the American eagle, the British lion, and a square-rigger labeled "Commercial Union." Both of these kerchiefs have been found printed in blue, red, or brown. In 1822 "Flag Handkerchiefs" were advertised in a New York newspaper.

No less than four different kerchiefs with the facsimile of the Declaration of Independence were made. Two were printed on silk and two on cotton. The two silk ones were made about 1820 in France. Both are based on William Woodruff's print of the Declaration of Independence. In the one made by H. Brunet et Cie, Lyon, France, the text of the Declaration is framed in an acorn wreath which contains seals of the thirteen states and portraits of Washington, Jefferson, and Adams. It has a border of small stars and is printed in black on white. The second kerchief design was also made in Lyon and is similar to the one described above except that it is printed in black on a yellow ground and has a border of laurel leaves. The cotton kerchief made in America in the early 19th century shows the text of the Declaration of Independence with a crest of laurel and oak branches and the Liberty Bell. The Border is composed of the coat of arms of each of the thirteen states and scrolls with names of Revolutionary generals and forts. It is printed in sepia on white. Another cotton kerchief which was probably printed in America in the early 19th century has a facsimile of the Declaration of Independence with an acorn border with the medallions of the thirteen states and a cresting made up of crossed flags, and trumpets and the portraits of Washington, Jefferson, and Adams. In the lower left-hand corner is a scene of "The Patriotic Bostonians discharging British ships in Boston Harbor" and in the right corner a scene of "Genl. Burgoyns surrender to Genl. Gates at Saratoga." The border is of anchors and cannon, and the kerchief is printed in sepia on a white ground. The same design is also printed in red on buff. Several other kerchiefs relating to Washington and American history were printed.

In 1804 or 1805 a memorial kerchief with a tomb and mourning figures and the words "In Memory of Major-General Alexander Hamilton" was printed in America. It is in sepia on a white ground. A printed silk kerchief with a portrait of Washington in a medallion supported by cornucopias, flags, and oak and laurel leaves, and a sunburst and star border with an outside oak-leaf border was printed in 1818 or 1819 in England.

A silk kerchief was printed in 1832 by M. Fithian of Philadelphia. It has the text of Washington's Farewell Address with a medallion portrait of Washington at the top and is printed in black on a white ground.

In 1889 an American kerchief with a bust of Washington surrounded by four shield emblems, laurel leaves, and ribbons, with the inscription "In God we Trust," was printed in red and black on a white ground. The design was based on a medal by Simon Benjamin Duviviar. A late portrait of Washington standing beside his horse is in a star-bordered medallion with two shields against a background of red and white stripes. This is a late-19th-century kerchief. Washington's portrait appears together with those of the King of Poland, Gen. Kosciusko, and Gen. Lafayette on a cotton kerchief made in France in the early 19th century. It is printed in pink on white and has embellishments of ribbons, tassels, roses, and wheat.

Five kerchiefs are known to have been printed with scenes and subject matter relating to the War of 1812. Several of these were printed in Scotland and some were also printed in America. One of the earliest is printed in maroon on a beige, cotton ground. At the top is the American eagle with portraits of Washington, Jefferson, and Madison and the inscription "Liberty & Independence Our Country's Pride & Boast." In laurel-circled medallions are scenes of eleven battles of the War of 1812 set upon a ground of stars and sprigs. In the medallion of the Battle of New Orleans "Glascow" and the engraver's name (which is illegible) are printed. This kerchief was made in Scotland in about 1815. A similar kerchief printed in sepia on white has "The Glorious Victory of New Orleans" as the central scene, and this is surrounded by seven scenes of naval battles. In the printed key of the scene is the name "C. Gray," a Scotch engraver who made kerchiefs with American scenes in the early part of the 19th century.

The cotton kerchief with the inscription "United States of America—Huzza For the Navy" has eight scenes of the War of 1812, including the Peace at Ghent and portraits of Perry and MacDonough. It was probably printed in America late in 1815 or 1816. Two silk kerchiefs were printed in America which relate to the War of 1812. The first, printed in remembrance of James Lawrence, has an urn and draped flags and naval emblems printed in black on white silk. It was drawn by N. W. Munroe and engraved on wood by C. Cobb.

On April 21, 1820, J. M'Laughlin at Washington printed a memorial to Stephen Decatur. It has a headpiece of ships and patriotic emblems and a poem and biographical sketch eulogizing Decatur. It is printed in black on white silk.

Various other events in American life and history have been recorded on printed kerchiefs. The Germantown Print Works, Philadelphia, printed

Cotton kerchief printed in maroon on beige ground. Portraits of Washington, Jefferson, and Madison and battle scenes of War of 1812, printed in Glasgow, c. 1815.

several kerchiefs in 1824. One has a center scene of Penn's Treaty with the Indians and Friends Meeting House, Philadelphia. A companion kerchief shows scenes of Lafayette in Philadelphia and New York. Both kerchiefs are printed in sepia on a white ground and both are marked "Germantown Print Works." A quilt is also in existence made up of kerchiefs printed at Germantown Print Works, although the works are not listed in any directories of that date. A silk kerchief was also printed at this time showing the "Arrival of Lafayette at Castle Garden." It has a design of crossed flags, eagle, and drum, a wreath with a sunburst, and the inscription "Welcome Lafayette." It is printed in tan on yellow and is similar to the badges and ribbons printed in New York for the Castle Garden celebration.

A kerchief with a portrait of Franklin and illustrations from *Poor Richard's Almanack* is printed in pink on white. It dates about 1800 and was probably made in France or England. Also of foreign make are the kerchiefs printed with the "Steam Frigate Fulton the First" and scenes depicting "American Sports." This kerchief was printed in pink and white and in sepia and white in about 1815–1820. At about the same date is the kerchief with scenes of commercial treaties with Europe. It has a floral wreath around a central scene and a floral border. It was printed in green, pink, brown, and yellow on a white ground. It was printed in England in about 1815, as was the kerchief with symbolic figures representing the Four Continents, which is printed in brown on a white ground. One of the handsomest kerchiefs was that showing the famous race between the horses Eclipse and Henry in 1823. It has three oval medallions with scenes from the first, second, and third heats, set on a ground of laurel leaves. Small medallions tell the story, and the border is of palm leaves. It is printed in red on a yellow ground.

In 1837 a silk kerchief was printed in New York with the farewell address of Andrew Jackson set in a flower-and-fruit border. It is printed in black on white silk. A silk kerchief was also printed in 1838 in celebration of the arrival of the steam packet *Sirius* from Dublin. It has a view in the center, an inscription, and a floral border and is printed in black on beige.

Two cotton kerchiefs were made in about 1850, one depicting the manufacture of paper, with scenes printed in lavender on white, and one illustrating the manufacture of silk, in pink on a white ground. Children's kerchiefs with picture alphabets and Sunday-school lessons were printed by the Boston Chemical Printing Company at about this date. They were printed in gray on white. A kerchief illustrating "The House that Jack

Built" was printed in pink on a white ground, and in the 1870s a kerchief with a multiplication table was printed in red on a white ground.

The various political campaigns were also commemorated in printed kerchiefs. In 1840 a Harrison kerchief with a log cabin in the center, a border of barrels, and the inscription "Hard Cider" was printed in red, black, and brown on a tan ground. A silk flag was also printed in red, white, and blue with "Harrison & Reform" inscribed in white stripes. In 1844 a cotton flag with a portrait of Henry Clay was printed in connection with his campaign. A flag with the inscription "Native Americans Beware of Foreign Influence" was also printed in 1844, and in 1845 President James K. Polk's first message to Congress was printed in blue on a white silk ground. The campaign of Zachary Taylor in 1848 occasioned the printing of five different kerchiefs. A cotton kerchief printed by Sarony & Major, New York, has a full-length portrait of Gen. Taylor and four Mexican War scenes from Currier & Ives. It is printed in brown and sepia. Another kerchief shows Sartian's engraving of Taylor with Mexican War scenes and a laurel-leaf border printed in sepia on white. The third kerchief shows the planting of the flag at Buena Vista and portraits of Gen. Taylor, Lt. Col. May, Gen. Wool, Gen. Scott, and Gen. Patterson in the border. It is printed in blue, sepia, and red on a white ground. A cotton broadside was printed by George F. Nesbitt in New York. It has the inscription "Democratic Whig Nominations / For President / Zachary Taylor / For Vice President / Millard Fillmore / For Governor, Hamilton Fish" printed in black on a white ground. A similar broadside was printed with the names of the aspirants for the offices of surrogate, register, and recorder of New York; and a third named the nominations for Congress and for the Assembly.

A silk kerchief was printed by Frederick Bauer & Co., Louisville, Kentucky, with an equestrian portrait of General Zachary Taylor and Mexican War scenes. The kerchief is inscribed "From a Daguerreotype taken by J. M. Hewett" and "Entirely of American Manufacture—Warranted fast colours." Kerchiefs also commemorate the campaigns of Cleveland, McKinley, and Theodore Roosevelt, and while these are devoid of artistic value they do have historical interest and as the years go by will become more valuable. The same is true of the kerchiefs made and sold at the various expositions. At present the only ones that are old enough to have value are those printed in connection with the Centennial Exposition at Philadelphia in 1875–1876. There were no less than six cotton kerchiefs with views of this event. One series had diagonal views of "Horticultural Hall," "Art Gallery," and "Main Exposition Hall," each set with different borders and printed in black on a white ground. These were 36 by 24 inches in size. Another kerchief had a medallion portrait of Washington inscribed "Centennial / International Exhibition / Philadelphia / 1876" and views of six exhibition buildings. It is printed in black on white and has a red border. Another kerchief has a view of the Centennial Art Gallery printed in black on white and has a red border.

A cotton American flag with the stars to form "1776/1876" was also printed at this time, as was a medallion portrait of Washington between two shields. Washington holds a message inscribed "Washington / Victory is / ours / Paul Jones." The medallion is blue, red, and sepia on a field of red and white stripes.

Old kerchiefs can be identified by the coarse hand-woven material and by the colors. The earliest were pink or red on white. Blue, green, purple, sepia, and brown were used later. The motifs of design and border decoration are also a key to the age and often to the nationality of the kerchiefs. However, the surest means of fixing a date is by a study of the portraits and scenes, which can usually be traced to an engraving of the period. Early kerchiefs are rare. Even those of the 19th century are comparatively rare, but considering their one-time universal popularity there must still be many stored away in attic trunks. But if you despair, start your collection with a Teddy Roosevelt, a Zachary Taylor, or a "Pavilions of the Nations / New York World's Fair 1939."

BIBLIOGRAPHY

Catalogue of American Scenes and Events on Textiles, September to November, 1941. New York Historical Society.
"Calico and Linen Printing in Philadelphia," by Harrold E. Gillingham. *Bulletin of The Historical Society of Pennsylvania*, vol. 52, April, 1928.
Painted and Printed Fabrics, by Henri Clouzot. The Metropolitan Museum of Art, New York, 1927.

❧ 19 ❧

American Samplers and Needlework Pictures

THE SAMPLER, made by children and young girls in their early teens, is the first record of needlework in America. The earliest samplers followed English patterns and displayed samples of drawnwork as well as embroidery stitches. Early samplers were made on long narrow strips of hand-woven linen about 8 inches in width. One characteristic of the 17th-century sampler is that it is always long and narrow. Although the average width is 8 inches, some are only 6 or 7 inches wide, and as long as 25 or 29 inches.

The earliest samplers were made up of alphabets and conventional fruit and flower borders, which included such motifs as the Indian pink, trefoil, strawberry, acorn, Tree of Life, the Stuart "S," pineapple, and fleur-de-lis. In addition to fruit and flower motifs, birds and animals are often found in conventional borders. The embroidery was done in linen or loosely twisted silk thread, which was hand-dyed, and the early sampler was worked in greens, blues, and browns, although some were all white. The stitches most often used in the 17th century were the angular cross-stitch and the tent or petit-point stitch. White samplers were made in satin stitch and the designs were geometric. The earliest and best-known American sampler is that made by Ann Gower, the wife of Governor Endicott. It was made in England in about 1610, is worked in eyelet and satin stitch, and has letters and borders of drawnwork at the bottom. It is in the collection of the Essex Institute in Salem. The sampler of Loara Standish is embroidered with letters and a verse and has borders of blue and brown. Another 17th-century sampler is that of Miles and Abigail Fleetwood. It was made in 1654 and in addition to alphabets and floral borders has this verse:

> In prosperity friends will be plenty
> But in adversity not one in twenty.

There are not more than a dozen American 17th-century samplers recorded and most of them are in museum collections, although as late as 1945 the sampler of Hannah Lindall, dated January 28, 1692, was sold in the Harold E. Gillingham sale in Philadelphia. All of the 17th-century American samplers found were made in New England and while the majority of the 18th-century samplers were also made in New England there were many made in Long Island, New Jersey, and Pennsylvania. The typical 18th-century American sampler is signed and dated and has several alphabets, sometimes as many as five. Toward the end of the 17th century the sampler became shorter and broader and in the 18th century such proportions as 16 by 18 inches, 16 by 11¾ inches, and even 13 by 13 inches square are the rule rather than the exception. Early in the 18th century a floral border began to be used as a frame around the sampler. Although there were many samplers made with reds and greens and various-colored threads, for the most part the coloring consisted of dull greens, blues, browns, and cream on a background of brown linen. Occasionally a background of mustard color, dark green, or blue is found. Sampler stitches now included cross-stitch, tent stitch, satin, rope, stem eyelet, chain, French knot, cat stitch, hem (long and short), tapestry, queen stitch, and many others. In addition to borders of fruit and flowers there were verses, usually of a religious nature, such as the Lord's Prayer, the Creed, the Ten Commandments, or the verse that starts:

> Jesus permit thy gracious name to stand,
> As the first effort of an infant's hand

Other verses dealt with the themes of death and sorrow, friendship, learning, needlework, love, and nature. About 1798 and a few years afterward patriotic subjects are found, including peace and war and the death of Washington.

Early in the 18th century several interesting subjects were introduced. They appear first as panels at the bottom of the sampler, but gradually take a place of prominence in the center of the sampler. One of the most important motifs is the Adam and Eve motif, which is seen on samplers as early as 1709. The figures are nude, as are the figures of Adam and Eve motifs in samplers dated 1741. However, in 1760 a quaint Adam and Eve in Quaker dress is seen on a sampler with a Brown University building and a scene of a doctor's gig and horse. Sometimes the sun and moon are shown, and the tree with forbidden fruit and the snake, and often men, stags, and other animals appear in the scene. A sampler dated 1788 has a scene of a cottage, deer, Adam and Eve, and two figures carrying a tree, together with flowers and cooing doves. Other Biblical characters represented on 18th-century samplers include Ashur and Elisha dancing and playing musical instruments on a sampler dated 1718, and in a 1760 sampler Caleb and Joshua carrying the grapes of Eshcol are shown. A scene of the Three Fates and the Garden of Eden is dated 1737. In about 1730 the shepherd and shepherdess, familiar in all 18th-century needlework, is represented on a sampler made in Pennsylvania. The hunting scene with men and dogs, trees, stags, and other animals is also characteristic of 18th-century samplers. It is used together with religious verses and alphabets. Birds, butterflies, lions, peacocks, rabbits, squirrels, turtles, cocks, and worms are also to be found on late 18th-century samplers. Around the middle of the 18th century, the house, which became so familiar in 19th-century samplers, was seen for the first time. Small brick houses, together with figures and animals such as domestic sheep, cows, ducks, and cocks, make up the scene. Public buildings were also shown, including many in Providence, Rhode Island, where such buildings as those at Brown University were introduced on samplers made at Miss Polly Balch's School. Buildings of Harvard, Yale, and Princeton universities and scenes of towns and villages are also embroidered on late 18th-century samplers. Flowers in a vase or in a basket were also motifs used in borders and even as the center of a sampler. One naïve sampler dated 1750 has a scene with trees and animals, and, on a mound or hill, a basket of flowers is represented larger than the tree. An unusual sampler made in York, Pennsylvania, is divided into squares which contain sprays of flowers alternating with pious sentiments and the name of the girl's parents and thus suggests the family-record samplers, so many of which were made in the late 18th and early 19th centuries.

By the 19th century the sampler is characterized by more naturalistic designs and the conception is more individual. The linen is often of a coarse, loose weave. A typical motif which appeared late in the 18th century is the house. There are representations of churches, public buildings, Solomon's Temple, the schoolhouse, and the child's own house, which is probably the most interesting, for it includes more individuality. There are cottage and barnyard scenes with domestic animals, castles with deer, and churches with angels. One sampler dated 1812 has a representation of an orphanage surrounded by lion rampant, fox, deer, and fowl. The cottage with birds and trees is a familiar scene, and the brown- or red-brick schoolhouse is

TOP: Silk chenille pastoral. Satin embroidered Washington memorial. CENTER: Needlework picture, c. 1754. Seat cover. BOTTOM: Sampler, 1826. Sampler showing New York City Hall, 1828.

combined with angels in flight, trees, and a verse or several alphabets. A castle or cottage with deer, dogs, birds, or shepherd and shepherdess are all combined on one sampler. From the beginning of the 19th century the schoolhouse became a familiar motif; however, it is not so individual or so interesting as the large Solomon's Temple with birds, trees, and peacock. The American eagle is often seen in 19th-century samplers above a farmhouse. Sometimes the eagle is naturalistic and sometimes it is represented with a shield and flags. In addition to all the other motifs alphabets and verses continued to occupy a part of the sampler, and the Adam and Eve and shepherd and shepherdess motifs continued to appear on samplers down to about 1830. Two types of samplers seen occasionally are the darning sampler, with specimens of various types of darning enclosed within a floral border, and the map sampler. Both types were popular in England but were not common in America. After 1830 the sampler deteriorated in workmanship and the designs were more realistic. Also fewer samplers were made, and after 1850 the making of samplers became a lost art.

The embroidered picture was another distinctive type of American needlework. It was first made in New England in the 18th century. Needlework pictures were worked in wool and silk on a linen ground. Landscapes with figures were produced chiefly in tent or petit-point stitch. The romantic subject matter was taken from engravings of English and French paintings. Often groups of figures were taken from several different engravings and combined in one needlework panel. In a Boston newspaper of 1757 "canvas pictures ready drawn" were advertised. The subject matter of 17th-century embroidered pictures was religious and was taken from Old Testament stories such as Abraham and Hagar, Abraham offering Isaac, and David and Bath-sheba. However, the 18th-century picture was not religious, but usually concerned itself with shepherds and shepherdesses and pastoral scenes. As early as 1730 a sampler signed and dated contained this subject, but most of the needlework pictures date around the middle of the century. The reclining shepherdess appears in a landscape with trees, sheep, lambs, a deer, birds, and a distant scene of a village. In another interpretation of the shepherdess there are flocks of birds and parrots, sheep, a shepherd with crook, and in the background a house. A shepherd and shepherdess picture which is probably later, but more original in conception, is the one in the Metropolitan Museum of Art. The shepherdess is standing and holds a branch in her hand; the shepherd with pipes sits on a ladder which is propped against a fruit tree; sheep, geese, dogs, and a turtle gambol amid the stylized hills; and birds and clouds fill the sky space. This "Bringing in the May" scene is a favorite with the 18th-century needlewoman. Groups of figures in a harvest scene were also worked in 18th-century New England needlework. Pastoral scenes by Jacques Stella (1596–1657) furnish the figures which are used in many of these American 18th-century embroidered pictures. Sometimes a group of figures is represented, and again only one figure is copied and the rest of the scene is original. Thus the quaint embroidery in the Newburyport Historical Society contains several typically American houses, a windmill, and a boy astride a goat, together with the decorative figure with a basket of flowers similar to the figure in the Stella pastoral. Another embroidered picture includes a man playing pipes and pastoral figures of a man, woman and deer, geese, birds, and flowers, and again a representation of a New England house.

The famous "Fishing Lady" embroidered pictures also have some of the same figures, including the pastoral couple by Stella and a boy riding a pony. In one panel is a shepherd and a woman spinning, and the center panel has the pond and fishing lady and her gallant companion. The foreground is a tapestry of birds, deer, dogs, and ducks on a pond, while no less than four New England houses are in the distance amid clouds, birds, parrots, and butterflies. Other pictures of the Fishing Lady panel without the other figures have been found. A pastoral scene worked in tent stitch on canvas shows a shepherdess with sheep, a house or castle in the background, and a man and dog. The faces are painted and appliquéd. The picture is in the Cleveland Museum and is dated 1758.

The famous scene of Boston Common worked by Hannah Otis in about 1745 is similar to the Fishing Lady picture, but in the Boston Common scene the Hancock House and other landmarks can be identified. However, the motifs of birds, strawberries, and trees are almost identical with those in Fishing Lady embroideries and may have been directed by the same New England embroidery teacher, the now famous Mrs. Condy, or Mrs. Hiller, who advertised in the Boston newspapers as follows: in 1742, "Mrs. Condy opens her school next Week and Persons may be supply'd with the Materials for the Work she teaches, whether they learn of her or not. She draws Patterns of all sorts, especially Pocket Books, House Wives, Screens, Pictures, Chimney Pieces, Escritoires, etc. for Tent-Stitch, in a plainer Manner, and cheaper than those which come from London." In 1747: "Patterns drawn by the late Susannah Condy for sale by Elizabeth Russel, her daughter-in-law." In 1748: "Mrs. Hiller designs to open a

TOP: Painted and embroidered satin pictures, 19th century. BOTTOM: Embroidered satin picture, c. 1740.

Boarding-School where they may be taught and may be supplied with Patterns in all sorts of Drawing and Materials for their Work."

In 1757 David Mason, japanner, advertised: "Drawings on Satin or Canvis for Embroidering." "Yellow canvas and canvas pictures ready drawn" were also advertised in newspapers at about this date. In 1800 J. M. Williams, R.A., of London, advertised in the Boston Gazette: "Designs and patterns of all kinds painted and outlined on silk or satin to fill up with needlework." In 1810 L. Lemet, the engraver, advertised in the *Albany Gazette*: "Framing of Needlework—He offers to paint the head gratis."

That silk embroideries on black and white satin were made before the middle of the 18th century is evidenced by the group in the Boston Museum of Fine Arts. These are especially interesting, for although such motifs as trees, birds, and mounds are stylized, the houses and figures and especially the sailing ship are local New England, and the conception of the designs is original. One panel might be called a sailor's farewell. The museum dates these silk embroideries 1740. A picture of "Abraham Offering Isaac" worked in silk on white satin is dated February 16, 1733. Also the "Story of Absalom," worked in satin stitch on black satin, was made in the mid-18th century. However, most of the embroideries on satin date from the late 18th and the first quarter of the 19th centuries. They were worked in flat silk stitches and French knots. Sky, faces, and other detail was painted on the silk background. Chenille was often used for more realistic effects on trees, grass, rocks, and animals such as sheep or dogs. Paintings and engravings by Carrington Bowles, Thomas Barker, and Bartolozzi, together with those of struggling artists, furnished the designs. However, such a book as R. Furber's *Flower Garden* was also "for working and painting in color" and Heckell's collection of flowers in baskets was "for drawing or needlework." Needlework pictures on satin with subjects from Thomas Barker include "Labour and Health," "Woodman and Wife," and "A Country Girl." A pair of oval needlework pictures on satin depict a boy shepherd and a girl shepherdess set in a frame of flower garlands. They are dated 1790.

Other needlework pictures on satin made in the first quarter of the 19th century include such subjects as "Cupid and Psyche," "Paul and Virginia," "Monument to General Daisey," "The Cottage Girl," "Woman with Harp," and "Mt. Vernon." Scenes of New York and other cities were also embroidered on silk. Silk pictures with sentimental subjects were also made as watch papers. These pictures usually had the sky and faces of figures painted in water color.

Embroidered pictures on satin were first made in America at the Moravian schools in Bethlehem, Pennsylvania. The flower embroideries in satin stitch on satin made by the Moravians were especially distinctive. The flowers were arranged in sprays, festoons, and garlands, and also in baskets, sometimes tied with ribbons. The flowers are usually naturalistic and so exquisitely embroidered that they would please even a botanist. Roses, carnations, and daisies are arranged in baskets or sometimes in a wreath around a pious verse. The Moravians also worked religious pictures, and such subjects as "Isaac and Rebecca," "Finding of Moses," "Cornelia and the Gracchi," "Christ and the Woman of Samaria" are often found.

Many paintings of Angelica Kauffman were copied in 19th-century stitchery, and shepherds and shepherdesses, boys and girls, maps and ships, and many places of historical interest such as Mt. Vernon, embroidered in long and short stitch, together with painting on satin backgrounds, were made between 1800 and 1830. Scenes of a shepherdess with staff and a piping shepherd continued in popularity. Some are on white satin, buttonhole-stitched into a background of black satin. Other scenes are surrounded by a border of naturalistic oak leaves. One early 19th-century child shepherdess with lamb has an embroidered border of vine and berries and festoons containing roses, tulips, and other flowers. A decorative shepherdess with three sheep is set against a landscape of chenille trees and water-color sky. Another shepherdess embroidered and painted by Laura Reed includes a realistic farmhouse and fence.

A few family registers were embroidered in silk on satin, but the most popular 19th-century theme worked on satin was the "Mourning Picture." These also originated with the Moravians and some were made as early as 1740, but the majority of these mournful scenes date between 1800 and 1830. The various engravings made in connection with the death of George Washington may have set the pattern for the popularity of the embroidered Mourning Picture. An engraving by Thomas Clarke of Boston, dated 1801, shows an obelisk under a weeping willow. On the obelisk is an oval portrait of Washington with cherubim and laurel wreaths and inscription and at the side of the monument is a figure of a man and two women. This is similar to the scenes shown on Mourning Pictures embroidered on satin. The scene usually has a tombstone with urn and inscription, dates, and a willow tree, with one or more figures of women mourning or carrying laurel wreaths for adorning the tomb. The embroidery is done on white satin in somber tones of gray and black or tan, blue, and green silk thread or silk chenille, with painted faces and sky. A unique Mourning Picture in the collection of the Metropolitan Museum of Art has a double obelisk with two urns. A beautiful Mourning Picture in the collection of the New York Historical Society has a border of naturalistic leaves, roses, morning glories, lilies of the valley, and cornucopias with fruit and wheat, which in color and technique shows Moravian influence. This was made by Eliza Kortright of 29 Broadway, New York City, and dated 1820.

Samplers and needlework pictures should be judged for the beauty of their design and the quality of the workmanship. Good examples have clear but mellow color and formal designs. Cross-stitch formed a square on the back of old samplers. Later designs became more naturalistic and less organized and the colors became monotone, and instead of fine hand-dyed silks and yarns, commercial threads were used. In late examples of samplers the canvas was no longer hand-woven.

BIBLIOGRAPHY

American Samplers, by Ethel Stanwood Bolton and Eva Johnston Coe. The Massachusetts Society of the Colonial Dames of America, 1921.

American Needlework, by Georgiana Brown Harbeson. Coward-McCann, Inc., New York, 1938.

"An Introduction to the Study of Eighteenth Century New England Embroidery," by Gertrude Townsend. *Bulletin of the Museum of Fine Arts,* Boston, vol. 39, April, 1941.

∞ 20 ∞

Ladies' Handwork in America in the 18th and 19th Centuries

As EARLY AS 1714 boarding schools of Boston were teaching "Flourishing Embroidery, and all sorts of Needle-work, also Filigrew, Painting upon Glass"; in 1716, "Feather-work and Turkey-work"; in 1742, "screens, Pictures, Chimney Pieces"; and in 1748, "Wax-Work, Japanning, Quill-work, Feather-work, Shell-work, Dresden flowering on Lawn and Muslin, and Tambour." One New York gentleman of the 18th century was so overcome by the amount of needlework done in his household that he wrote the following letter to the printer of the *New York Mercury*, and it was published October 16, 1758. Speaking of his wife he says:

> She calls up her Daughters at a certain hour and appoints them a task of needle-work to be performed before breakfast. We have twice as many fire-skreens as chimneys and three flourished quilts for every bed. Half the rooms are adorned with a kind of futile pictures which imitate tapestry. She has twenty coverns for side-saddles embroidered with silver flowers, and has curtains wrought with gold in various figures.

However, although needlework kept all early American women occupied, more needlework was made in New England in the 18th century than in any other part of the country. In addition to samplers and needlework pictures discussed in the preceding chapter, women were busy embroidering dresses, petticoats, waistcoats, bed hangings, cushions, and chair seats. Although some few articles of stump work and beadwork were made in America in the 17th century, the crewelwork of New England was really the first ornamental stitchery made in America. Bed hangings and bed-spreads as well as petticoats and mantel hangings made in the 18th century are preserved in museum collections, so we can judge the beauty of the work. Crewelwork was worked in wool and cotton thread on a ground of homespun linen. Some yarns were home-dyed, but the majority of them were imported from England. In 1743 "shaded crewels, blue, red, and other colours of worsteds" were advertised in a Boston newspaper. Clear bright blues, greens, yellows, browns, rose, peach, and sometimes Canton blue yarns were worked in oriental or Rumanian stitch together with outline, satin, chain, stem, herringbone, and darning stitches, as well as French knots. The patterns were similar to Jacobean embroideries but were more open. Oriental influence is seen in the trees, vases of flowers, and exotic animals. Patterns were also taken from pattern books of birds, flowers, and animals which were published in England late in the 17th century. Such birds as peacocks and macaws and animals such as dragons, monkeys, deer, squirrels, and even snails are found in crewel embroideries. Among the flowers were the carnation, rose, the Florentine artichoke, and the tulip. Certain designs in crewelwork are distinctly American such as the Pine Tree, the Oak, Bittersweet, Bellflower, and the Red-winged Blackbird. Fruit trees, berries, and grapevines seem to be taken from nature, as does the rising sun. Such designs as hearts, stars, and crowns probably have a religious origin. Among the most interesting motifs are the brook with fish, the deer, sheep, butterflies, and the quaint figures of women. Soldiers and the Battle of Bunker Hill were worked on a crewel bedspread made in 1776, and the Balloon Ascension of 1785 is seen on curtains of American crewelwork. Sets of chair seats have crewelwork designs of trees and animals. Turkey work or "carpet knotting" in imitation of carpets was also used for chair seats, bed and table covers, and rugs. The designs of turkey work were made up of zigzag lines mostly worked in red and greens, although blue, buffs, browns, magenta, and black were also used.

Quilting on white linen was also made early in the 18th century. Patterns included the Pineapple, Fern Leaf, Cornucopia, Baskets of Flowers, Pomegranate, Princess Feather, Vines and Grapes, Rope, Bellflower, and geometric patterns such as the Diamond Block, Cross Bar, Diagonal, Horizontal, and Basket weave. "Queen Charlotte's Crown" dates from 1770, and other quilting patterns include the Tree of Life, Acanthus, Oak Leaf, Pine Tree, Dove of Peace, Tide Mill, Splint, Star of Bethlehem, and the Eagle. Later patterns included "E Pluribus Unum," "Dolly Madison Star," "Starry Crown," "David and Goliath," and "Mrs. Cleveland's Choice." Certain patterns are peculiar to various sections of the country. The "Harvest Sun" and "Ship's Wheel" are from New England. The "Cactus Basket" and "Desert Rose" first made in 1800 are Western, as are the "Cowboy's Star" and "Arkansas Traveller" of 1860 and the Ohio pattern "Bear's Paw" made in about 1850. Some bedspreads as early as 1800 combine patchwork and quilting. Candle wicking with uncut knots was also made by 18th-century women, and patterns like the Basket of Flowers, Grape, and Tree of Life are early. Angular patterns and Eagles and Stars date about 1825.

Tambour was a chain stitch worked with a special hooked needle. The pattern was drawn on lace or wool and the finished material shows loops of thread or wool. This work, which was introduced in the 18th century, was popular with workers in needlework as late as 1850. Most of the tambour work preserved today is on lace or net, although an advertisement of 1773 says: "She works in Tambour ladies robes, ruffles, muffs, tippets, work bags, quadrille baskets, gentlemens waiscoats, knee garters, sword knots, etc. Also the Tambour completely taught in gold, silver, silk and cotton."

The needlework picture continued to be made down into the 19th century. Large pictures of George Washington, Benjamin Franklin, and Henry Clay in room settings with chairs, desks, and other furniture, were made in about 1830. Landscape and Biblical scenes and copies of pictures were also popular. Sentimental needlework pictures of children and animals and Italian villas, "The Sicilian Maid," "Scottish Chieftain," "Arabian Scout," "Mary Queen of Scots," and "Washington Crossing the Delaware" (after Leutze) were popular subjects between 1840 and 1860. Upholstery for chairs and stools was worked in designs of naturalistic flowers, leaves, wreaths, and baroque scrolls. About 1856 needlework canvas patterns and wools for working them were imported from Germany. The patterns were blocked for cross-stitch or needlepoint and painted in color on canvas and the work was popularly called Berlin Work. Chair seats, pillows, stools, fire screens, banners, and pictures were made in gaudy, brilliant, zephyr wools on canvas of various colors—white, black, or claret. Canvas was obtainable in cotton, wool, or silk, the silk being the best. Some Berlin Work was done on horsehair. The stitches used, while essentially a cross-stitch variation, were called Irish or Railroad, Turkish, Victoria, or Czar stitch according to the popular conversation of the day. Designs were typically Victorian and included horses, pet dogs—especially poodles, spaniels, and "pug" dogs —deer, parrots, birds and wreaths of flowers, roses, lilies, ivy, grapes, and autumn leaves. In addition to the larger articles of household usage, personal articles (such as railroad bags, note cases, tobacco bags, suspenders, pincushions, and shawl straps) were made and patterns for these were issued monthly by *Godey's Lady's Book* and other publications of the time.

Embroidery in cross-stitch on paper was also popular in the 19th century. Some pictures were worked on paper, but bookmarks and mottoes were made in such quantities that there are many to be found today, and collectors have found them a source of interest. Bookmarks have such inscriptions as "Forget Me Not," "I'll Keep the Place," "Love," "Amour," "Holy Bible," "Souvenir," "Sincerity," and "Look to Jesus." The designs include flowers, geometric borders, and a Cross and Bible. Bookmarks are backed with silk ribbon, which often hangs as fringe at the top and bottom of the bookmark. These were made between 1830 and 1900. Mottoes have such inscriptions as "Good Morning," with a cross-stitch of a cock; 'Old Oaken Bucket," with a picture of a well and bucket; and "What is Home Without a Mother" and its companion "What is Home Without a Father"; "Welcome"; "Home Sweet Home"; or there are religious mottoes such as "Jesus Saves," "Holy Bible," or a picture of lilies with the verse "They Toil Not Neither do They Spin." The designs include flowers, geometric borders, a Cross and Bible, and often a scene of a house or even a farm with figures and animals.

In addition to needlework, women of the 18th century made many other kinds of fancywork. As early as 1702 quillwork or paper filigree, or mosaic, as Mrs. Delaney called it, was made to decorate picture frames, boxes such as tea caddies, and coat of arms. Parchment or gilt and colored paper was cut in narrow (one-eighth-inch) strips and rolled into spirals or quills or cones, then one edge was glued to the background of the article being made—silk, wood, or paper. Filigree was used in figures and decoration in churches of the 16th century. In the 17th century it was used in the costumes of small wax figures and together with stump work on boxes and mirror frames. Pepys speaks of a basket made of paper filigree in 1663 and as early as 1710 filigree work was being taught in Boston private schools. A candle sconce with a walnut Queen Anne frame filled with a quillwork design of flowers is dated 1720. Similar work was used for fire screens, mirror frames, in frames for Wedgwood plaques, and as chimney pieces. Hatchments or family coat of arms were also made in filigree and large cabinets were covered with filigree work. In 1786 the *New Ladies' Magazine* published patterns for filigree tea caddies, chimney pieces, screens, cabinets, frames, and picture ornaments. The technique seems particularly suited to such small articles as tea caddies, and many of them were made. Against a background of wood and with insets of Wedgwood medallions, needlework, or painted ovals, the intricate lacework paper spirals made a beautiful pattern of gold, silver, and color that looks like delicate carving. Designs of flowers and leaves with birds and conventional spiral borders give the effect of gold and ivory carving. Colors most often used are red, blue, white, purple, and gold and silver. As late as 1811 Jane Austen mentions rolling the papers for a filigree basket, but filigree was probably not made after about 1820 and most of that found today dates from the 18th century.

Featherwork was also taught in the American private schools of the 18th century. This work had been introduced to Spain from Mexico and was used in religious triptychs as a background for carving. It was also used in 17th-century stump-work embroidery to give a realistic effect. Feathers were both sewn on and glued on. By the 18th century the collecting of feathers of exotic birds became a hobby, and tapestries were made of feathers of hummingbirds and other colorful and rare feathers. However, few pieces of this early handiwork are to be seen today. In the 19th century women again took up the hobby of featherwork. Feathers were collected and sometimes dyed and made into flowers by bending or curling them with a penknife and wiring them. Some flowers were made into wreaths and put under glass domes or framed, and others were used as bouquets in vases. Many of these feather-flower wreaths are to be found in attics today.

Flowers, wreaths, frames, and boxes were also made of shells. Small rice shells were pasted to cardboard and formed the background, and larger, more decorative, shells were used for roses or other flowers. Shell boxes are sometimes decorative, but the pasteboard animals, vases, and frames covered with shells are hardly to be commended. Wreaths of shell flowers were framed in walnut frames, and shell flowers in vases were put under glass domes. All of these articles are available today in antique shops. The shellwork of the 18th century made by Mrs. Delaney and other women was of finer workmanship and the shells were more carefully selected. Stands, lusters, mirror frames, and cabinets were sometimes covered with shellwork patterns of various colors, and shells were used to imitate enamel. Larger shells were used for cornices and grottoes. Some shellwork was made in molds, as evidenced by the following advertisement in a Boston newspaper of 1760: "Any person having moulds for Wax-Work or Shell-Work to dispose of, are desir'd to inform said Bramham or the Printers." Mrs. Abigail Hiller, one of the best-known teachers of Boston, taught "Wax-Work, Transparent and Filligree, Painting upon Glass, Japanning, Quill-Work,

TOP: White linen quilting, American, 18th century. BOTTOM: Crewelwork chair seat, 18th century.

Feather-Work, and Embroidering with Gold and silver" in Boston in 1748.

If we can judge from the wax figure of Reverend Joshua Gee dated 1748 in the Museum for the Preservation of New England Antiquities, the "Wax-Work" was figure work. The well-known wax figures and portraits by Patience Wright, John Christian Rauchner, and Reuben Moulthrop date from the 18th century. In 1772 Patience Wright went to England, where she made wax portraits of King George, Garrick the actor, Benjamin Franklin, and Mrs. Catherine McCauley. Wax figures of English characters were exhibited in New York in 1749, and at Vauxhall Gardens in 1768 wax figures and scenes, including fruit trees and "pieces of Grotto-Work and Flowers composed of Shells," were shown. Some of the figures were life-size, as were those of King George and Queen Charlotte exhibited in 1772, the representation of the banquet from Macbeth, and Harlequin and Columbine. In 1773 Mr. McNeill exhibited a piece of "Wax and Shell Work," the scene taken from Homer's *Iliad*, showing Hector and Andromache at the City Gate. Mr. McNeill also taught wax- and shellwork. As late as 1801 an exhibition of waxwork figures and heads in bas-relief were colored in natural tones, and much of the work was excellent.

In 1850 waxwork was revived, but instead of portraits and figures, wax flowers and fruit were made. Small flowers, fruit, and berries were molded by hand, but larger fruit and flowers were made by putting heated wax in a plaster mold. Wax dolls, sheep, and birds were also made in molds. In 1853 a *Hand-book for Modelling Wax Flowers* was published by J. & H. Mintorn, who also furnished patterns and molds for fruit and such bell-shaped flowers as violets, jasmine, moss rose, and China and Banksian roses. Molding sticks of different shapes and sizes were made of hard, smooth, turned wood. The stick gave support to the flower and a center for stamens. Wax was colored yellow, green, red, blue, and other colors by adding pigment to the wax before modeling, and flowers were also tinted and shaded by hand with brushes. These compositions of fruit and flowers were sometimes arranged in vases or baskets and put under a glass dome, and others were made in wreath form and framed. Favorite flowers were fuchias, passion flowers, convolvuluses, and orange blossoms. Some of the fruit compositions are of fine workmanship and worth collecting as specimens of Victorian workmanship.

Beadwork frames were made in the 17th and early 18th centuries and beadwork was used in stump-work embroidery and in other needlework as well as in pictures on boxes and book covers. However, 19th-century beadwork is the kind that is most available to the collector today. Purses, card cases, cigar cases and beadwork pictures with scenes of castles and Swiss chalets were popular. In 1818 Chez Martin, a shop in Paris, put out a pattern book of colored designs for beadwork purposes. Designs included flowers, landscapes with ruins and classic buildings, and scenes with ships, bridges, and a hunting scene. In the late 19th century beadwork mats and pincushions had Greek-key borders and fringed loops and patterns of crude birds and flowers. A brush holder in the shape of a shoe and heart-shaped pincushions were popular items, and both are found in considerable numbers today. The work on them is coarse and crude in color and design. Some of this work was made by Indians.

In *Godey's Lady's Book* of January, 1855, a new art work for ladies is described and illustrated. It is called "Potichimanie," and in spite of its fancy name is nothing more than decalcomanias glued on the inside of glass vases. However, the idea originated in Paris and must have had a widespread popularity because vases to be used were made at Sèvres and Clichy. Generally the shapes were good and were of Chinese inspiration, although some had Victorian fluted tops. Pictures to cut out and paste were also imported and included Dresden medallions, Chinese figures and flowers, Assyrian patterns from Nineveh, and Sèvres and Etruscan designs. One candlestick in an illustration in Mrs. Pullan's *Lady's Manual of Fancy Work* published in 1859 has borders of grapes and leaves and medallions of French buildings in deep blue and gold. Vases were blue and gold, pink and gold, and Etruscan dull red and black. Glass table tops were also made in Potichimanie. While many of the shapes and designs are really in good taste, such subjects as "Hiawatha's Wooing" and children rolling hoops, show that high standards did not apply to all Potichimanie, and it was not too many years before the process deteriorated into gumming cigar bands on the outside of brown jugs. Who knows, we may be collecting these jugs for the names of cigars no longer made! Yet that can be no worse than moss pictures against a painted sky, seaweed baskets, pine-cone or cut-leather picture frames, or pictures of Indian chiefs burnt with a needle on white pine!

But let us go back to 1800, when the education of young ladies at the Columbia House Boarding and Day School in New York City included "embroidery and tambour in gold, silver and colors, fillagree, artificial flowers, fancy baskets, netting, hair, print cloth and muslin work of very kind."

Hairwork was a popular form of jewelry decoration in America as early as the middle of the 18th century. It was at first used by jewelers in memorial rings, lockets, and brooches, with the hair of the deceased loved one arranged under glass and mounted with a circlet of gold or precious stones. Hair was also made into devices, figures, and landscapes upon a background of ivory. This type of work was done by artists who were also known as miniature painters and profile cutters.

On January 3, 1763, Charles Oliver Bruff, goldsmith and jeweler, advertised: "Mourning rings of all sorts, trinkets for ladies, plats hair in a curious manner in true lover's knot for buttons, rings or lockets." On February 8, 1762, Samuel Tingley, gold and silversmith, had stolen from his shop "one ring with four Diamonds and a flat stone with a little Hair under." On May 4, 1767, John Dawson, goldsmith and jeweler, advertised in the same paper: "He also plaits hair in the neatest manner to any size or shape, for rings or lockets, and forms it (after the new taste) to resemble Mocco." On August 6, 1772, Bennett & Dixon, jewelers, advertised in the *New York Journal or General Advertiser*: "Mourning rings, plain or set with any kind of stone with hair worked in landskips." And in the *New York Gazette and Weekly Mercury* for May 20, 1776, John Shaw, jeweler, advertises: "Cyphers in Hair done for Lockets, Rings, etc. etc." In the *New York Gazette and Weekly Mercury* for January 2, 1775, Whitehouse & Reeve advertised: ". . . have engaged a person from London that understands the art of working hair in sprigs, birds, figures, cyphers, crests of arms." In the *New York Daily Advertiser*, January 2, 1799, P. Parisien advertised miniature painting and "all kinds of devices neatly executed with real hair, mourning rings, lockets, etc. made to any fancy." In 1802 Parisien advertised that he would make a tour of the country making "Hair Devices." Parisien was still working in 1815 and was later elected to the National Academy of Design. A. Edouart was also doing hairwork or hair painting in 1815. He made portraits, landscapes, devices in human hair, and portraits of dogs and horses in their own hair. Breast pins with hair of a loved one under glass were also worn, and woven-hair bracelets with gold clasps were made as early as 1814.

John Ramage also painted memorial designs in water color and dissolved hair. Other 18th-century artists who did miniatures and hairwork

TOP LEFT: Paper filigree hatchment. TOP RIGHT: 19th century hairwork jewelry. MIDDLE LEFT: Vase, Potichimanie. MIDDLE RIGHT: Silk embroidery, metallic threads. BOTTOM LEFT: Portrait, Zachary Taylor, stuffed cloth and embroidery. BOTTOM RIGHT: Bead-and-wool wreath, waxed fruit under glass, late 19th century.

were Ezra Ames, Samuel Folwell, Edward G. Malbone, Francis Rabineau, Claudius Fallize, N. Hancock, and William Lovett. These men did both hair painting and "hair plaiting" for the backs of lockets or for use under glass in breast pins. Jewelers and goldsmiths did the same sort of work but also made bracelets, earrings, and brooches of plaited hair. In 1800 T. B. Dumontet had a hairwork and jewelry manufactory in Philadelphia and numerous jewelers in various parts of the country were doing the same kind of work. Both kinds of hairwork continued to be made as late as 1880.

Toward the middle of the century hairwork became so popular that several books were published. In 1840 *The Jeweller's Book of Patterns in Hairwork* was published in London. This contained copperplate engravings of devices and patterns in hair suitable for mourning jewelry, brooches, rings, guards, necklets, lockets, bracelets, miniatures, studs, links, and earrings. Several other books were published between 1860 and 1870. The 1859 *Godey's Lady's Book* printed directions for hairwork, and hairwork continued to be the fashion until the end of the century. Women made hairwork bracelets, earrings, pins, and other devices at home and took them to a jeweler for mounting, but it was probably not much before *Godey's* printed the directions in 1859 that it became a "pastime for ladies." In 1864 *Peterson's Magazine* included instructions in hairwork for the amateur.

Patterns included braiding, interlacing, and snakelike designs for bracelets, and chains. Motifs included feathers, flowers, hearts, crosses, bowknots, butterflies, and lettering such as "Sister," "Mother," "Love," "Friendship" and initials. Grapes, acorns, and vases were set together with gold leaves, hands, locks or snake heads. The designs were made with hair and gold threads over hollow forms. Forms also included small trinkets in hairwork such as those of gold and silver on charm bracelets today. Among these charms or trinkets in hairwork were horseshoes, swords, cannon, musical instruments, slippers, fish, skates, bird cages, teapots, chairs, bottles, steins, and letters of the alphabet. Braiding was described as "square chain braid, reverse chain braid, sixteen twist chain, striped snake chain braid and cable chain braid." Round and oblong beads were set in a chain with gold leaves. Memorial scenes included the tomb with figure and weeping willow, doves, wreaths of flowers and pansies. Watch chains were also woven with the hair of a deceased beloved.

CHAPTER

∽ 21 ∽

Paintings on Velvet

IF YOUR GREAT-GRANDMOTHER went to a young ladies' private school between the years 1800 and 1850 she learned how to do theorem or stencil painting. You may even own one of these old paintings on velvet of fruit or flowers or perhaps an imaginative landscape or family birth record. From the collector's standpoint these paintings are desirable because they are a naïve expression of American handicraft. The colors, mellowed with age, are soft and harmonious, and the designs are often excellent. The execution may not always be fine, but in the best paintings on velvet, the limitations of the process have produced pleasing results. The fact that the process was mechanical and the designs usually copied does not detract from their charm. Even so, no two velvet paintings are exactly alike.

These paintings, which were also done on silk, paper, and wood, were also known as Oriental Tinting or Poonah Work because the method employed originated in the Orient. Technically the process was mechanical, or theorematical. The paintings were done by using a number of stencils, known as theorems, a small theorem being used for each separate leaf or flower petal. The theorems were cut out of "horn" paper, which was made by coating ordinary drawing paper with linseed oil, then brushing it with turpentine or varnish. The stencil was placed on the material and the open parts were covered with paint. The paint of creamy consistency was applied with a stiff brush in a downward circular motion. The detail work was done with India ink and a fine sable brush.

So popular was this handicraft that many articles and books were published explaining how to paint with theorems and how to paint on velvet. The earliest book was J. W. Alston's *Hints to Young Practisioners in the Study of Landscape Painting*, which was published in London in 1804. Instruction in the *Art of Painting on Velvet* was added to the new edition in 1805 and also was included in the edition of 1820. The book gives detailed information about the preparing and mixing of colors and how to apply them to the velvet, but no information is given on making theorem patterns.

The following directions from Alston about the preparation of colors should be of some help in judging a fine old painting on velvet, for colors prepared with such care mellow with age, but do not fade as later commercial colors often do.

The following is from Alston's book:

Preparation of Colours

1. Gum Water—dissolve gum astragant (or dragon) in water to consistency of oil.
2. Yellow—boil French berries in pint of water, add alum.
3. Green—boil verdigris and cream of tartar in quart of water.
4. Crimson—carmine boiled in water and salammoniac added.
5. Rose colours—saffron flowers prepared in saucers and called saucer colour. Moisten with lemon juice.
6. Bright blue—1 pound indigo, 3 ounces oil of vitriol and water. Pale by adding water.
7. Dark blue—Prussian and water and salt.
8. Black—take common ink.
9. Paler black—genuine India ink.
10. Orange colour—saffron in water.
    Purple—logwood chips, water and alum. Add gum dragon to prevent from running.

Definite detailed instructions for mixing colors are given, such as "No. 2, 3, 8, & 10 for green for foregrounds." This explains why the colors in many velvet paintings are the same, since definite mechanical rules were followed. Alston also cautions that the first tint must dry before proceeding with the second, and the velvet must be brushed with a hand brush so that no dust will get in the paint.

Undoubtedly in most cases the teachers prepared the paint just as they usually furnished theorems for the pupils to use. This is the reason why so many velvet paintings are of the same subject and the same coloring. However, at a later date the colors were commercially prepared and sold in boxes or saucers, as is evidenced from the following advertisement in the *Boston Daily Advertiser*, January 1, 1816:

Painting on Velvet etc. Just opened at the Music Salon and Variety store over Messers. Callenders No. 40 Marboro St. Complete Boxes of Colours for painting on Velvet—also a variety of elegant velvet patterns etc. Superior water colours either in the single cake or in boxes from 25¢ to 2 dollars each. Sable, Camel's Hair, and Lead Pencils. Bristol boards, paper, gold Borders and ornaments together with an extensive assortment of high finished Drawings (most excellent studies) consisting of groups of Flowers, Single flowers, Landscapes and Fancy Pieces etc.

In the *New York Commercial Advertiser* of 1821, colors for painting on velvet are advertised by several stores as follows:

> E. B. Clayton No. 279 Broadway opposite Washington Hall has just received a few boxes English Colors for painting on Velvet warranted equal if not superior to any yet offered in this city.—June 20, 1821.
> Boxes of colors for Painting on Velvet. Pink or Carmine Saucers, Brushes for Painting on Velvet, etc. For Sale by A. T. Goodrich & Co., 124 Broadway.—May 17, 1821.
> Reeves Colours for Painting on Velvet with brushes etc. complete—Reeves' Ponah Colours with brushes palat etc. complete. Gallstone, Royal Blue, Carmine, Kings, Yellow, Lake—J. V. Seaman 296 Pearl St.—November 12, 1821.

Velvet especially for painting on was also advertised. In the *New York Evening Post,* October 6, 1818, the following appeared: "A few pieces of White Velvets for painting on for sale at 150 Broadway by Philbook & Peters."

The increase in the popularity of velvet painting is evidenced by the following advertisement in the *New York Commercial Advertiser,* February 12, 1830. "Painting Velvet. We have constantly on hand a choice assortment of white Genoa Painting Velvet—5'–8"; 3'–4" and 4'–4" wide. Doremus, Suydam & Nixon cor. Broadway & Courtland St."

Velvet painting was probably at its height of popularity in 1830. *Godey's Lady's Book* of that year gives directions for Oriental Tinting or Poonah Work. Mathew D. Finn wrote a book on theorem painting which was also published in 1830.

This book, which explains the theorematical system as "easy and possible of excution by a child," lists the necessary equipment as follows:

1. A good set of brushes—camel's hair pencils
2. Paint in cups or plates
3. Gold shell for ornaments
4. Pencil and bodkin for tracing
5. Bristol board for drawing
6. Pasteboard for theorems
7. Oiled tissue for sketching
8. Black paper
9. Horn paper for patterns
10. Theorems to draw by

The list of colors needed includes light chrome green, light chrome yellow, Prussian blue, Antwerp blue, Vandyke brown, purple brown,

Indian red, India ink, flake white, lampblack, powdered carmine, gold shell—gum tragacanth for mixing.

Directions include keeping the brush dry, working in a circular motion, and commencing with the deepest shade. Patterns or theorem of a pheasant and rosebud are included.

Painting on velvet was taught in most private schools for girls from about 1810 to 1840. Although according to Alston's book, velvet painting was done in England and possibly in America before 1810, no signed pieces have been found before that date and I have found no newspaper notices of painting on velvet prior to that of the Columbian Academy of Painting in the *New York Commercial Advertiser*, November 5, 1810. "Painting and Drawing—Anatomy. Pieces executed in the new and very improved manner of Painting on Silk worthy of the attention of the Ladies both on account of its economy as well as its excellence."

After 1810 we find many advertisements of young ladies' schools which refer to painting on velvet.

Mrs. Byron's Boarding School for Young Ladies at Greenwich mentions painting on velvet, plain sewing, and fine needlework, together with reading, arithmetic, history, French, music, and dancing, as taught in 1812. Mrs. Rowson's Academy in Boston taught needlework, drawing and painting on wood, velvet, etc., according to the *Boston Daily Advertiser*, Mar. 20, 1813.

Velvet painting was taught at Mrs. Leary's in Newark, New Jersey, in 1828 and at the Skaneateles Female Seminary in 1830. In answer to a notice which I ran in the *Skaneateles Press* I have had several letters telling me about paintings still owned by families in that vicinity. These were undoubtedly supervised by the teacher at the old Skaneateles Female Seminary.

Mrs. Almira Phelps, who was vice-principal of Troy Female Academy, which must have included velvet painting in its course of studies, writes in *The Female Student* in 1836, "Velvet, Chinese painting etc. are methods by which handsome pictures are made but they are almost wholly mechanical operations and neither afford evidence of genius nor have they a tendency to refine and elevate the taste."

The process of velvet painting is also closely linked with stencil work on tin and wood furniture. In fact, when Hitchcock and other furniture factories began using stencils they employed women to do the work, and undoubtedly many were trained in the young ladies' schools of the era.

Paintings on velvet. TOP LEFT: Rare flowers in basket. Landscape with figures, also rare.

Although the subject matter of painting on velvet includes still life, landscapes, and figures, still-life subjects were most popular and are most frequently found today. They include fruit or flowers in a basket or tipped bowl. Fruits pictured are grapes, peaches, pears, cherries, and, in the larger paintings, watermelon. Some of these are similar to the James Peale still-life oil painting on canvas of fruit in a bowl which was painted about 1820. Sometimes the fruit is on a platter or there may be a cup or pitcher of pottery. One large still life has a blue and white pottery pitcher showing the willow pattern. Sometimes a bird or parrot or butterfly is added to the composition. Another popular subject was flowers. Single moss roses, lilies, and a wreath or garland of flowers were usually executed on small pieces of velvet, while larger pieces were used for flowers in a bowl or in a formal urn. Sometimes a bird or butterfly is included with the flowers. A rare still life of shells and seaweed is in the collection of Helena Rubenstein.

Landscapes are rarer than fruit or flowers. These are usually imaginative and often include figures. Subjects include Spring, Dog in Landscape, Lady of the Lake, Castle of Udolpho, the rare "Liberty in form of Goddess of Youth giving support to Bald Eagle," and one of figures illustrating a quotation from Homer. Biblical scenes are rare, but include such subjects as Ruth and Boaz, and Ruth and Naomi.

Portraits or figure groups are rare, but one of a governess and children and another of two children have been found. These must have been executed by experienced artists, since there is considerable detail drawn by hand.

Mourning scenes, family registers, quilts, and fire screens were also painted on velvet but they are extremely rare. A large mourning scene of a church, figures, tombstones, and trees is owned by Aline Bernstein. One painting of the scene is in black and white and grays and is especially beautiful in tone contrasts. Another painting of the same scene is in aurora shades and dull blue and green.

Few velvet paintings are signed, but enough are signed to give us some information regarding dates. No signed piece has been found dated before 1810 or after 1830. Some are signed in needlework stitches and some with pen and India ink. Names of the painters are not very important, since we know that velvet painting was done by almost every girl who went to private school between 1810 and 1840 and by many other persons as well —even by men. However, the list taken from *American Primitive Painting* by Jean Lipman, to which I have added a few names, may be of some interest.

PAINTERS ON VELVET

Charlotte Adams, Amenia, N.Y., 1830. Still life
Salome Barstow, Mass., 1820. Still life
Lucy Bartlett, Mass., 1830. Memorial
Martha Stuart Beers, New Lebanon, N.Y., 1830. Still life
Mary Bradley Lee, Mass., 1830. Still life
Hannah P. Buxton, N.Y., 1820. Memorial
Elizabeth Potter Clark, New London, Conn., 1830. Still life
Harriet B. Clarke, New York, 1820. Memorial
Maria Cole, Cheshire, Mass., 1830. Still life
Eleanor L. Coward. Still life
Mary B. Davis, 1820. Fruit basket, parrot and butterfly.
Polly C. Dean, Mass., 1820. Memorial
Mathilda A. Haviland. Still life
Lydia Hosmer, Concord, Mass. Still life
Mary Ann Kimball, Pa., 1825. Memorial
J. McAuliffe, 1830. Genre
Ann Elizabeth Salter, Mass., 1810. Memorial
Sarah F. Terry, Mass. Still life
Mrs. Boutwell, 1830
Sarah Hancock, 1822. Still life
Noone Family Register, c. 1837

Landscape and figure subjects are rare and valuable. Memorials are not so rare but are desirable and difficult to find. Still-life subjects are the most available and when good in composition and workmanship are desirable for a collection.

To be of value in a collection a velvet painting should be in good condition. Grayed color does not detract from its value, but too many age spots or tears in the velvet reduce the value. The velvet background is usually browned or tanned with age, but the colors should be rich and the composition good in design and execution. A comprehensive collection should include still life, landscape, and figure compositions and might include theorems on paper as well.

BIBLIOGRAPHY

American Primitive Painting, by Jean Lipman. Oxford University Press, New York, 1942.
"Paintings on Velvet," by Louise Karr, *The Magazine Antiques,* September, 1931. Collection of Aline Bernstein.

22

American Ornamental Painting of the 18th and 19th Centuries

IN EARLY AMERICA commissions for portraits and easel pictures were few; nevertheless the painters had plenty of work to do, since there was constant demand for inn and shop signs, coat of arms, coach painting, "shew boards," sailing pictures, banners, masons' aprons, fire buckets and, later, fire hats and fire engines. There were also household articles such as furniture, trays, mirrors, clocks, and bandboxes to be decorated. Many of these articles made in the 18th and 19th centuries are to be found today, and whether they were painted by coach or ship painters, japanners, glaziers, or artists, they are of interest to the present-day collector. As popular antiques, closely related to the life of the people, they tell us a great deal about the craftsmen who made them and the persons who first owned them.

Old tavern and shop signs of the 18th and early 19th centuries are particularly interesting. The earliest American tavern signs were made in the 17th century, but few exist today. In subject matter the early tavern signs followed those of England, and we find such names as "King's Arms" in Boston in 1642, and "King's Head," "Queen's Head," and references to the crown and to many British heroes such as "Vernon's Head," "Cromwell's Head," "Marquis of Rockingham," and "King of Prussia." After the siege of Quebec, General Wolfe taverns became popular. After the Revolution taverns took the names of Washington, Franklin, Lafayette, Hamilton, John Hancock, and other American heroes. Heraldry also played a part in the names of inns, and we find the crown especially popular between 1718 and 1777. There was the "Rose and Crown," dating from 1725, the "Hat and Crown," "Crown and Beehive," "Crown and Razor," and "Three Crowns." The sign of the British Union Jack was popular before 1776, but after the Revolution the flag of the thirteen states, the arms of the United States, the Eagle, the Goddess of Liberty, Liberty Pole, Liberty Cap, and the arms of the various states gained attention. Religion also played a part in early signs, and we find such signs as "St. George," the "Gilt Bible," "Bible and Anchor," and "Good Samaritan." Flower and tree signs included the orange tree, logwood tree, coconut tree, locust stump, pine tree, green bush, wheat sheaf, bunch of grapes, pineapple, and bluebell. Animals and birds also were often used on American tavern signs. The earliest were the lion, the fox, and, in 17th-century New York, the "Blue Dove" and the "Wooden Horse," 1641. In 18th-century New York there was a "Black Horse Tavern"; in 1714 "Fighting Cocks"; "Coach and Horses," 1733; "Bull's Head," 1755; "Dog's Head in Porridge Pot," 1730. Other 18th-century New York taverns included such names as the Griffin, Leopard, White Swan, and Red Horse. In 18th-century Philadelphia there was a yellow cat, a dolphin, and a fighting cock. In Providence, Rhode Island, there was a golden fox in 1768 and a black horse in 1762 and a greyhound in 1772. Other animals on American signs of the 18th century included a crow, three cranes, unicorn, and white hare. Tavern signs of the 19th century include "Coach and Horse," "Eagle," "Temperance," "The Jolly Sailor," "Noah's Ark," "Steamboat," "Oxen and Eagle," "Bull's Head," "Indian Chief," and "Indian on Horseback," which is at Anawan House, Rehoboth, Massachusetts.

Shop signs usually contained a symbol of the trade and this was often cut in profile, so, generally speaking, there was less decorative painting than on the tavern signs. One of the earliest trade signs was at William Bradford's printing shop in New York in 1693, which was the "Sign of Bible." Another early sign was the shoe sign in Providence, Rhode Island, in 1718. It had black and red shoes painted on a white ground and was cut in scroll-work outline. Coaches were made at the "Sign of the Chair-Wheel" and "The Riding Chair." At the "Sign of the Platter" J. Leddell made pewter in New York in 1744. Mary Jackson made brass articles at the "Brazen Head" in Boston. Upholstery was made at the "Sign of the Royal Bed" in Philadelphia and at the "Crown and Cushion" in New York. Compasses were sold at the "Sign of Quadrant and Surveying Compass," watches at the "Sign of the Dial," keys at the "Golden Key" or "Sign of the Lock," and hardware at "Cross Keys & Crown." A tailor worked at the "Sign of Hand and Shears," a weaver at the "Sign of the Stocking," and an oysterman at the "Dish of Fry'd Oysters."

Early American signs were usually of wood, painted in bright colors, and often had borders of carving or of painted decoration. Tavern signs usually were painted with the name and owner of the tavern and the date, while trade signs had the name of the trade and the owner's name. Signs were held in place by iron brackets and sometimes scrolls of decorative wrought iron were placed at the sides of the sign. Some early signs were made entirely of iron or other metal. The wooden signs were made in various shapes. Some of the earliest, as the sign of the "Rose and Crown," 1725, were framed in a square frame of turned moldings; others of this sort had a triangular pediment within which was painted the date and name or initials of the owner. Turned spindles and curved pediments made a frame for other early signs. Sometimes the oval with the painting was set within a frame of four turned spindles, and some signs had curved swan's-neck pediments similar to those on early mirrors. Some 18th-century signs were decorated by "strewing smalt," which was a sanding process done with ground glass.

There is no record of the 17th-century sign painters, and the earliest sign painter of the 18th century was the now well-known Joseph Badger of Massachusetts (1708–1765). Throughout his life Badger painted houses, signs, and coat of arms, as well as portraits, in the vicinity of Boston. Although no ornamental painting in existence is known to be the work of Badger, there are many Badger portraits in American museums today. There were also many other ornamental painters who advertised in 18th-century Boston newspapers. In 1713 Nehemiah Partridge advertised "all sorts Japanning, Painting, Dials made." John Adams and Mr. Stanbridge also advertised as painters, and in 1750 Samuel Hely. In 1761 John Gore painted coaches and carpets and Daniel Carter, Thomas Craft, Jr., and George Killicup also did "carpet and all sorts of painting." William Fullerton and George Mason, "limner, portraits, and crayon," and Christian Remick, who painted coat of arms and sea pictures and is well known for his "Blockade of Boston," all did ornamental painting in Boston in the 1760's. Thomas Johnston sold colors, made charts, painted coat of arms, and engraved portraits and music, and Dunlap mentions a Jones who painted signs in Boston, and John R. Penniman, who did signs and clock faces for Willard in 1812.

In the *Pennsylvania Gazette*, March 20, 1739, the following advertisement appeared: "John Winter—Painter at the Sign of the Easy Chair—Coach, coat-of-arms, signs, shewboards, writing ornaments. 'Sign of King's Arms' to sell." In 1740 Gustavus Hesselius, now well known for his portraits, advertised in the *Philadelphia Gazette*: "Coats of arms on coaches, chaises, or any kind of ornamenting, Landskip, sign, show Boards, ship and house painting, gilding, pictures cleaned." Other Philadelphia sign and ornamental painters were Joseph Boehm, John Walters—miniature painter, Alexander Christie, and John Justice, who conducted a painting school and also painted "Houses, Signs, Flags, Drums, and Fire buckets." William Matthews painted signs, houses, ships, transparencies, and fire buckets in 1796, and in the early 19th century David Claypoole Johnston did wood and copper engraving and painted door plates, and Isaac Weston, Nathaniel Grogan, and Christopher Wispart painted coaches, signs, and fire buckets in 1785. The best known Philadelphia sign painter was George Rutter, who in 1782 advertised "sign, shewboards, Landscapes, carriages, Fire buckets in gold or blue sand or other ways." In 1785 Rutter had as a partner Martin Jugiez; in 1796 he was in partnership with the well-known painter Matthew Pratt, and they advertised "portrait and ornamental painting, emblematical, Masonic, Historical, Allegorical, devices, Regimental colors, and standards, ships, Flags, Drums, and every other decoration of that kind on linen, silk, or bunting. Fire buckets, coffin plates, drums and colors for militia of Different States." Those associated with the firm were Matthew Pratt, George Rutter, William Clarke, and Jeremiah Paul. When business was dull in about 1790, Matthew Pratt had painted his first tavern sign, called "The Representation of the Constitution of 1788." It contained portraits of the men composing the convention, including Washington and Franklin, and the verse:

> Those 38 great men have signed a powerful Deed
> That better times to us, should very soon succeed.

Pratt also painted the "Fox Chase" for a tavern on Arch Street. The scene was of a gentleman on horseback with fox and hounds. The "Ship in Calm" scene with Neptune was painted for Lebanon Gardens on South and 10th Streets, and the "Game Cock" for a beerhouse on Spruce Street.

In the 19th century John A. Woodside, a New York painter, restored this sign. Woodside also painted a sign with a scene of the signing of the Declaration of Independence for the Union Hotel and was considered the best sign painter of his time. Although these signs were famous and hung for many years, none exist today. However, the painter John Neagle in the 19th century said, "I remember many signs for public houses painted by Pratt." It was generally known that Philadelphia signs were remarkable for the skill with which they were designed and executed. John Wesley Jarvis, who also painted signs at the beginning of the 19th century, says:

In my school boy days the painters of Philadelphia were Clark, a miniature painter, Galagher (Gullagher) a painter of portraits and signs. . . . Jeremiah Paul—another who painted red lions and black bears as well as beaux or belles was old Mr. Pratt and the last was Rutter an honest sign painter who never pretended or aspired to paint the human face divine except to hang on the outside of a house: these worthies when work was plenty—flags and fire buckets, engines and eagle in demand used to work in partnership and I worked for them all.

This is quoted from William Dunlap, who says that he himself painted his first portrait on a sign in London. John Fanning Watson in the *Annals of Philadelphia* mentions the "Bulls Head Sun" sign painted by Bernard Wilton in 1760 and "The Fiddler" and a cask-of-beer sign said to have been painted by Benjamin West. Watson also says that George Rutter painted the finger boards at the corners of the house numbers and remembers "The Last of the Mohicans" as one such decoration. He remembers such other Philadelphia signs as a portrait of Franklin, "Sir Walter Raleigh Smoking," "The Fox Chase," "Stag Hunt," and a portrait of Koulikhan. Jeremiah Paul painted a sign of Washington and later did a portrait of the Washington family, but he was not above doing the lettering job on the books in Stuart's portrait of Washington. In 1809 Jacob Eicholtz, the coppersmith of Lancaster, who is also known for his portraits, painted a portrait of Pitt on a sign in Lancaster.

Painters in New York City did not give as full description of their work in the newspapers and we seldom find mention of signs. The earliest advertisement was that of Gerardus Duyckinck, who "continues to carry on the Business of his late Father (Gerret) deceas'd viz limning, Painting, Varnishing, Japanning, Gilding, Glazing and Silvering of Looking-Glasses. He also will teach any young Gentleman the art of Drawing, with Painting on Glass." Other early New York ornamental painters were John Earl; John Humble; John Watson; Joseph Woodruff; John Baldwin; and Flagg and Searle, who did ship and coach painting in 1765; John Delamontaine; Thomas and James Barrows mentioned by Dunlap; John Haydock; Peter Noire, "sign, ship, and House Painting"; Christian Livingston; Jacobus Tiedeman; Sebastian Guebel, "coach painter and gilder—quantity of beautiful furniture, elegantly painted, and varnished in the Japan Taste"; William Dowall and William Williams—1769—"at Rembrandt's Head,

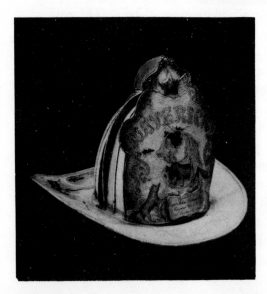 

TOP: Painted fire buckets, 18th and 19th centuries. CENTER: Painted keg used in Erie Canal ceremonies, 1825. Painted fire helmets, 19th century.

undertakes painting in general viz; History, Portraiture, landskip, sign painting, lettering, gilding and strewing smalt. N.B. He cleans, repairs and varnishes any old pictures of value and teaches the art of drawing." In 1746 Williams taught Dunlap in Philadelphia, and in 1794 he painted a portrait of Washington. Stephen Dwight also taught art, painted portraits and historical scenes, and carved and did "all sorts of house, ship, and cabinet work in New York in 1763." Dunlap records that Abraham Delanoy, Jr., a portrait painter who studied with West, also painted signs, and Delanoy advertised "most kinds of painting done." In 1824 H. S. Mount, a brother of William Sidney Mount and himself a member of the National Academy, was a sign painter in New York.

At the end of the 18th century and during the first quarter of the 19th, Albany was a flourishing city with craftsmen such as pewterers, braziers, looking-glass makers, and ornamental painters. As early as 1790 an unnamed miniature painter from Europe advertised in the *Albany Gazette*. Thomas P. Jones came from Philadelphia in 1808 to cut profiles in Albany, and Q. Schipper from Holland did likenesses in colored crayons. In 1805 John P. Bone advertised carving and gilding, and in 1806 John Clark did coach painting, gilding, and ornamenting. Joseph Burton also did painting and glazing. L. Lemet, who advertised in New York City as a partner of St. Memin, was in Albany in 1805 and advertised "Picture and Looking Glass Frames. Every description of ornamental work, gilt, carved or plain" and in 1810 "Crayon, engraving, and Drawing School." In 1809 J. & T. Gladding, Gilders & Glaziers, advertised "Coach, sign and ornamental painting, Profiles cut and painted on Glass." And on July 7, 1809, J. L. D. Mathews, "Sign and Ornamental painter and Gilder," advertised: "Drawing taught: Architectural, Hand Sketching, Landscape, Painting." From 1797 Thomas Russell, painter and glazier and dealer in artists' supplies, advertised ship, house, and sign painting at the "Sign of Raphael's Head." In 1793 Ezra Ames advertised:

Painting, Portrait, and Sign painting, Gilding, Limning. The subscriber solicits the patronage of the admirers of the Fine Arts of Painting Portraits, Miniatures and Hair devices. From the encouragement he has already received, he flatters himself of giving general satisfaction. Signs, Coaches, Chaises, Sleighs, Standards, painted in the best manner.

In 1799 Ames moved his shop to the "Sign of Raphael's Bust," so that it seems likely that he painted this sign, which is illustrated in the *Albany Gazette* from about 1798 through 1810. Also Ames probably did the more elaborate ornamental work for Thomas Russell even before he shared his shop.

The manuscript correspondence and the account books of Ezra Ames (1790–1826), part of which is in the New York Historical Society, give us a definite record of the painting done by this portrait and ornamental painter. The account books mention all sorts of painting, including furniture staining, house painting, portraits, and "lettering plate for coffin." But it is his ornamental painting in which we are particularly interested because it also tells the story of the other ornamental painters of the time. Although the existing paintings known to have been painted by Ames are all portraits, except for a landscape of Lake George, his account books between 1790 and 1801 contain much mention of decorative painting and comparatively little about portraits. However, there are a number of miniatures recorded, including a hairwork miniature painted in 1792. Ames painted, gilded, and lettered many signs, including a brazier's sign, for which he was paid £1 16s. in 1791. Later signs included one with a picture of Pocahontas and a Darby and Joan. The early signs were decorated with gold leaf. Ames also painted sleighs and chaises. For painting "Landscape and cyphers on back of chaise" Ames was paid 3s. An item of "painting 2 cherubs" was £1 16s., a portrait, 10s., and a miniature 18s. Ames also worked in Worcester, Massachusetts, for several years and during this time he painted clock faces, and gilded clock cases and figures for Moses and Benjamin Willard. In 1801 Ames painted picture frames for the Honorable George Clinton. He also painted and gilded mirror frames, wooden boxes, carpets, sun blinds, drums, tea canisters, tin tea chests, and tin chandeliers. Ezra Ames was a man of some standing in the community and probably the best painter, for we find in his account book that he painted standards of colors for the cavalry and the state, caps and buckets for the fire-engine company, and portraits of senators. Ames was a Mason and he did considerable work for the lodge, such as painting aprons in silk and satin, banners and carpets, and "a Masonic certificate" and engraving a "Masonic Meddle." In 1794 he painted a "carpet for Pittstown Lodge." In 1796 Masonic items recorded include "Night Templar—Mason 1 c. Aprons 2. 1 Royal Arch Do.—2/ 1 Master Do. 1/12; Masonic Certificate." In 1797 Ames painted a "Solomon's Temple and Jerusalem," which may have been for a Masonic Solomon's Chapter. He also painted and papered a lodge room and painted another Masonic carpet in 1799, and as late as 1825 an item in his account book reads: "Masonic Royal Arch robes furnished for Solomon's Chapt. Poukipsie." Painted carpets or floor cloths were made in America as early as the 17th century. They are of two kinds, the earliest type being made of sailcloth painted on both sides and padded between. They were painted in designs of checks, plain or marbled, circles in squares, and other geometric patterns. In addition to painting, Ames also did engraving of brass knockers, medals, silver spoons, sugar tongs, snuffboxes and even portraits.

In Hartford, Connecticut, the sign and ornamental painters that are on record because of their advertisements in newspapers are J. Grimes, "house, ship and sign painting," 1797; S. Blydenburg, "sign painting and ornamental painting," 1799; Abner Reed, copperplate engraving, sign painting, gilding, 1803; and Mr. Hill, "sign and fancy painting, profiles." Reuben Moulthrop, the well-known miniature painter, advertised painting and waxwork in 1793. Signs in the collection of the Rhode Island Historical Society at Providence include an eagle and shield with grapes, a gun, sword, cannon and cannon balls, which is signed "Rice." William Rice painted in New England in the early 19th century. Another sign of the Center Hotel has an eagle and shield with arrows and olive branch and is signed "Brown." Still another eagle sign, dated 1829, is signed by E. R. Michele Felice Corné, the Italian refugee who painted scenic walls in houses in Salem and Providence from 1799 to 1845, as well as portraits, tavern signs, ships, landscapes, and historical scenes. William Mason painted signs and did woodcuts in Hartford.

Advertisements in the *Maryland Gazette* and the *South Carolina Gazette* reveal quite a list of ornamental painters working in that part of the country in the 18th century. As early as 1737 B. Roberts was painting "portraits, Heraldry and Landscapes for Chimney pieces." In 1752 A. Pooley painted "History, Alter Pieces, Landscapes, Views of own houses, signs" in Maryland. A great deal of Sheraton furniture in the vicinity of Baltimore was decorated with paintings of historic houses, ruins, flowers, and musical instruments by John Barnhart, John & Hugh Findlay, and others. Also painting in Baltimore was J. Stevenson, who in 1773 advertised: "History portrait, and miniatures for rings, and bracelets, landscapes, perspective of towns, painting on silk and satin. Hairwork and Fan painting." Jeremiah Theus, who painted a portrait of Washington, also painted "Crests and coat-of-arms for coaches or chaise." Other Baltimore painters were James Campbell, coach, sign, house and ornamental painting in 1785; Barkley, Hugh, O'Meara, Patrick, "sign painting, floors, transparent blinds, rural scenes for chimneys" in 1792; Boyle, William & Co., house, ship, sign, carpet, "Fancy Painting" in 1792; James Walker, at the "Sign of the Painting Muse," who painted "coach, sign, floor, fire, and candle sconces"; Mr. Murray, who painted signs, and Tilyard, who painted signs in about 1810 and of whom Sully said: "His attempts at portraits are admirable." Painters working in South Carolina in the 18th century include Wayne and Ruger, who advertised "signs and floor painting" in 1768; Thomas Booth, "coach, sign, and house painter," 1768; George Flagg, a nephew of Washington Allston, "Heraldry and coach painting" in 1772; Sebastian Martin; Ann Hawes; Milling and Oliver, "House Signs" in 1781; None, Walsh and Dixon, "ships, signs, house" in 1783; P. Tylsho, "horse and coach"; James Campbell, "coach, sign, House, Landscape, and ornamental"; Jonathan Badger, "ship, sign, glazier, gilder," 1792; and Warwell, who painted "History, Alter, Sea, Flowers, Fruit, Heraldry, Coaches, Window blinds, chimney blinds, skreens, Deceptive Temples, Triumphal Arches, Obelisks, Statues for Groves and Gardens." Warwell was eulogized as "a noted limner."

Early American coaches were also painted with coat of arms and gilt decoration and sometimes more elaborate ornamentation. Washington's coach is said to have been decorated with cupids and festoons and wreaths of flowers. At least we have evidence that many painters of considerable ability worked at coach painting. Among them were Edward Hicks, the well-known primitive painter, James Frothingham, John Neagle, Ezra Ames, who painted coaches in Albany, and others listed before in this chapter. The early coachmakers of New York—James Hallet, Samuel Lawrence, and Elkanah and William Deane—did their own carving, painting, gilding, and japanning. In 1794 coach and sign painting was done in New Brunswick, New Jersey, by William Lawson, Jr.; Andrew Ryder, who also painted chairs; and Francis Rabineau, limner, who did "Miniature painting, crayon, coach and chair painting and painting of every description."

Leather fire buckets were used in New York and other early American cities as early as the 17th century. The first buckets were ordered abroad, but by 1658 American shoemakers were making fire buckets of hand-sewn tanned sole leather. These were marked with the mark of the house and the city arms. By 1812 the number of fire buckets was reduced, but they were still in use as late as 1840. Fire buckets were marked with the name, initials, or number of the owner. Many were decorated with coat of arms, eagles, portraits, figures, and other insignia. In 1741 new leather buckets in New York were ordered marked "City of N. York." The first known decorator of fire buckets was Evert Duyckinck, glazier, who marked fire buckets in New York in 1658 with the city coat of arms and a number. There were a dozen or so painters and glaziers in New York in the 18th century who advertised painting of various sorts, including coat of arms. It is strange that they do not mention painting fire buckets, since no less than six Philadelphia painters between 1785 and 1792 advertised fire-bucket painting. George Rutter "painted and ornamented" fire buckets and in 1785 he advertised that he could furnish and paint buckets with the arms of the various states. John Fenno made leather buckets in Boston in 1794. In 1815 Craft & Faxon, harness makers in Boston, made "buckets for fire engines and fire societies" and Samuel Perkins advertised painting fire buckets.

In 1740 the leather fireman's cap was invented. It was round with a high crown and a narrow brim and usually had the number painted on a separate piece of leather at the front. The stove pipe hat was developed after the Revolution. These flat-top hats were used principally for parades and were usually decorated with numbers, insignia, and even portraits, together with fancy gilt decoration. The eagle and portraits of Lafayette, Lincoln, and other well-known men are found on old hats. Hat fronts and presentation shields were also decorated with painting, as well as gold, stitching, and metal ornaments. Paintings included portraits of patriotic characters, well-known landmarks, and scenes and pictures of engines and flags. A plate from the Hancock Engine Company, New York, has a painting of the Hancock house and the Washington hose has a portrait of Washington. These were all painted by artists of some ability, even though the leatherwork was done by saddlers until almost the middle of the 19th century. Fire-cap makers in New York in the 19th century were Matthew Du Bois, who set up a factory in 1824, John Wilson, John W. Towt, William Baudoine, George Henry Ramppen, Robert Roberts, William Hinton, and Henry T. Gratacap, who opened his own factory in 1836. For thirty-two years Gratacap manufactured the caps for New York firemen and also for those of other cities. Gratacap was succeeded by Cairns & Brothers. There are a few old fire hats on the market today and fire buckets are also available, but there are so many collectors in the field already that the beginner can only hope to get some of the less decorative pieces.

TOP: Shop sign, late 19th century. BOTTOM: New England inn signs, early 19th century.

From 1796 on fire engines were often lavishly decorated. The first decorated engine in New York was Engine No. 15, which had a wreath of roses painted on its back and on its panels. Sometimes as many as four painted panels decorated one engine. In the 19th century fire-engine painting was a means of livelihood to many artists and even the best did not refuse a commission to paint a panel or "back." These backs were made of mahogany and were usually removed when the engine went to a fire. They were used on parade and often used in the decoration at a fireman's ball. Sometimes the painting was allegorical or patriotic, and quite often it included landscapes and nude figures. The panel on the Franklin Fire Engine Company which was given to them in 1835 was a picture of Franklin, the boy printer. Other paintings included an Indian chief and his squaw, firemen rescuing a woman, the Burning of Troy, Bunker Hill Monument, Hercules, Slaying the Lion, and portraits of Clinton and Jefferson. The Aqueduct at Little Falls was painted on the condenser of the Clinton Engine in New York when it was in the Erie Canal Celebration in 1825. The portrait of the actor Edwin Forrest was on another, while the Tammany Tiger decorated the "Big Six." The painting of a nude woman tied to a horse decorated the engine of the Mazeppa Hose Company. This was painted by the artist A. P. Moriaority in 1851. Moriaority also painted "The Guardian Angel" and "Repose" on the panels of Hose Company No. 9. Thomas Grenell, scenic artist, painted the Clinton Engine with the bust of De Witt Clinton receiving a floral crown from the Genius of Agriculture. At the right is a view of Albany and at the left the Erie Canal. Other fire-engine paintings included Othello's Courtship and Lawrence's Monument, a portrait of Thomas Jefferson signing the Declaration of Independence, Helen of Troy, Neptune, Commerce, and Udora. The pictures on the Niagara Engine Company in New York were originally painted by Thorp and Thomas Grenell, a well-known scenic painter who also painted panels of the "Birth of Venus" and "The Translation of Psyche" on the Americus Engine in 1849. The panels on the Niagara Engine were three views of Niagara Falls and one of a volcano at sea. After the engine was damaged in a fire in 1853 Hoffman redecorated it with four scenes: "Venus Rising from the Sea," "Joy and Sorrow," "Trojan Fugitives," and a view of Niagara Falls. Another American artist who decorated fire engines was Henry Inman, who also painted a fire-company banner which was later engraved on firemen's certificates. John Quidor, a member of the National Academy, decorated the Columbian Engine with an Indian Chieftain and his squaw. William H. Philip painted the "Battle of Bunker Hill" and "Washington at the Battle of Monmouth" on the panels of Hose Company No. 3's cart, and John A. Quigg painted views of the clipper *Contest* and the yacht *America* on another New York fire engine. Other artists who decorated fire engines were Theodore Pine, Joseph H. Johnson, L. Ayer, and David Reut Etter, who decorated panels for the Franklin Fire Engine of Philadelphia in about 1830.

The above notes only list the paintings on New York fire engines and, while few others are recorded, such cities as Boston, Philadelphia, Washington, Chicago, and others, also had decorations on their equipment and many of them must be in existence today in private families, in fire companies, or in private museums. Also, it is not impossible for such paintings to come to light at any time in secondhand stores or warehouse sales, and you may be the lucky finder.

Banners and standards of colors for the army were painted by hand as late as 1820. These included flags, the arms of the states, and other patriotic insignia. Masonic banners were hand painted, and the various trade organizations, such as the pewterers, coopers, tanners, chairmakers, and stonecutters, also had hand-painted banners, which were used at their meetings and at the various patriotic parades in the 18th and early 19th centuries. Banners with emblematical paintings were carried by all the various organizations marching in the Erie Canal Celebration parade in New York. The New York Horticultural Society banner was painted by Thomas Grenell, and the booksellers and stationers carried a banner with a design of books and the Torch of Knowledge painted by Inman, the well-known engraver. Early scene painters in New York included John Joseph Holland, Hugh Reinagle, John Evers, and William Strickland.

Another type of ornamental painting done in the 18th and early 19th centuries is what was known as transparencies. Transparencies were made on linen, silk, or gauze and painted with oil colors diluted with turpentine, printer's oil, or burnt linseed oil. The cloth was first primed with a mixture of flour and water and size. This was put on the cloth, which was first stretched on a frame. When the priming coat was hard, the picture was sketched and painted on. Window blinds and transparencies for illumination were made in the same way except that for outdoor paintings the cloth was waxed, and wax and turpentine were mixed so that they would stand dampness. Window shades were usually painted on hollands linen. The designs were patriotic and allegorical as well as scenic. When the shades were drawn in the daytime a transparent picture was seen in the room, while at night the picture was seen from the outside. After 1830 these shades were made in factories and sold in stores, but before that time they were painted to order by ornamental artists. In 1825 a Clinton Window Curtain was advertised. Other blinds were made with portraits of Lafayette, Washington, Jefferson, and other heroes. In the 1840s and 1850s such patterns as Indian, Gothic, Bouquets, Landscapes, Battle of Bunker Hill, Washington and Jefferson, and Grecian Fount were available. Painted shades were also still made to order for Masonic temples, steamboats, and private individuals. Painted curtains with fringe and tassel design and a landscape between were also in demand. Early shades were painted and stenciled, but later they were done by lithographic printing. "Window Shades—J. B. Woodford—Scripture Views, Vignettes, Landscapes, Corinthian Columns, Doric, Ionic, Roman, Grecian, Gothic, Plain Scrolls neatly executed—Also Vignettes on pure white grounds."—*New York Commercial Advertiser*, April 17, 1845.

Transparencies were used for illumination in national celebrations from about 1780 when, during the Peace Celebration, Alexander Quesnay de Glovay put transparent pictures in his windows in Philadelphia. The subject of these transparencies was allegorical and patriotic and depicted General Washington trampling British Pride underfoot. The artist, Charles Willson Peale, took the idea and painted three transparencies for his own windows the next night. These pictures included portraits of Cornwallis, Washington, Rochambeau, and Lafayette and were afterwards exhibited many times. In 1782 Congress commissioned Peale to paint transparencies for the State House Yard for the celebration of the birth of the Dauphin of France, and in December, 1783, Peale was commissioned to make the Triumphal Arch for the peace celebration. It had a transparency on each column. The whole arch burned as Peale was lighting it. Peale also painted a transparency at the celebration of the new constitution and also filled his windows with transparencies at the death of Washington. And in 1804 Peale painted an "Apotheosis of General Washington" at the Peale Museum in celebration of the Louisiana Purchase.

The transparencies on the Lafayette Arch in Philadelphia in 1824 were painted by Sully, Peale, and Strickland, a scenic artist. At Washington's inauguration the transparent paintings exhibited in various parts of New York City were equal to any before seen in America. The Fort at Broadway had a transparency representing the virtues Fortitude, Justice, and

Wisdom. At Vauxhall Garden on July 4, 1798, a transparent painting by Joseph Snyder was shown. A transparent portrait of Jefferson was exhibited in New York at his inauguration. In July 4, 1807, Vauxhall Garden exhibited a 60-foot transparency of New York City and Bay during the British evacuation of the city in 1783. At a ball of the City Assembly in 1812, J. J. Holland, a scene painter and friend of Dunlap's, painted a transparency with the "Guerriere and Constitution," the "Capture of the Macedonian," and the "Defeat of the Frolic by the Wasp." In the minutes of the Common Council of New York City it was "ordered that a warrant issue for $200 in payment of the Transparencies prepared and used at the late dinner in celebration of our naval victories, and that said paintings be considered the property of the Common Council." "Perry's Victory" was displayed at the City Hall on October 23, 1913, and Tammany Hall displayed a transparency of Harrison and an Indian, while the Theatre exhibited a picture of the "Hornet and the Peacock."

On February 14, 1815, the following appeared in the *New York Evening Post:* "Transparent Paintings. Will be executed at No. 1 Murray St. Size and device should be sent as early as possible—Jarvis." In the *New York Evening Post* for Feb. 28, 1815, along with a description, the names of the painters are given: "6 transparencies for Eastburn, Kirk & Co. were painted by Jarvis. Transparencies at the *New York Gazette* were painted by Holland & Smith, J. J. Astor's by Alex Gesselain." Transparencies were also painted by Parisien, the miniature painter. The City Hall was decorated with large allegorical transparencies of the Genius of America and the City Arms and also a huge American Eagle with transparencies of Columbia and Britannia on its wings. These were painted by Holland, Smith, Robertson, and Dunlap. Washington Hall displayed a Temple of Fame with a portrait of Washington (the same as exhibited annually). Tammany Hall displayed a transparency of an emblematic design of Columbia, History, and Fame. The Mechanics Bank transparency included the Hammer and Hand. Other transparencies followed the patriotic theme with Columbia, Britannia, Eagles, Ship Models, Liberty, Peace, and Plenty.

Duncan Phyfe showed a transparent lantern spelling the names of Washington and naval heroes strung across the street. Mrs. Fowler, who conducted a drawing academy, painted a transparency representing the goddess of painting, and a Mr. Crawford, a portrait painter, displayed a transparency painted by himself. On November 14, 1815, upon the arrival of Decatur, the front of the Theatre displayed a naval transparency of the successes of Decatur. This was painted by Charles Wesley Jervis. When Lafayette visited New York in 1824 transparencies were again displayed on public buildings. In the *New York Commercial Advertiser*, August 16, 1824, mention is made of the transparency at Chatham Garden painted by H. Reinagle, Esq. In 1815 Reinagle conducted an academy of drawing and painting at his house in Albany. At the dinner at Washington Hall and at the French dinner given in Lafayette's honor, transparencies were displayed as a part of the ceremony and at the ball at Castle Garden a transparency of La Grange, Lafayette's home, was displayed. The decorations, including the transparency, were executed by H. Reinagle, Grenell and H. Ritter. On July 4, 1825, transparencies at Castle Garden were painted by Boudet, Grenell & Co. They included one picture 30 feet by 12 feet by Mr. Boudet, of Washington and Lafayette on horseback and a distant view of Yorktown. The transparency was on view for several days for a fee of 25 cents. At Vauxhall Garden the transparency depicted the "Surrender of Cornwallis," taken from the engraving. At the Grand Canal Celebration on September 8, 1825, many transparencies were again displayed in New York at Peale's Museum, Scudder's Museum, and the Park Theatre. The subject matter included canal boats, Buffalo, Indian chiefs, portraits of Clinton, and emblematic devices. At the City Hall the transparency included views of the Erie Canal and names of the worthies together with emblematical devices on the columns. On September 13, 1825, six transparent paintings were displayed at Castle Garden. They were painted by Mr. Boudet, and included the coat of arms of the states; "Lady of the Lake"; "America Welcoming Strangers to her Happy Shore"; "Bolivars Camp"; "Washington and Lafayette at Yorktown"; "Decatur revenging the murder of his Brother"; and "King Pepin evincing muscular strength in killing a lion at a Bull Fight." In October Mr. Boudet exhibited a transparency of "The Treaty of William Penn with the Indians." A transparency of "View of the Falls of Mt. Ida" was painted by Hugh Reinagle. In 1826 Peale's Museum exhibited "the Grand transparent Orrery 27″ in circumference." William Dunlap gives us the names of other painters of transparencies in his *Diary of William Dunlap*, Philadelphia, June 23, 1833— "Longacre when a boy with Murray was sent to assist B(arralet) in painting a transparency commemorative of Perry's Victory. B. took snuff and told stories instead of working."

Probably the only American transparency in existence today is the one at the New York Historical Society which was painted for the dinner held there in celebration of the semicentennial anniversary of the first inauguration of George Washington on April 30, 1839.

In the course of the evening a fine transparency representing old Federal Hall formerly standing at corner of Wall & Nassau Streets—the scene of Washington's inauguration was disclosed by the withdrawal of a curtain at the upper end of the hall and produced a brilliant effect. The figures of Washington and Chancellor Livingston were seen on the balcony, the one laying his hand upon the book, while the other administered the oath of office in the presence of a vast concourse of people. The painting was extremely well executed and taking the company by surprise, drew forth long and loud applause. The hall was decorated with copies of Stuart's portraits of five presidents painted by Stuart himself.

There is no record of the name of the painter of this transparency, but Thomas Grenell, Hugh Reinagle, or Inman may have done it.

Banners and transparencies were used as late as the political elections of 1856, and Isaac Augustus Wetherby advertised in the *Davenport Gazette* that he would paint banners and transparencies for either party. Theater curtains and drops were made as transparencies and such a drop showing a scene of a city is in the collection of the Rhode Island Historical Society. It was painted in the first part of the 18th century.

❧ 23 ❧

American Mirrors and Picture Frames, 1700–1850

THE MIRROR which we take for granted today was almost unknown before the 17th century, and then the small bits, hardly large enough to see one's face in, were carefully treasured. One inventory of 1660 reads: "boxed mirror."

Mirrors are listed in American inventories of the 17th century, but it was not until the 18th century that mirrors were made in America and then the glass was imported from England. Although the glass used at that time was much smaller than the present-day glass, it was the important part of the mirror. The styles of American mirrors followed those of England and were introduced by English workmen in this country. Generally speaking, American mirror styles are from Queen Anne to Victorian. However, museums contain mirrors of the William and Mary period with a wide square frame and circular top. These frames, usually made of olive or walnut, are often decorated with inlay of flowers and birds, or the circular top may be cut in openwork designs. They date from 1680 to 1700. Occasionally a mirror had a wide needlework frame or a frame of beadwork or papier-mâché or lacquer. Although some few mirrors of this style may have been made in America, they are not in the shops today, and the earliest American mirrors to be found are those of Queen Anne style, which were made from about 1710 to as late as 1765. In the 18th century American mirrors were usually made in Boston, New York, Philadelphia, Baltimore, and Charleston. By the 19th century, however, there were looking-glass makers in such places as Worcester and Newburyport, Massachusetts; Newark, New Jersey; and towns as far west as Ohio and Missouri and as far south as Louisiana.

As early as 1715 William Randle had a looking-glass shop in Boston

and made mirrors of these early types. By 1729 James Foddy from London
had set up business in New York. His advertisement appears in *The New
York Gazette*, October 6, 1729.

James Foddy, Looking Glass maker, late from London hath brought a Parcel of
very find Pier glasses, sconces with fine Brass Arms; Dressing Glasses also of Sundry
Sorts, in Glass-Frames, Glass and Gold Frames, Gold Frames, Japann'd, Wallnut and
Olive Wood Frames. He is likewise in a readiness to new quick-silver and take the
stains out of Old Looking-Glasses, which will render them as good as ever. He also
undertakes to square, Diamond Cut and Polish Old Looking-glasses and converts
them to the best use.

Foddy went to the West Indies after a few months and did not return to
New York until 1737. In the meantime Gerardus Duyckinck in 1735 had
opened a shop. The *New York Weekly Journal*, January 6, 1735: "Lookin-
glasses new silvered, and the Frames plaine Japan'd or Flowered also all
manner of painting done."

Queen Anne mirror frames were usually made of walnut or walnut
and gilt combined, although some were completely gilt. The glass of the
earliest Queen Anne mirrors was made in two sections and the top section
was cut with a design of leaves or flowers and the frame was made in cyma
curves often topped by a cresting with cutout designs. The frames are
usually walnut veneer, but the cresting is solid walnut. Some mirrors have
a line of gold inside the frame and at the top of the cresting, and a gold shell
or a pierced gilded design is set in the center of the cresting. Some Queen
Anne mirror frames are lacquered. By 1750 similar frames were made with
the glass in one piece. These frames are of wider proportions. Gilt frames
with a cresting at both the top and the bottom and a cartouche between
the top scrolls are dated 1725 to 1750 and are similar to the later scroll
pediment Chippendale mirrors.

Fretwork mirrors of the Queen Anne and Chippendale periods are
the most available of all early mirror types. They are made of walnut and
mahogany often veneered on pine. These mirrors have a top and bottom
fretwork. The top fretwork has a scroll design; and often a carved shell,
flower, or bird is set in the center, or such a design may be applied to the
wood. There is usually a small gilded molding around the inside of the
frame. The earliest mirrors of this type have cyma curves at the tops of
their frames and the glass may be made in two parts. Later fretwork mirrors
have strings of carved leaves or flowers at their sides, and on some mirrors
the top fretwork becomes a scrolled pediment and a carved eagle is placed

in the space between the scrolls. Fretwork mirrors made between 1780 and 1790 have cyma curves on their inner edges and their gilded designs are incised in the wood. They usually have a pheasant at the top, carved strings of flowers and leaves at their sides, and branches of gilt leaves incised in the crestings at both the top and the bottom. Many of them are so similar, especially in the design of the gilt decoration, that they seem to be the work of one man or of one shop. These fretwork mirrors were made from 1725 down to 1800. Their beauty depends largely upon the design of the fretwork and the fineness of the general proportions of the mirror.

The typical Chippendale scroll pediment mirror was made of walnut or mahogany with bandings of gold around its edges and a cartouche, bird, or carved gold flower set between the scrolled pediment at the top of the frame. Carved strings of leaves, flowers, or draperies are usually at the sides of the frame. This type of mirror was also made in pier-glass sizes. These mirrors date between 1750 and 1775 and were also called Georgian. The most typical Chippendale mirror was of gilt and the frame was completely carved in leaves, flowers, and cartouches, which displayed a galaxy of C curves and rococo forms. Often an outer frame made up of carved sections and mirrors surrounded the center mirror. These mirrors were made of pine and date from 1755 to 1780. Two of the best-known American makers of mirrors of the Queen Anne and Chippendale types were Henry Hardcastle and Stephen Dwight, carvers, who had shops in New York in 1755 and until 1774. In 1765 James Strachan, carver and gilder from London, had a shop in New York where he "makes and sells all sorts of Picture and Glass Frames, Tables, Gerendoles, brackets and Candle stands carved and gilt, in Oil or burnish'd Gold."

In 1769 Minshall, carver and gilder from London, established a shop in New York and advertised from then until 1775. In the *New York Journal or General Advertiser*, March 16, 1775, he describes his stock:

An elegant assortment of Looking-Glasses in oval or square ornamental frames ditto mahogany. The greatest variety of girandoles ever imported to this city. . . . Birds and baskets of flowers for the top of bookcases or glass frames. . . . Also an elegant assortment of frames without Glass. Any Lady or Gentleman that have Glass in old Fashioned frames may have them cut to ovals or put in any pattern that pleases them best. The above frames may be finished white, or green and white, purple or any colour that suits the color of the room, or gilt in oil or burnished gold equal to the best imported.

In the *New York Journal or General Advertiser* in 1769 Nicholas Bernard, carver, advertised an assortment of looking glasses "with carved,

TOP LEFT: Mirror, gilt frame, 1790–1800. RIGHT: Mirror, walnut and gilt, 1760–1775. BOTTOM LEFT: Gilt mirror, 1790–1800. BOTTOM RIGHT: Queen Anne mirror, walnut veneer and gilt, 1740.

and carved and gilt Frames, do. Pediments and plain Mahogany and Walnut; also Dressing Glasses, Girondoles."

Stephen Whiting of Boston advertised "Piedmont, Sconce and Pier looking glasses" in 1749. Also he manufactured frames to suit the buyer. In 1774 Whiting was importing "sconce and pier looking glasses in Walnut, Mahogany, oval frames in the newest taste neatly carved and gilt."

The best-known maker of this period, whose frames of various types are identified today, is John Elliott of Philadelphia (1753–1776). He made mahogany and walnut Queen Anne frames with a crested top and the glass in two sections. He also made mahogany and walnut fretwork looking-glass frames, and mirrors with a scrolled pediment and a carved gold eagle. He also made "pier, sconce, swinging, dressing and pocket mirrors." Mirrors by Elliott are to be found in several museums. His fretwork mirrors were plain and inexpensive, and this style continued to be made by his son until 1809. Mirrors have also been found with the label of James Reynolds, carver and gilder of Philadelphia (1756–1794), and of Jonathan Gostelowe, cabinetmaker of Philadelphia.

The mention of oval mirrors in the advertisements of the late 18th century probably refers to mirrors of the Adam style. Adam mirrors were also made in rectangular shape. They were carved, gilded, and fluted; with urns, honeysuckle, and other classic motifs. The festoons and strings of flowers (husks or paterae) were so delicate that they could not be carved in wood, but were made of plaster composition. Adam mirrors influenced the Hepplewhite style of mirror of a few years later. These mirrors, however, are usually rectangular, but they have the draperies and leaves of composition and use the classic vase form. Often several ears of wheat are set in the vase. Many of the frames have rosettes at the corners and the edges of the frame may have a border of carved leaves or a ropelike design. One of the most popular types of Hepplewhite mirrors had a cresting of agricultural implements, including a scythe and rake and a basket of fruit, or a pair of cornucopias filled with fruit. Another looking glass of this period has a glass painting of Washington set within a cresting of laurel leaves and a stylized bowknot. These mirrors of the Hepplewhite period date from 1790 to 1815 and may be similar to the looking glasses in an advertisement of 1797: "Looking glasses with white panel and festoon ornaments."

Another type of mirror made at about this date was similar to the Chippendale scroll pediment type of mirror but it was more delicate in proportions and detail. The gilt scroll pediment holds a vase with flowers, wheat, or an eagle at its top, and there is also often an inlaid American eagle or inlaid vertical bars in the wood of the pediment. Carved and gilt leaves drop at the sides of the mirror, but the fretwork at the bottom is plain. The frames are usually made of veneered mahogany and date from 1790 to 1800. The Metropolitan Museum owns one such mirror, which has a painted glass panel of a waterfront scene.

In 1797 Josiah Bumstead of Boston advertised "mahogany and gilt looking glasses from two to one hundred dollars per pair. A few very elegant with gilt frames." In 1799 in Boston, "Dearborn, Carver and Real Gilder in Burnished Gold," advertised "Oil, Japan or Burnish Looking glasses, Gerondoles, Picture frames. . . . Gold Enamel on glass. Very complete assortment of mahogany framed looking glasses all sizes—American manufacture." The variety of size as listed in an advertisement of 1794 suggests looking glasses for various purposes and various size rooms.

37 by 18 inches	30 by 14 inches
30 by 18 inches	27 by 16 inches
29 by 18 inches	23 by 14 inches

From 1795 to 1850 and after, mirrors were a common household item and were so numerous that only those of fine workmanship or of particularly rare design or historical interest are worth collecting. Sheraton-type mirrors were made from 1795 to 1820. This type of mirror was architectural in design. They are rectangular with columns, often following the Greek orders, and have a heavy pediment at the top which is decorated with balls, acorns, fluting, rosettes, or carved acanthus leaves. There is a panel of glass or wood at the top of the glass. The most interesting mirrors of the Sheraton period are those which have patriotic paintings on the panel. These paintings include scenes from the War of 1812, with the various combats of the *Constitution* and *Guerriere* and Perry's Victory on Lake Erie. These scenes are often labeled. Other panels contain portraits of Washington, eagles, and symbols of Liberty or festoons of flowers. Similar English mirrors had scenes of classic ruins and landscapes. Rare Sheraton mirrors have two columns at each side with panels of glass between, which may be decorated with a floral or leaf design. These date between 1790 and 1810, while the patriotic scenes date from shortly after the War of 1812 to 1820. Some Sheraton frames have a panel of crisscross line design while others have objects such as draperies, flowers, grapes, or classic figures in low relief composition. Some mirrors have a panel of wood and also similar frames are made entirely of mahogany and are not gilded.

The majority of the men who made these mirrors were painters as well as gilders, and sometimes also carvers. For example, "Cotton & Corless, Painters, Japanners, and Gilders—Looking glass frames—Carving" of Philadelphia advertised from 1794 to 1796. John Beath of Boston in 1794 advertised: "Looking glasses, picture frames and ornament done in burnish gold and silver." Bernard Cermenati of Newburyport, Massachusetts, made Sheraton gilded frames with white panels with painted decoration from 1800. And John Doggett of Roxbury, Massachusetts, made a Sheraton mirror which is in the Metropolitan Museum and is dated 1815. From Doggett's account book of the years 1802 to 1809 we find that he was not only a cabinetmaker but a carver and gilder as well, although he did not usually do the painting, for he had several artists in his employ, such as John R. Penniman, who painted panels for his mirrors. In 1809 he charged $125 for a mirror and frame 44 by 29 inches. Earps & Company of Philadelphia also made mirrors of this type between 1814 and 1824 and some have been found with these labels. In this period the American looking-glass makers no longer followed English models but developed a style of their own. Many of the mirrors have elaborately painted glass panels of cities, buildings, and memorials to Washington as well as scenes of the War of 1812. The urns, columns, and other carvings are delicate and well modeled.

In the *Connecticut Courant* of 1815 the following advertisement describes looking-glass frames of that date: "Pillared and plain mahogany. Walnut framed,—Statia." Empire-style mirrors are heavier and less elegant in appearance, although they have some of the same features as the Sheraton period mirrors. The columns are larger and heavier and the design is nonarchitectural.

Often there is a turned column across the top of the frame instead of a pediment. The painted glass panel is seen on many Empire mirrors but the scene is often genre instead of patriotic, although an eagle tops the pediment on mirrors made by William Wiswell in Worcester, Massachusetts, in 1830. A familiar type of Empire mirror is decorated in black and gilt or black and maple with wide plain frames. These are similar to the later Victorian mahogany veneer frames, which are rectangular and may be hung vertical or horizontal. An advertisement of 1827 reads "Looking glasses for mantel, Pier and Toilet in Pine, Mahogany, Maple, and gilt frames."

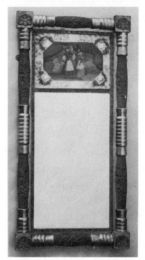

TOP: 19th-century gilt mirrors with painted panels. CENTER LEFT: Courting mirror. CENTER: Late 19th-century gilt and wood with painted panel. RIGHT: Early 19th-century gilt with small decorated panel. BOTTOM: Pair of Bull's Eye Mirrors.

Mahogany oval veneer frames are also Victorian, as are black-walnut frames with a gilt inner border. These were made with two glasses and were often 5 feet in height. Huge gilt mirrors with elaborately carved composition crests were made to hang over Victorian mantels or over low marble-topped tables. Pairs of small oval gilt mirrors with a decoration of applied gilt composition flowers were also used in Victorian homes late in the 19th century. Oval Victorian frames with carved rococo designs and fruit, grapes, and leaves, all decorated in gilt, show French influence. These mirrors are too numerous and too poor in design or workmanship to interest the serious collector, although they do fit in with the decoration of Victorian rooms.

Convex Empire mirrors, both with and without candle brackets, are of French origin and date from about 1800 to 1820. They all have heavy gold frames both with and without carving of laurel leaves or a border of gold balls. At the top there is usually a carved eagle on a rock pedestal, a shell or basket of fruit, or a pair of dolphins; and at the bottom and sides are leaves and shells of carved wood and composition. When brackets for candles are attached at the sides or bottoms these mirrors are known as girandoles.

Convex mirrors of similar design had been made in England since about 1720. However, the name "girandole" was not used until the oval sconced mirrors of Adam's time and the elaborate carved and gilt rococo girandoles of Chippendale's time. It should be remembered that girandoles were mentioned in American newspapers as early as 1765 and 1769. They may have been of the convex type or they may have been of Chippendale design or perhaps early convex girandoles.

Two other types of mirrors should be mentioned in speaking of collecting American mirrors. While they were not made in America, they were brought here by sea captains. The Bilboa mirror (1780–1810) was made in Bilboa, Spain. The distinguishing characteristic of these mirrors is that the frame is made up of pieces of various colored marbles glued on a wooden frame. It has moldings of gilt and a gilt cresting after the designs of Adam and Hepplewhite.

Courting mirrors with painted glass frames and a glass cresting similar in shape to early William and Mary crestings were brought from China by New England sea captains in about 1800. They are small, about 15 inches in height, and usually come in a wooden box. Tiny mirrors of both Bilboa and Courting types are also found.

It is difficult to find really fine old mirrors. Many have had their glasses replaced, but more serious still they have been cut down and remodeled. However, in some cases even the remodeling goes back to the late 18th century. Mirrors of the 19th-century types are plentiful, especially the simple types of cruder workmanship. Even if the painting on the glass panel is poor and harsh in color there is often a primitive charm. These mirrors were often made in rural districts and may be classed as provincial. Pennsylvania Dutch mirrors with fluted columns and pediments and a bright scene painted on the glass panel are crude in workmanship. Sometimes the wooden frame is decorated with a spattered paint design.

Small provincial mirrors of the Queen Anne or Chippendale fretwork type are also to be found in the shops today. Simple rectangular mirrors of curly maple are also available today. Curly maple mirror frames were mentioned on the label of Thomas Nott of Philadelphia as early as 1790.

All types of mirrors from Queen Anne to late Empire were also made in horizontal form for use above mantels. Usually the glass is in three sections, with the larger section in the center. One of the loveliest mirrors of this type is the Sheraton double-column mirror with architectural pediment and balls, and an upper section of crisscross lattice-work. These horizontal mirrors are not so plentiful as the vertical mirrors. Dressing glasses, with one or more drawers, made to set on a dressing table, were made from 1710 and have mirrors attached which follow the designs of the various styles from Queen Anne down through Empire.

Since early advertisements tell us that the looking-glass maker was also the picture-frame maker, picture frames are logically treated in this chapter. The frames in the earliest inventories are black ebony or olive wood. In the 18th century black wood frames continue to be popular, but there is usually a carved gilded border near the glass or perhaps two gilt borders. The early mezzotints, such as that of Dr. Cotton Mather by Peter Pelham which hangs in the Metropolitan Museum of Art, were framed in this manner. Needlework pictures of the 18th century are also found in old frames of this type. Late in the 18th century frames of carved wood completely covered with gold leaf were made. Some of these are almost as elaborate as the Chippendale carved mirrors of the same date. Gradually as the designs became more delicate plaster replaced the wood carving. In 1791 James Smith of Baltimore advertised himself as a "picture frame maker, carver and gilder—Looking Glasses." In 1791 William Faris advertised in the *Maryland Journal*: "Silvering and framing plates, carving and gilding frames. Picture frames of any dimension or pattern—plain carved, black or gilt."

In Philadelphia in 1793 John Eckstein & Son at their "Looking Glass Warehouse" "Execute orders on frames for looking glasses, paintings—plain or gilt."

In Charleston, North Carolina, in 1797 Cotton & Stattler made "looking glass frames, girandoles, paintings, needlework framed in burnish, old gold, black & gilt."

Burnished gold frames were also imported from London and Amsterdam. Carvers, gilders, and cabinetmakers combined framing pictures until the end of the 18th century.

By 1800 small frames were made of gold leaf, and often a gold and black glass border with designs and the name of the subject or the artist was painted in gold on the glass. This style continued until the middle of the 19th century. When John Beath of Boston advertised in 1794 he may have referred to ornament on glass: "Picture frames and ornament done in burnished gold and silver."

Victorian mirror and picture frames were often of papier-mâché decorated and sometimes inlaid with mother-of-pearl. However, plaster and gilt was the favorite decoration for the Victorian frame, and the oval shape was especially popular at this time. Later walnut oval frames of turned wood with a plain gold border near the glass were favorite frames for family photographs. Frames were also sanded and marbled and plain gold frames often had a stenciled design. The large frames for portraits and large paintings usually continued to be made of gold and plaster composition. Simple provincial frames are of narrow walnut or mahogany veneer or pine, painted and decorated.

Late Victorian frames were also made of brown composition similar to that of daguerreotype cases. Also frames were made of brown Rockingham-type pottery, and walnut tricktrack frames with crudely carved leaves at the corners were typical frames for small pictures in the 1770s.

BIBLIOGRAPHY

American Antique Furniture, by Edgar G. Miller, Jr. M. Barrows & Company, Inc., New York, 1937.

❧ 24 ❧

American Paper Hangings and Wallpaper-covered Bandboxes

EARLY AMERICAN WALLPAPERS and wallpaper-covered bandboxes, particularly those with historical scenes, offer an interesting and comparatively inexpensive field for the antique collector, and for the researcher, too, for to date few exact data have been uncovered. Several writers have recorded the names of the first "paper stainers" or wallpaper manufacturers, but just which maker manufactured a certain pattern or at what date the pattern was first made is not often known.

However, wallpaper was made in considerable quantities in 18th-century America, and there were early makers in Philadelphia, Boston, and New York as well as in a few other towns. Plunket Fleeson of Philadelphia is credited with making the first wallpaper in America in 1739. Other early makers in Philadelphia were Ryves and Fletcher, 1775, which became Ryves, Ashmead, and Poyntell in 1787; Joseph Dickinson in 1784; Le Collay and Chardon in 1789; Samuel Law & Co., 1790–1816; and Burrill and Carnes in 1790. In 1791 Burrill and Carnes advertised "Festoon and common borders." The advertisement also mentions that they marked their papers "Burrill and Edward Carnes." There were forty workmen in the factory and over 600 patterns of paper when the factory was taken over by Chardon and Anthony in 1794. Another early wallpaper maker in Philadelphia was Thomas Hurly, who operated a paper hangings manufactory from 1803 to 1816. The Philadelphia Directory of 1812 lists Orth and Kean, and Anthony Chardon, paper-hanging manufacturers. The directory of 1816 lists Henry T. Virchaux as operating a paper-hanging manufactory and John Simpson, James Mitchell, Samuel Laws, G. & F. Dedaker, John Chambers, and Joseph Bastian as paper stainers. F. Gerhard was a marble papermaker and paper hanger. We also find that stationers and upholsterers are often listed as wallpaper stainers. In 1820 John Howell, who had been an early paper stainer of Albany, New York, was operating a wallpaper factory in Philadelphia. Mackay and Dixey made wallpaper in Springfield, East Jersey, in 1790, and Asa Smith worked in Baltimore from 1800 to 1810.

Painted paper was for sale in Boston stationers' shops as early as 1700, but it was 1760 before Jonathan and John Amory manufactured the first wallpaper in Boston. Nothing is known about the papers which they made, but we do have a record in the inventory of John Welsh, Jr., who had a paper-staining manufactory in Scots Court, Boston, in 1786. The inventory includes "a set of prints of Quaker figures; a set of Diana; Fantail; Oval & slack; Green figure; Slack; Pin oval; Sprig; fantail borders; canopy borders; scroll." It also included printing and painting tables, bags of colored flocks, refuse, and odd balls of painted paper. In 1789 a notice in the *Independent Chronicle* stated that Moses Grant "càrries on the paper staining manufactory of John Welsh jun." Joseph Hovey, paper stainer and linen printer advertised in the *Independent Chronicle*, Boston, July 15, 1790: "Plain blues, greens, Brocade, Velvet, and Chintz figures with handsome Festoon Patch, and carved work Borders, elegant panel papers for wainscoting and stair cases. Beatiful Flower Pots for Chimney boards—all prints executed at manufactory 10% cheaper than elsewhere." In 1790 Prentis & May also advertised in Boston newspapers "plain blue green, buffs and pink with frosted spangled festoon, patch, carved work and common borders. Large figured papers from 2 to 17 colors—Fifty different patterns." May continued the business alone in 1791 and made "a rich variety of papers with every different order of architecture; and festoon borders from 20″ to 1″, variagated papers on the subjects of War, Peace, Music, Love, Rural Scenes, etc., Chintz patterns common, Tutanick, Tuscan, Dorick, Gothick, and Composite Orders."

Ebenezer Clough operated the Boston Paper Staining Manufactory in 1795 and the Rev. William Bentley records that a paper mill at Newton, Massachusetts, was making paper for blocks and stamps used for hangings. Other early makers of wallpaper in Boston include Moses Grant; Josiah Bumstead & Son, who operated a paper-staining business from 1798 to 1831; and J. W. Thacher, who had a paper manufactory in 1799. William Marshall, paper stainer, worked in Boston from 1820 to 1830 and advertised "Forest Paper of various patterns and shades" in 1823. In 1765 John Rugar of New York produced several patterns to show at the meeting of the Society for Promoting the Arts, although few individual paper stainers are listed in New York directories before 1800. From 1805 to 1810 John Colles had a paper-hanging manufactory at 42 Pearl Street, New York. Other 18th-century makers of American wallpaper included Robert Long, Newburyport, Massachusetts, 1798; Mills and Webb, Hartford, Connecticut, 1793; and Thomas Webb, Albany, 1794. Albany continued as an early center of wallpaper making. In 1803 J. Howell & Son, who had operated a paper-hanging and trunk manufactory in New York City, opened a factory in Albany, and in 1804 E. Pemberton advertised in the Albany newspapers: "Manufactures and keeps on hand a large assortment of Paper Hanging with elegant festoon and other borders." Early American wallpapers owned by Cooper Union Museum include patterns of checks, blocks, diamonds, sprigs, rosettes, and stripes. The predominating colors are blue, green, dull red, tan, and black. These early patterns were cut on a wood block and stamped with distemper and oil paints. The paper stainer did this work but did not make the paper and probably did not make the blocks. From 1800 the number of manufacturers increased until in 1824 there were more than sixty wallpaper manufacturers in America.

By 1812 Hartford, Connecticut, had become a center for wallpaper manufacture. Such firms as I. & J. Bolles, Zechariah Mills and Edward Danforth, later Mills and Danforth, and Woodbridge and Putnam were making landscape, draperies, stripes, and pillar designs. Mills and Danforth advertised "Landscape figures" in 1814 and Woodbridge and Putnam in 1816 advertised "over 2,000 patterns—Landscape figures, draperies, stripes, pillars, and set figures." Accompanying the advertisement is a cut of trees and three sheep, which was a decorative motif generally used around this date. In 1818 Woodbridge and Putnam advertised "satin grounds" and "vines" in addition to the before-named patterns and "Pattern Books sent to order." George Putnam advertised in the *Connecticut Courant*, May 30, 1820: "Has just manufactured a few new figures of paper hangings among which is a very beautiful view of sea and rocks with a castle erected upon them. Ships at anchor and a pilot boat under full sail." This view is to be found on many bandboxes made between 1820 and 1830. On August 29, 1820, George Putnam advertised bandboxes as follows: "George Putnam has just manufactured a large quantity of bandboxes of various sizes. Orders for any part of the Country, size, pattern, or quantity." In 1821 the firm name was Jones & Putnam, and in 1823-1824 the name was Putnam & Roff. This firm under its various names made the only bandbox papers that we can definitely identify as to maker and date. The "sea and rocks" paper was used on bandboxes, together with other patterns. Another bandbox has an eagle with ribbons printed with "Putnam and Roff, Paper Hanging and Band Box Manufact. Hartford, Con."

Paper hangings were manufactured in New Bedford, Massachusetts, in 1814 by John Perkins. He advertised "Elegant landscape, Large and small curtain, and Drapery patterns with curtain and lace figured borders to match. Entry and panel papers. Plain green, blue, orange." In 1817 Perkins had 4,500 rolls of paper hangings on hand, and in 1819 he advertised landscape and other patterns at 30c to 50c a roll. "Borders and paper for Window Curtains, plain and figured of a thick and durable quality. Any part of roll not used may be returned. Same rate as he sells to venders in Boston and New York." In 1828 Perkins advertised "Ready made paper curtains, plain and figured—Bandboxes." In 1832 the New Bedford Bandbox Manufactory was operated by Joseph L. Freyan. Joseph S. Tillinghast, Union Street, New Bedford, was an importer of French paper hangings and a bandbox manufacturer. His label is found on the Erie Canal Box. This paper was undoubtedly made soon after the Erie Canal was finished in 1825 and may have been made in France. French papers were especially popular for fireplace boards, and French, English, and Italian scenic papers were also popular in America. French papers with vases of flowers were advertised for covering fireplace boards. While these boards were usually covered with floral paper, a fireplace board in the Pennsylvania Museum has a scene of the Narrows, Fort Hamilton. Bandboxes covered with wallpaper, and small fancy boxes covered with floral and geometric patterns of wallpaper and marble papers, were used in America from late in the 18th down to the late 19th century. The first of these fancy boxes came from France, as is evidenced from an advertisement in the *Philadelphia General Advertiser*, 1790: "Francis De L'Orme, Upholsterer from Paris, makes pasteboard boxes of all shapes and sizes." De L'Orme worked in Philadelphia and later North Carolina. The little boxes were used for powder, patches, handkerchiefs, gloves, sewing materials, and sweets. Some had feet and were trimmed with gold and silver papers. Later some were mounted with prints, painted glass covers, and velvet stenciled with such inscriptions as "Friendship." Some were lined with diaper papers, but they were usually lined with old newspapers, and this gives us a clew to when and where they were made. Many found in the shops today have newspapers of Philadelphia and other Pennsylvania towns dating between 1820 and 1830.

Bandboxes probably were not covered with wallpaper in America much before 1800, although John Fisher advertised bonnet and bandbox boards for sale in Baltimore in 1789. The fragment of paper from the bandbox of Abigail Adams (1765-1818) now preserved in Cooper Union Museum was one of the earliest boxes. However, the paper may have been made in France, as many of the papers covering the earliest bandboxes certainly were made in France. Such designs as women and mountebanks, fountains and classic temples, mythological scenes, exotic birds, and Italian gardens were probably made in France. Papers with pastoral scenes, Napoleon and soldier, and Napoleon on horseback also may have been made in France. The early pineapple, baskets of fruit and flowers, and other early floral patterns were probably French, too, although we cannot be certain.

Whether the papers made in America were original designs or copies of French designs or who designed such papers as Clayton's Ascent and Castle Garden we do not know. Of course they were adaptations from prints of the era, but that Putnam and Roff employed a local designer at their factory is evidenced by the bandbox paper with the eagle and ribbon scroll. One of the earliest bandbox papers has a design of an urn and eagle. This was probably made in America around 1810. Generally speaking, the pastorial scenes and classic landscapes were among the earliest bandbox designs. The majority of the wallpapers with historical scenes date after 1820. Usually each bandbox had two designs, one on the top and one on the sides, and the combination of designs varies on different boxes. Thus one bandbox with a design of Castle Garden is found with a landscape on the cover and another has a design of two Victorian dogs on the cover.

The foundation of the majority of wallpaper bandboxes is cardboard, but Hannah Davis, the well-known bandbox maker of East Jaffrey, New Hampshire, made nailed wooden boxes of spruce shavings and covered them with wallpapers. She went into the woods and selected her trees, bought them and had them cut, and then she nailed them while green. The logs were cut and stood on end on a platform and a machine with a sharp blade, run by foot power, cut off thin slices about ⅛ inch thick, which served as the sides of the boxes, the small slices for ribbon and trinket boxes, the large slices for hatboxes. The bottoms of the boxes were made of pine. The bandboxes were usually lined with newspapers and marked with a printed label: "Warranted Nailed Band Boxes manufactured by Hannah Davis East Jaffrey, N. H." These boxes cost from 12 cents to 50 cents for the largest. Hannah Davis had a peddler's cart and a sleigh (for winter) and peddled her boxes throughout New England. She worked from about 1818

TOP: Advertisement, *The Evening Gazette*, Boston, April 10, 1830. BOTTOM LEFT: Blue Bandbox, "H. Barnes, Philadelphia." CENTER: Napoleon at St. Helena, blue ground, Hannah Davis. RIGHT: New York Harbor, Castle Garden, Trinity Church, City Hall. All early 19th century.

to 1863. The exact date of any of her boxes is usually determined by the date of the newspaper lining. Not all unmarked wooden bandboxes can be attributed to Hannah Davis, however. Nicholas Brower, bandbox maker of New York City, was at one time a cooper and a Windsor-chair maker, so it is very probable that his bandboxes were made of wood.

Below is a short check list of early bandbox makers of Philadelphia, Boston and vicinity, and New York as found in city directories, in newspaper advertisements, and on labels on bandboxes.

NEW YORK BANDBOX MAKERS

Charles Cox, Band Box Mfg., 96 Bowery, 1807–1811
Catherine Adriance, bandbox maker, 282 Greenwich, 1811–1814; 55 Bowery, 1815–1818
John Brower, bandbox maker, 161 William, 1814
Samuel Brower, bandbox maker, 127 William, 1815–1826
Nicholas B. Brower, bandbox maker, 60 Fulton, 1819; 132 William, 1820; 110 Fulton, 1825–1826
Thomas Day, bandbox and trunk maker, 55 Nassau, 1818–1820
Thomas Day, Jr., bandbox manufacturing, 82 Fulton, 1821–1822; listed as paper hanger, 1825–1826
Jane Wright, bandbox maker, 168 Fulton, 1826–1827; 155 Fulton, 1828–1837
Day & Parsell, bandbox makers, 38 Division St., 1838–1841
Tirzah Day, bandbox maker, 369 Pearl St., 1838–1841
Joseph Biele, fancy box maker, 45 Gold St., 1830–1831

PHILADELPHIA BANDBOX MAKERS

Frederick Comerlo, bandbox maker, 67 Coates, 1805–1807
Ursula Comerlow (widow), bandbox maker, 67 Coates, 1808–1817
Edwards Rushton, bandbox maker, 93 N. Front, 1813–1824
Mrs. Maddin, bandbox maker, 1816
Jane Rushton (widow), bandbox maker, 93 N. Front, 1825–1833
Maria Moore, bandbox maker, 122 New, 1823–1833
Margaret Bartlett, bandbox maker, 66 Coates, 1825–1833
Benjamin Wade, paper box maker, 1816–1819
Nicholas Kline, bandbox maker, 1829–1833
Gabriel Moore, bandbox maker, 25 Laurel, 1829–1836
Henry Barnes, bandbox maker, 18 Strawberry, 1829–1830; 33 Jones Alley, 1831–1836
James Winter, scourer and bandbox maker, 37 Mulberry, 1829–1836
D. N. Carvalho, marble and fancy paper manufacturing, 1835–1836
Jesse Baker, paper box manufacturer, 21 Bank St., Philadelphia

BOSTON & NEW ENGLAND

Kilby Page, paper hanging, 71 Washington St., Boston, 1820–1831

Jesse P. Hurlbert, pasteboard, bandbox, and paper hangings, fancy boxes, bonnet, hat,
   boxes, fire boards, Boston, 1829 and 1830
John C. & Charles Cook, paper hangings, 220 Washington St., Boston, 1831–1835
Mark Worthley, fancy boxes, 119 Washington, Boston, 1835–1845
Joseph S. Tillinghast, bandbox manufacturer, Union St., New Bedford, 1825–1830 (?)
H. G. Hinckley, manufactory of hat, cap, muff, and bandboxes, Hartford, 1847–1850
Henry Gladding, bandboxes and fancy boxes, New Haven, 1849

The following is a list of all known bandbox designs, together with
descriptions, approximate dates, and makers' names where known.

HISTORICAL SCENES

Clayton's Ascent. On sides, scene of balloon, houses, and trees printed in pink,
white, and green on tan ground; also found on canary yellow and ultramarine
grounds. Inscription: "Clayton's Ascent." On cover of box a village scene and large
telescope pointed at moon, on which garden scene is depicted. Inscription: "A Peep
at the Moon." Border on edge of cover of fuchsialike flowers in blue, pink, and white.
C. 1835–1840. Also found with pigeon and rooster on sides.

Grand Canal. Canal locks, boats, and figures of men printed in black, brown, red,
and white on blue ground. Inscription: "Grand Canal." Cover of box conventional
flower, scrolls, and grapes; also found with scene of President Jackson on cover.
Border on edge of cover guilloche design in tan and yellow. 1825–1835.

Canal and Landscape. Scene along canal printed in blue, brown, and green on
yellow ground on sides of box. No inscription. Cover of box has scene of trees and
classic temple. Narrow border of bellflowers on edge of cover.

Castle Garden. On sides scene of Castle Garden from Battery Park after print
showing promenade deck. Printed in rose, white, dark green on blue ground. Inscription: "Castle Garden." On cover landscape with buildings and daisy border. Border
on cover small sawtooth design. Also found with dogs on cover. Box all wood. Also
found with wooden top and bottom and pasteboard sides. C. 1835–1836.

Engine 13. Fire engine and firemen extinguishing flames on burning houses
printed on sides and top in pink, red, and white on yellow ground. Border on edge of
cover scroll in green, white, and red. Label: H. Barnes & Co. Philadelphia, 33 Jones
Alley, Fancy and Ribbon boxes. (Cooper Union.) 1831–1836. On blue ground with
scene of fire engine and coaching scene in pink, white, and dark green on blue
ground. Same scene with Castle Garden on cover, no label. (New York Historical
Society.)

Capitol at Washington. Capitol building and lawn and trees printed on top and
sides of box in olive, pink, and white on chartreuse ground. (Cooper Union.) Printed
in rose, white, and dark green on blue ground. (New York Historical Society.) C.
1830–1835.

Sandy Hook. Marine scene with sailboat and lighthouse printed in pink, white,
and brown on a dark-blue ground on sides and cover. Inscription: "Sandy Hook."
C. 1830–1835.

Capitol at Albany. Scene of Capitol on blue ground on sides. Cover of large roses
and green garden temples in rose and white against blue ground. C. 1830–1835.

Windmill and Railroad. Landscape of windmill and horse-drawn railroad cars loaded with wood printed in red and green on canary-yellow ground on sides of box. Cover of box scene of house and trees set in border of daisies. Border of tassels on edge of cover. C. 1830.

New York Post Office. Scene of pink brick buildings on blue ground on sides and cover of box. Also found with Deaf and Dumb Asylum on cover. C. 1830–1840.

Deaf and Dumb Asylum. On yellow ground on cover. On sides, scene of rhinoceros and hunters on foot and horseback with bows and arrows. Printed in green, pink, and brown on yellow ground. Box in Cooper Union has written inscription inside cover: "Rosanna Carmany 1836." C. 1830–1836.

"Port of Buffaloe on Lake Erie." Scene of lake with steamboat and inscription on sides of box. Cover has sea and rocks with castle and sailboat. Port of Buffalo also used together with scene of University of Middletown, Conn. Label on box owned by Gertrude Bilhuber: "J. Wright, Paper Hanging Warehouse and Bandbox Manufacturer, 168 Fulton St., N.Y., 1826–1827." Paper possibly made by George Putnam or Putnam & Roff, Hartford, Conn.

City Hall, N.Y. Scene of City Hall with garden triangle, fountain, and iron railings.

Merchants' Exchange, N.Y. Blue ground printed in pink, green, and white. Inscription: "Merchants Exchange."

Holts' Hotel, N.Y. Yellow ground. Cover is floral design. Sides of box have six-story building printed in brown and white. C. 1835–1840.

Scenes of Washington's Life. Cream ground and scenes in scrolls, including portrait of Washington, Washington Crossing Delaware, Battle of Monmouth, Surrender of Cornwallis and Entrance into New York. C. 1800–1815.

"Prosperity to Our Commerce and Manufacturers" and scene of large sailing vessel printed on yellow ground on cover. Sides of box floral scrolls enclosing lilies and leaves and printed in pink, white, and olive on yellow ground. C. 1815–1820.

Napoleon Battle Scene. Scene of Napoleon and soldiers printed in white and green and enclosed in frame of white lace and flowers on tan ground. All-wood box with Hannah Davis label on cover. Lined with 1833 newspaper. C. 1830–1835.

Napoleon at St. Helena. Scene of Napoleon and soldier and log of wood set in medallion of white scrolls. Printed in pink, white, and green on blue ground. Same scene on cover. All-wood box with Hannah Davis label. Lining of *New Hampshire Observer,* Portsmouth, December 29, 1830. Also found on cardboard box with 1831 newspaper lining. C. 1830–1835.

Surrender of Cornwallis. Chartreuse-green ground printed in browns and lavender. Scenes of Cornwallis and battlefield with soldiers in line formation. Fragment in Cooper Union. C. 1805–1815.

Urn and Eagle. Printed in blue and chartreuse on tan ground. C. 1810–1815.

Eagle on Trunk. Eagle with olive and laurel branches and ribbon with inscription "Putnam and Roff Paper Hanging and Band Box Manufact. Hartford, Con." Printed in green and rose on turquoise-blue ground. Border on cover repeat of circle and dot. 1823–1824.

British Queen. Entrance of ship *British Queen* to New York harbor in 1839. Scene outlined in red on chartreuse ground. C. 1840–1845.

Harrison Log Cabin. Scene of log cabin and cider barrel and two men—one a lame soldier. Steamboat on river marked "Ohio." Bright-blue ground printed in pink, yellow, and green. Cover scene of rocks, castle, and sailboat. C. 1840.

Zachary Taylor. Scene of camp with tents and General Taylor on horseback printed in rose, white, and green on blue ground on both top and sides of box. Box in New York Historical Society has label: "N. G. Hinckley, Hartford, Conn. Manufacturer of Hat, Cap, Muff and Band Boxes." C. 1847–1850.

New York Scenes. Harbor, Castle Garden, Wall Street, Trinity Church, and City Hall scenes from early prints set in framework of flowers, foliage, and fretwork, printed in blue and brown on light-blue ground. Probably English paper. C. 1840–1850.

Gallipoli and Istanbul. Scenes of towns and ships printed in brown, blue, and red on gray ground in repeat allover pattern on sides and cover of box. C. 1855–1860.

MYTHOLOGICAL, ORIENTAL, AND PASTORAL SCENES

Woman in Chariot with Horses. Scene of woman in Roman chariot drawn by horses against background of trees printed in rose, brown, and green on shaded blue and tan ground. Same scene on sides and cover of box. Small border of white flower and leaves on edge of cover. Inside box printed pamphlets giving names of vestry of Trinity Church dated March 25 and 28, 1812.

Woman in Chariot. Medallion of woman in chariot printed in green, rose, and white on light-blue ground and enclosed in white conventional foliage frame. Same scene on sides and cover of box. Wooden box lined with newspaper *Repository and Observer*, 1827. Label on inside cover:

Woman in Chariot Drawn by Griffons. Scene printed in pink, red, and olive green, against blue field. Same scene on sides and cover. C. 1830.

WARRANTED
NAILED
BAND BOXES
MADE BY
HANNAH DAVIS
JAFFREY

Oriental Figure with Camel. Oriental scene with camel and ruins printed in pink, red, and olive on yellow ground on sides of box. Cover of box has sprays of flowers. C. 1830.

Roses and Tempietto. Scene of classic figure in garden with Greek garden temple and large pink roses printed in pink and green on blue ground. Same scene on slides and cover. C. 1830.

Tempietto and Obelisk. Landscape scene with classic Greek garden tempietto, obelisk, trees, and bird printed in chartreuse, magenta, and blue on yellow ground. Same scene on sides and cover of box. C. 1840.

Tempietto with Figure. Garden scene with trees, classic figure, and garden temple printed in brown, pink, green, and white on blue ground on sides of box. Cover of box scene of rocks, castle, and sailboat. Small border of scrolls on edge of cover. C. 1830.

Cherub and Goat. Classic scene of trees, figures, doves, vases, and child with wings riding goat printed in pink, white, green, on blue ground on sides and cover of box. C. 1830.

Orientals and Dog. Three men in oriental costume on stage with dog with curtain drapery printed in pink, green, and white on blue ground on box cover. On sides of box scene of millpond, mill, and other buildings printed in pink, green, and white on blue ground. C. 1830–1840.

Charlatans and Women. Garden scene of women and clowns performing; printed in pink, green, and brown on blue ground in frame of white guilloche design. Lining, Philadelphia newspapers. 1839 and 1840.

TOP LEFT: Macaws, blue ground. TOP RIGHT: Clayton's Ascent, yellow ground. CENTER LEFT: Castle Garden, blue ground. CENTER RIGHT: Zachary Taylor, blue ground. BOTTOM LEFT: Capitol at Washington, blue ground. BOTTOM RIGHT: Fire Engine 13, blue ground.

Man, Woman, and Orientals. Man and woman in costume of 1835 and two men in Turkish costume printed in brown, pink, and white on blue ground on sides of box. Buildings in frame of daisies on cover of box. C. 1835–1840.

Shepherd and Flock. Scene with shepherd, sheep, and cows printed in pink, green, and white on blue ground on sides of box. Scene of men in oriental costume on cover. Small dot and circle border on edge of cover. C. 1830.

Garden Scenes. Two men holding girl on chair in medallion with decorative foliage and birds. *Man and girl on garden bench*—background buff, figures buff and bronze green. Hannah Davis label.

Garden Scene. Girl under tree being presented with bouquet of flowers by boy in medallion with dotted background, blue and white. Tall box with same scenes on top and sides. Label: Mark Worthley, Hand and Fancy Paper Box Manufacturer, 185 Washington St., Boston. C. 1835–1845.

Garden Scene. Woman with watering can and young man in knee breeches and cummerbund, wearing wide-brimmed flat hat with feather, resting one hand on shovel and other arm around maiden, set in foliage medallion printed in green, rose, and white on blue ground. All-wood box in Museum for Preservation of New England Antiquities has Hannah Davis label. C. 1830–1840.

Sheep. Pastoral medallion of sheep in framework of white lacelike scrolls printed in green, rose, and white on blue ground on sides and cover of wood bandbox. Label of Hannah Davis, Village Improvement Center, Jaffrey, N.H.

ANIMALS AND HUNTING SCENES

Hounds and Rabbits. Scene with large hounds chasing rabbits against a background of trees. Printed in pink, white, brown, and green against a blue field. Same scene on sides and cover of box. Small border of guilloche pattern in pink and yellow on edge of cover. C. 1840.

Dog and Stag. Scene of dog and stag printed in brown, tan, and white on blue ground on cover. Scene of horse and rider in same colors on sides of box. Small border of brown and yellow scallops on edge of cover. C. 1830.

Coach and Horses. Scene of coach loaded with baggage printed in pink and chartreuse green on bright yellow ground. Cover has scene of giraffe and men in Eastern costume. C. 1830. Also cover of rocks, castle, and sailboat. Coach and Horses also found on small oval box.

Coach and Horses. Printed in pink, red, and white on a blue ground. C. 1830.

Stag Hunt. Men and women on horses printed in pink, brown, and white on a yellow ground on sides of box. Cover of box is scene of dogs chasing ducks. Small border on edge of cover of blue leaves and berries. C. 1830.

Hunting Scene. Scene of men, horses and dogs, and fanciful landscape with alligators printed in green, yellow, and white on a blue ground. Cover of box is scene of terrace, river, and steamboat. C. 1830.

Hunters and Dog. Scene of hunters and dog printed in white, brown, and green against a yellow ground on sides of box. Scene of hunters at lunch on cover of box. C. 1830.

Squirrels. Scene of large squirrels against trees printed in red, green, and white against a chartreuse ground on sides of box. Cover of box is scene of houses and trees in border of daisies. C. 1830–1840.

Cows Grazing. Landscape with ruins and cows grazing printed in pink, white, and green on chartreuse yellow ground on sides of box. Cover design is of roses with grape border, with small border on edge of box of scallops in blue and rose. C. 1830.

Two Men in Boat. Two men in rowboat against background of trees and houses printed in pink, white, and green on tan ground on sides and cover of box. Border on edge of cover circle and dot pattern is yellow and pink. C. 1820.

Farmhouse. Scene of farmhouse, barns, pigs, and poplars and other trees printed in brown and white on blue ground on top and sides of bandbox. C. 1840–1850.

Woman on Horse. Medallions of woman on horse, man standing within framework of twisted foliage printed in pink, green, and white on blue ground. Pennsylvania newspaper of 1840 used as lining.

DECORATIVE BIRDS AND FLOWERS

Parrots. Parrots and palm trees in flower printed in magenta and green on mustard ground on top and sides of box. Same design in rose, white, and green on blue ground on sides of box. Cover of box is shepherdess and goat. Border on cover guilloche pattern. Newspaper lining in New York Historical Society dated 1826. C. 1820–1830.

Macaws and Vases of Flowers. Blue ground, printed in blue, green, and brown. Hannah Davis label.

Macaws. Macaws on branches printed in blue, brown, and white on yellow ground on sides and cover of box. Newspaper inside cover (New York), 1826.

Peacocks. Design of peacocks, flowers, and grape leaves printed in rose, white, brown, and green on blue ground. C. 1840.

Ruffed Grouse. Design of large grouse, trees, and hilly ground printed in red, white, and green on blue ground. Label: H. Barnes, 33 Jones Alley, Philadelphia, 1831–1836.

Swans. Scene of swans on pond with background of buildings printed in white, green, and brown on blue ground. C. 1840.

Basket of Fruit and Flowers. Large basket of fruit and flowers and figures of man and woman printed in white, green, and brown, on a blue ground on sides of box. Cover has patched Clayton's Ascent and scene of boat and sea serpent. C. 1835–1840.

Flowers and Drapery. Design of flowers and festoons of fringed drapery printed in pink, olive, and white on yellow ground. Blue dot and circle border on edge of cover. C. 1820–1830.

Damask Pattern. Allover pattern of conventional flowers in green, yellow, and orange on sides of box. Cover is same pattern in blue. Probably English paper. C. 1820–1830.

Moss Rose. White rose in diamond repeat framed in white scrolls printed in white, green, and pink on a blue ground. Lined with newspaper dated 1845. All-wood box. Label: Hannah Davis.

Pink Camellia. Large flowers and green leaves set in framework of white scrolls on yellow background. Label: Hannah Davis. C. 1840.

Large Pineapple. Design of large pineapple and leaves in yellow, rose, and green, on blue ground. Label: Hannah Davis. C. 1830.

Geometric floral pattern of leaves and flowers printed in browns and greens on light-green ground. Inside of box lined with design of dogs in front of church and sheep in front of castle, printed in rose, green, and white on buff ground. Hannah Davis label. 1820–1830.

English Chintz Pattern. Conventional flowers, bird, snake, and Chinese figure of man with hat, printed in pink, white, and yellow on dark blue. C. 1820.

Geometrical floral design. On light-green ground printed in browns and greens. Inside box are scenes of dogs and church and sheep and castle printed in rose, green, buff, and white on yellow ground. Hannah Davis label.

Top Hat. Bandbox in shape of top hat covered in striped paper of gray, red, and white foliage. C. 1830.

Wm. A. Shute, Caps, Hats, Fur Goods, 173 Washington St., Boston. Trade box with black top hats printed on blue glazed ground. Not wallpaper. C. 1850–1860.

John C. & Charles Cook, Importers & Manufacturers of Paper Hangings, Borders & Chimney Board Prints, 220 Washington St., Boston. Trade box with design of umbrella and hats. C. 1831–1833.

Reception of General Jackson at New Orleans. 1815–1830.

Washington at Mt. Vernon. 1830–1840.

Battle of Chapultepec. Soldier with American flag charging parapet. Gray ground figures of soldiers in blue, red, and white. 1848.

Certain designs are rare and thus bring a high price. Perhaps the most valuable box is the Putnam & Roff box with the "Eagle on Trunk" design and the maker's name, which gives us the date of the box. Any box with a design or maker's name that may be identified is of special interest. Thus the "Sea and Rocks" design is especially interesting although fairly common, because we know it was first made by George Putnam in 1820. Other early and rare patterns are "Woman in Roman Chariot," "Surrender of Cornwallis," "Eagle and Urn," "Prosperity to Our Commerce and Manufacturers," and "British Queen." Boxes for three-cornered hats covered with plain or conventional repeat patterns are rare, although not necessarily early. A tricornered box covered in plain blue glazed paper in the Museum for the Preservation of New England Antiquities has a label of S. M. Hurlberts, Pasteboard, Band Box and Paper Hangings Manufactory, 25 Court Street, Boston. This box is dated about 1820–1826. All wood boxes made by Hannah Davis are perhaps the most sought-after bandboxes, although, except for the Napoleon scenes, the majority of Hannah Davis boxes are covered with floral papers. To date no boxes have been found with early Philadelphia or New York makers' labels and no papers with the maker's name, although we have evidence that some makers marked their papers. Most of the designs on bandboxes were made expressly for use on bandboxes and thus fragments of papers have a place in a bandbox collection when properly framed and mounted. Bandbox paper is usually a little thinner than wallpaper.

Collections of bandboxes studied:

Cooper Union Museum for Decorative Arts
New York Historical Society
Village Improvement Center, Jaffrey, New Hampshire
Collection of Miss Gertrude Bilhuber

BIBLIOGRAPHY

Historic Wallpapers, by Nancy Vincent McClelland. J. B. Lippincott Company, Philadelphia, 1924.

Old Time Wallpapers, by Kate Sanborn. Literary Collector Press, 1905.

New York, Philadelphia, Boston, Hartford, Albany, New Bedford, Baltimore, Salem, and Providence newspapers.

Directories of Philadelphia, New York, and Boston.

Index